Daily STRENGTH for Daily NEEDS

by
Mary Wilder Tileston

This special edition was printed by the
Billy Graham Evangelistic Association

Daily Strength for Daily Needs by Mary Wilder Tileston
is a work in Public Domain

Cover photograph taken by Nina Engen
Foreword by Ruth Bell Graham
Editing, typesetting, cover design
© 1994 Billy Graham Evangelistic Association

Bible verses taken from the King James Version of the Bible

ISBN: 0-913367-35-4

Printed in the United States of America

FOREWORD

Years ago the discovery of Mary Wilder Tileston's *Joy and Strength* enriched my life.

Later I found she had compiled another book, *Daily Strength for Daily Needs,* which was published in 1891—another classic that should never go out of print.

In this volume also, the compiler lists authors in the back of the book, along with the dates when these people lived and other pertinent information, so that one becomes acquainted with saints of another generation.

May this book supply *Daily Strength for Daily Needs* along the pathway of your life, as it has mine.

Ruth Bell Graham
Montreat, July 1994

PREFACE

This little book of brief selections in prose and verse, with accompanying texts of Scripture, is intended for a daily companion and counselor. These words of the goodly fellowship of wise and holy men and women of many times, it is hoped may help to strengthen the reader to perform the duties and to bear the burdens of each day with cheerfulness and courage.

M. W. T.

JANUARY 1

They go from strength to strength.
                    —Psalm 84:7

First the blade, then the ear, after that the full corn in
the ear.
                    —Mark 4:28

BUILD thee more stately mansions, O my soul,
   As the swift seasons roll!
   Leave thy low-vaulted past!
Let each new temple, nobler than the last,
Shut thee from heaven with a dome more vast,
   Till thou at length art free,
Leaving thine outgrown shell by life's unresting sea!
               O. W. HOLMES

High hearts are never long without hearing some new call, some distant clarion of God, even in their dreams. Soon they are observed to break up the camp of ease, and start on some fresh march of faithful service. They do the good only to see the better, and see the better only to achieve it. They are too meek [to demand the service of others], too faithful for remorse, too earnest for repose. Their worship is action, and their action is ceaseless aspiration.

          J. MARTINEAU

JANUARY 2

The Lord shall preserve thy going out and thy coming in from this time forth, and even for evermore.
—Psalm 121:8

Lord, Thou hast been our dwelling-place in all generations.
—Psalm 90:1

WITH grateful hearts the past we own;
The future, all to us unknown,
We to Thy guardian care commit,
And peaceful leave before Thy feet.

P. DODDRIDGE

We are like to Him with whom there is no past or future, with whom a day is as a thousand years, and a thousand years as one day. We do our work in the great present, leaving both past and future to Him to whom they are ever present. We fear nothing, because He is in our future as much as He is in our past, as much as, and far more than, we can feel Him to be in our present. Partakers thus of the divine nature, resting in that perfect All-in-all in whom our nature is eternal too, we walk without fear, full of hope and courage and strength to do His will, waiting for the endless good which He is always giving as fast as He can get us able to take it in.

G. MACDONALD

JANUARY 3

As thy days, so shall thy strength be.
—Deuteronomy 33:25

Sufficient unto the day is the evil thereof.
—Matthew 6:34

———— ❧ ————

OH, ask not thou, How shall I bear
   The burden of to-morrow?
Sufficient for to-day, its care,
   Its evil and its sorrow;
God imparteth by the way
Strength sufficient for the day.
J. E. SAXBY

———— ❧ ————

He that hath so many causes of joy, and so great, is very much in love with sorrow and peevishness, who loses all these pleasures, and chooses to sit down upon his little handful of thorns. Enjoy the blessings of this day, if God sends them; and the evils of it bear patiently and sweetly: for this day only is ours; we are dead to yesterday, and we are not yet born to the morrow. But if we look abroad, and bring into one day's thoughts the evil of many, certain and uncertain, what will be and what will never be, our load will be as intolerable as it is unreasonable.

JEREMY TAYLOR

JANUARY 4

If ye then be risen with Christ, seek those things which are above, where Christ sitteth on the right hand of God.
—Colossians 3:1

OH, empty us of self, the world, and sin,
And then in all Thy fullness enter in;
Take full possession, Lord, and let each thought
Into obedience unto Thee be brought;
Thine is the power, and Thine the will, that we
Be wholly sanctified, O Lord, To Thee.

C.E.J.

Take steadily some one sin, which seems to stand out before thee, to root it out, by God's grace, and every fibre of it. Purpose strongly, by the grace and strength of God, wholly to sacrifice this sin or sinful inclination to the love of God, to spare it not, until thou leave of it none remaining, neither root nor branch.

Fix, by God's help, not only to root out this sin, but to set thyself to gain, by that same help, the opposite grace. If thou art tempted to be angry, try hard, by God's grace, to be *very* meek; if to be proud, seek to be *very* humble.

E. B. PUSEY

JANUARY 5

That He might present it to Himself a glorious church, not having spot, or wrinkle, or any such thing; but that it should be holy and without blemish.
—Ephesians 5:27

Ye also, as lively stones, are built up a spiritual house.
—1 Peter 2:5

❧

ONE holy Church of God appears
    Through every age and race,
Unwasted by the lapse of years,
    Unchanged by changing place.
          S. LONGFELLOW

❧

A temple there has been upon earth, a spiritual Temple, made up of living stones; a Temple, as I may say, composed of souls; a Temple with God for its light, and Christ for the high priest; with wings of angels for its arches, with saints and teachers for its pillars, and with worshippers for its pavement. Wherever there is faith and love this Temple is.

J. H. NEWMAN

To whatever worlds He carries our souls when they shall pass out of these imprisoning bodies, in those worlds these souls of ours shall find themselves part of the same great Temple; for it belongs not to this earth alone. There can be no end of the universe where God is, to which that growing Temple does not reach—the Temple of a creation to be wrought at last into a perfect utterance of God by a perfect obedience to God.

PHILLIPS BROOKS

JANUARY 6

But of him are ye in Christ Jesus, who of God is made unto us wisdom, and righteousness, and sanctification, and redemption.

— *1 Corinthians 1:30*

MEANWHILE with every son and saint of Thine
    Along the glorious line,
Sitting by turns beneath Thy sacred feet
    We'll home communion sweet,
Know them by look and voice, and thank them all
    For helping us in thrall,
For words of hope, and bright examples given
To shew through moonless skies that there is light in heaven.

J. KEBLE

It is right that we should have an aim of our own, determined by our individuality and our surroundings; but this may readily degenerate into exclusive narrowness, unless it has for a background the great thought that there is a Kingdom of God within us, around us, and above us, in which we, with all our powers and aims, are called to be conscious workers. Toward the forwarding of this silent, ever-advancing Kingdom, our little work, whatever it may be, if good and true, may contribute something. And this thought lends to any calling, however lowly, a consecration which is wanting even to the loftiest self-chosen ideals. But even if our aim should be frustrated and our work come to naught, yet the failure of our most cherished plans may be more than compensated. In the thought that we are members of this Kingdom, already begun, here and now, yet reaching forward through all time, we shall have a reserve of consolation better than any which success without this could give.

JOHN CAMPBELL SHAIRP

JANUARY 7

The exceeding greatness of His power to us-ward who
believe, according to the working of His mighty power.
—Ephesians 1:19

THE lives which seem so poor, so low,
    The hearts which are so cramped and dull,
The baffled hopes, the impulse slow,
    Thou takest, touchest all, and lo!
They blossom to the beautiful.

                SUSAN COOLIDGE

A root set in the finest soil, in the best climate, and blessed
with all that sun and air and rain can do for it, is not in so sure a
way of its growth to perfection, as every man may be, whose
spirit aspires after all that which God is ready and infinitely
desires to give him. For the sun meets not the springing bud that
stretches towards him with half that certainty, as God, the
source of all good, communicates Himself to the soul that longs
to partake of Him.

                WM. LAW

If we stand in the openings of the present moment, with all
the length and breadth of our faculties unselfishly adjusted to
what it reveals, we are in the best condition to receive what God
is always ready to communicate.

                T. C. UPHAM

JANUARY 8

As we have therefore opportunity, let us do good unto all men.

—Galatians 6:10

Let brotherly love continue.

—Hebrews 13:1

I ASK Thee for a thoughtful love,
    Through constant watching wise,
To meet the glad with joyful smiles,
    And to wipe the weeping eyes,
And a heart at leisure from itself,
    To sooth and sympathize.

A. L. WARING

Surely none are so full of cares, or so poor in gifts, that to them also, waiting patiently and trustfully on God for His daily commands, He will not give direct ministry for Him, increasing according to their strength and their desire. There is so much to be set right in the world, there are so many to be led and helped and comforted, that we must continually come in contact with such in our daily life. Let us only take care, that, by the glance being turned inward, or strained onward, or lost in vacant reverie, we do not miss our turn of service, and pass by those to whom we might have been sent on an errand straight from God.

ELIZABETH CHARLES

Look up and not down; look forward and not back; look out and not in; and lend a hand.

EDWARD E. HALE

JANUARY 9

*And in every work that he began in the service of the house
of God, and in the law, and in the commandments, to seek his
God, he did it with all his heart, and prospered.*
　　　　　　　　　—2 Chronicles 31:21

What shall we do, that we might work the works of God?
　　　　　—John 6:28

GIVE me within the work which calls to-day,
　To see Thy finger gently beckoning on;
So struggle grows to freedom, work to play,
　And toils begun from Thee to Thee are done.
　　　　　　　　J. F. CLARKE

God is a kind Father. He sets us all in the places where He
wishes us to be employed; and that employment is truly 'our
Father's business.' He chooses work for every creature which
will be delightful to them, if they do it simply and humbly. He
gives us always strength enough, and sense enough, for what He
wants us to do; if we either tire ourselves or puzzle ourselves, it
is our own fault. And we may always be sure, whatever we are
doing, that we cannot be pleasing Him, if we are not happy ourselves.

J. RUSKIN

JANUARY 10

Because Thy loving-kindness is better than life, my lips shall praise Thee.

—Psalm 63:3

Whosoever shall seek to save his life shall lose it; and whosoever shall lose his life shall preserve it.

—Luke 17:33

O LORD! my best desires fulfil.
   And help me to resign
Life, health, and comfort, to Thy will,
   And make Thy pleasure mine.

WM. COWPER

What do our heavy hearts prove?—that other things are sweeter to us than His will, that we have not attained to the full mastery of our true freedom, the full perception of its power, that our sonship is yet but faintly realized, and its blessedness not yet proved and known. Our consent would turn all our trials into obedience. By consenting we make them our own, and offer them with ourselves again to Him.

H. E. MANNING

Nothing is intolerable that is necessary. Now God hath bound thy trouble upon thee, with a design to try thee, and with purposes to reward and crown thee. These cords thou canst not break; and therefore lie thou down gently, and suffer the hand of God to do what He please.

JEREMY TAYLOR

JANUARY 11

I will be glad, and rejoice in Thy mercy; for Thou has considered my trouble; Thou hast known my soul in adversities.
—Psalm 31:7

NAY, all by Thee is ordered, chosen, planned—
Each drop that fills my daily cup; Thy hand
Prescribes for ills none else can understand.
    All, all is known to Thee.

A. L. NEWTON

God knows us through and through. Not the most secret thought, which we most hide from ourselves, is hidden from Him. As then we come to know ourselves through and through, we come to see ourselves more as God sees us, and then we catch some little glimpse of His designs with us, how each ordering of His Providence, each check to our desires, each failure of our hopes, is just fitted for us, and for something in our own spiritual state, which others know not of, and which, till then, we knew not. Until we come to this knowledge, we must take all in faith, believing, though we know not, the goodness of God towards us. As we know ourselves, we, thus far, know God.

E. B. PUSEY

JANUARY 12

Let the words of my mouth, and the meditation of my heart, be acceptable in Thy sight, O Lord, my strength, and my redeemer.

—Psalm 19:14

THE thoughts that in our hearts keep place,
   Lord, make a holy, heavenly throng,
And steep in innocence and grace
   The issue of each guarded tongue.

T. H. GILL

There is another kind of silence to be cultivated, besides that of the tongue as regards others. I mean silence as regards one's self,—restraining the imagination, not permitting it to dwell overmuch on what we have heard or said, not indulging in [daydreaming], whether of the past or future. Be sure that you have made no small progress in the spiritual life, when you can control your imagination, so as to fix it on the duty and occupation actually existing, to the exclusion of the crowd of thoughts which are perpetually sweeping across the mind. No doubt, you cannot prevent those thoughts from arising, but you can prevent yourself from dwelling on them; you can put them aside, you can check the self-complacency, or irritation, or earthly longings which feed them, and by the practice of such control of your thoughts you will attain that spirit of inward silence which draws the soul into a close [fellowship] with God.

JEAN N. GROU

JANUARY 13

Speak not evil one of another, brethren.
—James 4:2

Let all bitterness, and wrath, and anger, and clamor, and evil speaking, be put away from you, with all malice.
—Ephesians 4:31

⸙

IF aught good thou canst not say
   Of thy brother, foe, or friend,
Take thou, then, the silent way,
   Lest in word thou shouldst offend.
ANONYMOUS

⸙

If there is any person to whom you feel dislike, that is the person of whom you ought never to speak.

R. CECIL

To recognize with delight all high and generous and beautiful actions; to find a joy even in seeing the good qualities of your bitterest opponents, and to admire those qualities even in those with whom you have least sympathy,—be it either the Romanist or the Unitarian,—this is the only spirit which can heal the love of slander and of calumny.

F. W. ROBERTSON

JANUARY 14

Thy servants are ready to do whatsoever my lord the king shall appoint.

—2 Samuel 15:15

I LOVE to think that God appoints
   My portion day by day;
Events of life are in His hand,
   And I would only say,
Appoint them in Thine own good time,
   And in Thine own best way.

               A. L. WARING

    If we are really, and always, and equally ready to do whatsoever the King appoints, all the trials and vexations arising from any change in His appointments, great or small, simply do not exist. If He appoints me to work there, shall I lament that I am not to work here? If He appoints me to wait indoors to-day, am I to be annoyed because I am not to work out-of-doors? If I meant to *write* His messages this morning, shall I grumble because He sends interrupting visitors, rich or poor, to whom I am to *speak* them, or 'show kindness' for His sake, or at least obey His command, 'Be courteous'? If all my members are really at His disposal, why should I be put out if to-day's appointment is some simple work for my hands or errands for my feet, instead of some seemingly more important doing of head or tongue?

               F. R. HAVERGAL

JANUARY 15

For this is the will of God, even your sanctification.
—1 Thessalonians 4:3

BETWEEN us and Thyself remove
   Whatever hindrances may be,
That so our inmost heart may prove
   A holy temple, meet for Thee.

LATIN MANUSCRIPT OF
15TH CENTURY

Bear, in the presence of God, to know thyself. Then seek to know for what God sent thee into the world; how thou hast fulfilled it; art thou yet what God willed thee to be; what yet lacketh unto thee; what is God's will for thee *now;* what thing thou mayest *now* do, by His grace, to obtain His favour, and approve thyself unto Him. Say to Him, 'Teach me to do Thy will, for Thou art my God,' and He will say unto thy soul, 'Fear not; I am thy salvation.' He will speak peace unto thy soul; He will set thee in the way; He will bear thee above things of sense, and praise of man, and things which perish in thy grasp, and give thee, if but afar off, some glimpse of His own, unfading, unsetting, unperishing brightness and bliss and love.

E. B. PUSEY

JANUARY 16

God, even our Father, which hath loved us, and hath given us everlasting consolation, and good hope through grace, comfort your hearts, and stablish you in every good word and work.

—*2 Thessalonians 2:16, 17*

WHEN sorrow all our heart would ask,
We need not shun our daily task,
   And hide ourselves from calm;
The herbs we seek to heal our woe
Familiar by our path way grow,
   Our common air is balm.

J. KEBLE

Oh, when we turn away from some duty or some fellow-creature, saying that our hearts are too sick and sore with some great yearning of our own, we may often sever the line on which a divine message was coming to us. We shut out the man, and we shut out the angel who had sent him on to open the door. . . . There is a plan working in our lives; and if we keep our hearts quiet and our eyes open, it all works together; and, if we don't it all fights together, and goes on fighting till it comes right, somehow, somewhere.

ANNIE KEARY

JANUARY 17

Beloved, think it not strange concerning the fiery trial which is to try you, as though some strange thing happened unto you: but rejoice, inasmuch as ye are partakers of Christ's sufferings.

—1 Peter 4:12, 13

WE take with solemn thankfulness
Our burden up, nor ask it less,
And count it joy that even we
May suffer, serve, or wait for Thee,
   Whose will be done!

J. G. WHITTIER

Receive every inward and outward trouble, every disappointment, pain, and uneasiness, temptation, darkness, and desolation, with both thy hands, as a true opportunity and blessed occasion of dying to self, and entering into a fuller fellowship with thy self-denying, suffering Saviour. Look at no inward or outward trouble in any other view; reject every other thought about it; and then every kind of trial and distress will become the blessed day of thy prosperity. That state is best, which exerciseth the highest faith in, and fullest resignation to God.

WM. LAW

JANUARY 18

Thou shalt rejoice in every good thing which the Lord thy God hath given unto thee.
                                   —Deuteronomy 26:11

Rejoice evermore. In everything give thanks.
                                   —1 Thessalonians 5:16, 18

❧

GRAVE on thy heart each past 'red-letter day'!
Forget not all the sunshine of the way
By which the Lord hath led thee; answered prayers,
And joys unasked, strange blessings, lifted cares,
Grand promise-echoes! Thus thy life shall be
One record of His love and faithfulness to thee.

F. R. HAVERGAL

❧

Gratitude consists in a watchful, minute attention to the particulars of our state, and to the multitude of God's gifts, taken one by one. It fills us with a consciousness that God loves and cares for us, even to the least event and smallest need of life. It is a blessed thought, that from our childhood God has been laying His fatherly hands upon us, and always in benediction; that even the strokes of His Hands are blessings, and among the chiefest we have ever received. When this feeling is awakened, the heart beats with a pulse of thankfulness. Every gift has its return of praise. It awakens an unceasing daily converse with our Father,—He speaking to us by the descent of blessings, we to Him by the ascent of thanksgiving. And all our whole life is thereby drawn under the light of His countenance, and is filled with a gladness, serenity, and peace which only thankful hearts can know.

H. E. MANNING

JANUARY 19

Let the heart of them rejoice that seek the Lord.
—Psalm 105:3

The joy of the Lord is your strength.
—Nehemiah 8:10

BE Thou my Sun, my selfishness destroy,
Thy atmosphere of Love be all my joy;
Thy Presence be my sunshine ever bright,
My soul the little mote that lives but in Thy light.

GERHARD TERSTEEGEN

I do not know when I have had happier times in my soul, than when I have been sitting at work, with nothing before me but a candle and a white cloth, and hearing no sound but that of my own breath, with God in my soul and heaven in my eye. . . . I rejoice in being exactly what I am,—a creature capable of loving God, and who, as long as God lives, must be happy. I get up and look for a while out of the window, and gaze at the moon and stars, the work of an Almighty hand. I think of the grandeur of the universe, and then sit down, and think myself one of the happiest beings in it.

A POOR METHODIST WOMAN,
18TH CENTURY

JANUARY 20

The Lord taketh pleasure in His people: He will beautify the meek with salvation.

> —Psalm 149:4

SEND down Thy likeness from above.
   And let this my adorning be:
Clothe me with wisdom, patience, love,
   And lowliness and purity.

> JOACHIM LANGE

It is not in words explicable, with what divine lines and lights the exercise of godliness and charity will mould and gild the hardest and coldest countenance, neither to what darkness their departure will consign the loveliest. For there is not any virtue the exercise of which, even momentarily, will not impress a new fairness upon the features; neither of them only, but on the whole body the moral and intellectual faculties have operation. All the movements and gestures, however slight, are different in their modes according to the mind that governs them—and on the gentleness and decision of right feeling follows grace of actions, and, through continuance of this, grace of form.

> J. RUSKIN

There is no beautifier of complexion, or form, or behaviour, like the wish to scatter joy and not pain around us.

> R. W. EMERSON

JANUARY 21

Even the youths shall faint and be weary, and the young men shall utterly fall; but they that wait upon the Lord shall renew their strength; they shall mount up with wings as eagles; they shall run, and not be weary; and they shall walk and not faint.

—Isaiah 40:30, 31

LORD, with what courage and delight
   I do each thing,
When Thy least breath sustains my wing!
   I shine and move
   Like those above,
   And, with much gladness
   Quitting sadness,
Make me fair days of every night.

                H. VAUGHAN

Man, by living wholly in submission to [God's divine influence], becomes surrounded with, and creates for himself, internal pleasures infinitely greater than any he can otherwise attain to—a state of heavenly Beatitude.

                J. P. GREAVES

By persisting in a habit of self-denial, we shall, beyond what I can express, increase the inward powers of the mind, and shall produce that cheerfulness and greatness of spirit as will fit us for all good purposes. We shall not have lost pleasure, but *changed* it; the soul being then filled with its own intrinsic pleasures.

                HENRY MORE

JANUARY 22

Then shall we know, if we follow on to know the Lord.
—Hosea 6:3

AND, as the path of duty is made plain,
May grace be given that I may walk therein,
   Not like the hireling, for his selfish gain,
With backward glances and reluctant tread,
Making a merit of his coward dread,—
   But cheerful, in the light around me thrown,
   Walking as one to pleasant service led;
   Doing God's will as if it were my own,
Yet trusting not in mine, but in His strength alone!

J. G. WHITTIER

It is by doing our duty that we learn to do it. So long as men dispute whether or not a thing is their duty, they get never the nearer. Let them set ever so weakly about doing it, and the face of things alters. They find in themselves strength which they knew not of. Difficulties which it seemed to them they could not get over, disappear. For He accompanies it with the influences of His blessed Spirit, and each performance opens our minds for larger influxes of His grace, and places them in communion with Him.

E. B. PUSEY

That which is called considering what is our duty in a particular case, is very often nothing but endeavoring to explain it away.

BISHOP BUTLER

JANUARY 23

If thou draw out thy soul to the hungry, and satisfy the afflicted soul; then shall thy light rise in obscurity, and thy darkness be as the noonday; and the Lord shall guide thee continually.

—Isaiah 58:10, 11

———————— ❧ ————————

IF thou hast Yesterday thy duty done,
   And thereby cleared firm footing for To-day;
Whatever clouds make dark To-morrow's sun,
   Thou shalt not miss thy solitary way.

J. W. VON GOETHE

———————— ❧ ————————

O Lord, who art our Guide even unto death, grant us, I pray Thee, grace to follow Thee withersoever Thou goest. In little daily duties to which Thou callest us, bow down our wills to simple obedience, patience under pain or provocation, strict truthfulness of word and manner, humility, kindness; in great acts of duty or perfection, if Thou shouldest call us to them, uplift us to self-sacrifice, heroic courage, laying down of life for Thy truth's sake, or for a brother. Amen.

C. G. ROSSETTI

JANUARY 24

I will bless the Lord, who hath given me counsel.
—Psalm 16:7

Not slothful in business; fervent in spirit; serving the Lord.
—Romans 12:11

MINE be the reverent, listening love
   That waits all day on Thee,
With the service of a watchful heart
   Which no one else can see.

               A. L. WARING

   Nothing is small or great in God's sight; whatever He wills becomes great to us, however seemingly trifling. Once the voice of conscience tells us that He requires anything of us, we have no right to measure its importance. On the other hand, whatever He would not have us do, however important we may think it, is as nought to us. How do you know what you may lose by neglecting this duty, which you think so trifling, or the blessing which its faithful performance may bring? Be sure that if you do your very best in that which is laid upon you daily, you will not be left without sufficient help when some weightier occasion arises. Give yourself to Him, trust Him, fix your eye upon Him, listen to His voice, and then go on bravely and cheerfully.

               JEAN NICOLAS GROU

JANUARY 25

If ye know these things, happy are ye if ye do them.
—John 13:17

Therefore to him that knoweth to do good, and doeth it not,
to him it is sin.

—James 4:17

WE cannot kindle when we will
   The fire that in the heart resides,
The spirit bloweth and is still,
   In mystery our soul abides:
But tasks in hours of insight willed
Can be through hours of gloom fulfilled.

MATTHEW ARNOLD

Hurt not your conscience with any known sin.

S. RUTHERFORD

Deep-rooted customs, though wrong, are not easily altered;
but it is the duty of all to be firm in that which they certainly
know is right for them.

JOHN WOOLMAN

He often acts unjustly who does not do a certain thing; not
only he who does a certain thing.

MARCUS ANTONINUS

Every duty we omit obscures some truth we should have
known.

JOHN RUSKIN

JANUARY 26

O the depth of the riches both of the wisdom and knowledge of God! how unsearchable are His judgments, and His ways past finding out!
> *—Romans 11:33*

It doth not yet appear what we shall be.
> *—1 John 3:2*

NO star is ever lost we once have seen,
We always may be what we might have been.
Since Good, though only thought, has life and breath,
God's life—can always be redeemed from death;
And evil, in its nature, is decay,
And any hour can blot it all away;
The hopes that lost in some far distance seem,
May be the truer life, and this the dream.

A. A. PROCTER

St Bernard has said: 'Man, if thou desirest a noble and holy life, and unceasingly prayest to God for it, if thou continue constant in this thy desire, it will be granted unto thee without fail, even if only in the day or hour of thy death. If God should not give it to thee then, thou shalt find it in Him in eternity: of this be assured.' Therefore do not relinquish your desire, though it be not fulfilled immediately, or though ye may swerve from your aspirations, or even forget them for a time. . . . The love and aspiration which once really existed live forever before God, and in Him ye shall find the fruit thereof; that is, to all eternity it shall be better for you than if you had never felt them.

J. TAULER 1290-1361

JANUARY 27

For thus saith the high and lofty One that inhabiteth eterni-
ty, whose name is Holy; I dwell in the high and holy place,
with him also that is of a contrite and humble spirit, to revive
the spirit of the humble, and to revive the heart of the contrite
ones.

—*Isaiah 57:15*

WITHOUT an end or bound
Thy life lives all outspread in light;
   Our lives feel Thy life all around,
Making our weakness strong, our darkness bright;
Yet is it neither wilderness nor sea,
But the calm gladness of a full eternity.

F. W. FABER

O Truth who art Eternity! And Love who art Truth! And Eternity who art Love! Thou art my God, to Thee do I sigh night and day. When I first knew Thee, Thou liftedst me up, that I might see there was somewhat for me to see, and that I was not yet such as to see. And Thou streaming forth Thy beams of light upon me most strongly, didst beat back the weakness of my sight, and I trembled with love and awe: and I perceived myself to be far off from Thee in the region of unlikeness.

ST. AUGUSTINE

JANUARY 28

O fear the Lord, ye His saints; for there is no want to them that fear Him.

—Psalm 34:9

Thou openest Thine hand, and satisfiest the desire of every living thing.

—Psalm 145:16

WHAT Thou shalt to-day provide,
   Let me as a child receive;
What to-morrow may betide,
   Calmly to Thy wisdom leave.
'Tis enough that Thou wilt care;
Why should I the burden bear?

J. NEWTON

Have we found that anxiety about possible consequences increased the clearness of our judgment, made us wiser and braver in meeting the present, and arming ourselves for the future? . . . If we had prayed for this day's bread, and left the next to itself—if we had not huddled our days together, not allotting to each its appointed task, but ever deferring that to the future, and drawing upon the future for its own troubles, which must be met when they come whether we have anticipated them or not—we should have found a simplicity and honesty in our lives, a capacity for work, an enjoyment in it to which we are now, for the most part, strangers.

F. D. MAURICE

JANUARY 29

*I the L*ORD *will hold thy right hand, saying unto thee, Fear not; I will help thee.*
$$—Isaiah 41:13$$

Show Thy marvellous loving-kindness, O Thou that savest by Thy right hand them which put their trust in Thee.
$$—Psalm 17:7$$

I TAKE Thy hand, and fears grow still;
   Behold Thy face, and doubts remove;
Who would not yield his wavering will
   To perfect Truth and boundless Love?
                S. JOHNSON

Do not look forward to the changes and chances of this life in fear; rather look to them with full hope that, as they arise, God, whose you are, will deliver you out of them. He has kept you hitherto,—do you but hold fast to His dear hand, and He will lead you safely through all things; and, when you cannot stand, He will bear you in His arms. Do not look forward to what may happen to-morrow; the same everlasting Father who cares for you today, will take care of you to-morrow, and every day. Either He will shield you from suffering, or He will give you unfailing strength to bear it. Be at peace then, and put aside all anxious thoughts and imaginations.

FRANCIS DE SALES

JANUARY 30

If I take the wings of the morning, and dwell in the uttermost parts of the sea; even there shall Thy hand lead me, and Thy right hand shall hold me.

—*Psalm 139:9, 10*

———————— ✦ ————————

I CANNOT lose Thee! Still in Thee abiding,
   The end is clear, how wide soe'er I roam;
The Hand that holds the worlds my steps is guiding,
   And I must rest at last in Thee, my home.

E. SCUDDER

———————— ✦ ————————

How can we come to perceive this direct leading of God? By a careful looking at home, and abiding within the gates of thy own soul. Therefore, let a man be at home in his own heart, and cease from his restless chase of and search after outward things. If he is thus at home while on earth, he will surely come to see what there is to do at home,—what God commands him inwardly without means, and also outwardly by the help of means. Then let him surrender himself, and follow God along whatever path his loving Lord thinks fit to lead him: whether it be to contemplation or action, to usefulness or enjoyment; whether in sorrow or in joy, let him follow on. And if God do not give him thus to feel His hand in all things, let him still simply yield himself up, and go without, for God's sake, out of love, and still press forward.

J. TAULER

JANUARY 31

In all thy ways acknowledge Him, and He shall direct thy paths.

—Proverbs 3:6

He leadeth me.

—Psalm 23:2

IN 'pastures green'? Not always; sometimes He
Who knoweth best, in kindness leadeth me
In weary ways, where heavy shadows be.

So, whether on the hill-tops high and fair
I dwell, or in the sunless valleys, where
The shadows lie, what matter? He is there.

HENRY H. BARRY

The Shepherd knows what pastures are best for his sheep, and they must not question nor doubt, but trustingly follow Him. Perhaps He sees that the best pastures for some of us are to be found in the midst of opposition or of earthly trials. If He leads you there, you may be sure they are green for you, and you will grow and be made strong by feeding there. Perhaps He sees that the best waters for you to walk beside will be raging waves of trouble and sorrow. If this should be the case, He will make them still waters for you, and you must go and lie down beside them, and let them have all their blessed influences upon you.

H. W. S.

FEBRUARY 1

Now the God of patience and consolation grant you to be like-minded one toward another, according to Christ Jesus.
—Romans 15:5

Let patience have her perfect work.
—James 1:4

MAKE me patient, kind, and gentle,
　　Day by day;
Teach me how to live more nearly
　　As I pray.

　　　　　　　　SHARPE'S MAGAZINE

The exercise of patience involves a continual practice of the presence of God. We may come at any moment from an almost heroic display of good temper, and [find that] it is a short road to unselfishness, for nothing is left to self; all that seems to belong most intimately to self, to be self's private property, such as time, home, and rest, are invaded by these continual trials of patience. The family is full of such opportunities.

　　　　　　　　F. W. FABER

FEBRUARY 2

Now we exhort you, brethren, warn them that are unruly, comfort the feeble-minded, support the weak, be patient toward all men.

—*1 Thessalonians 5:14*

THE little worries which we meet each day
May lie as stumbling-blocks across our way,
Or we may make them stepping-stones to be
   Of grace, O Lord, to Thee.

A. E. HAMILTON

We must be continually sacrificing our own wills, as opportunity serves, to the will of others; bearing, without notice, sights and sounds that annoy us; setting about this or that task, when we had far rather be doing something very different; persevering in it, often, when we are thoroughly tired of it; keeping company for duty's sake, when it would be a great joy to us to be by ourselves. [This is] besides all the trifling untoward accidents of life; bodily pain and weakness long continued, and perplexing us often when it does not amount to illness; losing what we value, missing what we desire; disappointment in other persons, wilfulness, unkindness, ingratitude, folly, in cases where we least expect it.

J. KEBLE

FEBRUARY 3

Search me, O God, and know my heart; try me, and know my thoughts; and see if there be any wicked way in me, and lead me in the way everlasting.

—Psalm 139:23, 24

SAVE us from the evil tongue,
From the heart that thinketh wrong,
From the sins, whate'er they be,
That divide the soul from Thee.

ANONYMOUS

Such as are thy habitual thoughts, such also will be the character of thy mind; for the soul is dyed by the thoughts. Dye it then with a continuous series of such thoughts as these: for instance, that where a man can live, there he can also live well.

MARCUS ANTONINUS

Who is there that sets himself to the task of steadily watching his thoughts for the space of one hour, with the view of preserving his mind in a simple, humble, healthful condition, but will speedily discern in the multiform, self-reflecting, self-admiring emotions, which, like locusts, are ready to 'eat up every green thing in his land,' a state as much opposed to simplicity and humility as night is to day?

M. A. KELTY

FEBRUARY 4

If any man offend not in word, the same is a perfect man,
and able also to bridle the whole body.
> *—James 3:2*

Set a watch, O Lord, before my mouth; keep the door of my
lips.
> *—Psalm 141:3*

WHAT! never speak one evil word,
   Or rash, or idle, or unkind!
Oh, how shall I, most gracious Lord,
   This mark of true perfection find?
> C. WESLEY

When we remember our temptations to give quick indulgence to disappointment or irritation or unsympathizing weariness, . . . and how hard a thing it is from day to day to meet our fellow-men, our neighbours, or even our own households, in all moods, in all discordances between the world without us and the frames within, in all states of health, of solicitude, of preoccupation, and show no signs of impatience, ungentleness, or unobservant self-absorption,—with only kindly feeling finding expression and ungenial feeling at least inwardly imprisoned;—we shall be ready to acknowledge that the man who has thus attained is master of himself, and in graciousness of his power is fashioned upon the style of a Perfect Man.

J. H. THOM

FEBRUARY 5

Blessed are they that keep judgment, and he that doeth righteousness at all times.

—Psalm 106:3

Thou shalt be steadfast, and shalt not fear: because thou shalt forget thy misery, and remember it as waters that pass away.

—Job 11:15, 16

IN the bitter waves of woe,
   Beaten and tossed about
By the sullen winds that blow
   From the desolate shores of doubt,
Where the anchors that faith has cast
   Are dragging in the gale,
I am quietly holding fast
   To the things that cannot fail.

WASHINGTON GLADDEN

In the darkest hour through which a human soul can pass, whatever else is doubtful, this at least is certain. If there be no God and no future state, yet, even then, it is better to be generous than selfish, better to be chaste than licentious, better to be true than false, better to be brave than to be a coward. Blessed beyond all earthly blessedness is the man who, in the tempestuous darkness of the soul, has dared to hold fast to these venerable landmarks. Thrice blessed is he, who, when all is drear and cheerless within and without, when his teachers terrify him, and his friends shrink from him, has obstinately clung to moral good. Thrice blessed, because *his* night shall pass into clear, bright day.

F. W. ROBERTSON

FEBRUARY 6

Whoso putteth his trust in the Lord shall be safe.
                    —Proverbs 29:25

*I will cry unto God most high; unto God, that performeth
all things for me.*

                    —Psalm 57:2

ONLY thy restless heart keep still,
  And wait in cheerful hope; content
To take whate'er His gracious will,
  His all-discerning love hath sent;
Nor doubt our inmost wants are known
  To Him who chose us for His own.
                    G. NEUMARCK

God has brought us into this time; He, and not ourselves or
some dark demon. If we are not fit to cope with that which He
has prepared for us, we should have been utterly unfit for any
condition that we imagine for ourselves. In this time we are to
live and wrestle, and in no other. Let us humbly, tremblingly,
manfully look at it, and we shall not wish that the sun could go
back its ten degrees, or that we could go back with it. If easy
times are departed, it is that the difficult times may make us
more in earnest; that they may teach us not to depend upon ourselves. If easy belief is impossible, it is that we may learn what
belief is, and in whom it is to be placed.

                    F. D. MAURICE

FEBRUARY 7

Obey my voice, and I will be your God, and ye shall be my people: and walk ye in all the ways that I have commanded you, that it may be well unto you.

—Jeremiah 7:23

AND oft, when in my heart was heard
Thy timely mandate, I deferred
The task in smoother walks to stray;
But thee I now would serve more strictly, if I may.

W. WORDSWORTH

Pray Him to give you what Scripture calls 'an honest and good heart,' or 'a perfect heart;' and, without waiting, begin at once to obey Him with the best heart you have. Any obedience is better than none. You have to seek His face; obedience is the only way of seeing Him. All your duties are obediences. To do what He bids is to obey Him, and to obey Him is to approach Him. Every act of obedience is an approach—an approach to Him who is not far off, though He seems so, but close behind this visible screen of things which hides Him from us.

J. H. NEWMAN

As soon as we lay ourselves entirely at His feet, we have enough light given us to guide our own steps; as the foot-soldier, who hears nothing of the councils that determine the course of the great battle he is in, hears plainly enough the word of command which he must himself obey.

GEORGE ELIOT

FEBRUARY 8

He leadeth me beside the still waters. He restoreth my soul;
He leadeth me in the paths of righteousness for His name's
sake.

—Psalm 23:2, 3

HE leads me where the waters glide,
  The waters soft and still,
And homeward He will gently guide
  My wandering heart and will.

J. KEBLE

Out of obedience and devotion arises an habitual faith, which
makes Him, though unseen, a part of all our life. He will guide
us in a sure path, though it be a rough one: though shadows
hang upon it, yet He will be with us. He will bring us home at
last. Through much trial it may be, and weariness, in much fear
and fainting of heart, in much sadness and loneliness, in griefs
that the world never knows, and under burdens that the nearest
never suspect. Yet He will suffice for all. By His eye or by His
voice He will guide us, if we be docile and gentle; by His staff
and by His rod, if we wander or are wilful. Any how, and by all
means, He will bring us to His rest.

H. E. MANNING

FEBRUARY 9

*I was afraid, and went and hid thy talent in the earth: lo,
there thou hast that is thine.*

—*Matthew 25:25*

TIME was, I shrank from what was right,
    From fear of what was wrong;
I would not brave the sacred fight,
    Because the foe was strong.

But now I cast that finer sense
    And sorer shame aside;
Such dread of sin was indolence,
    Such aim at heaven was pride.

J. H. NEWMAN

If he falls into some error, he does not fret over it, but rising
up with a humble spirit, he goes on his way anew rejoicing.
Were he to fall a hundred times in the day, he would not
despair,—he would rather cry out lovingly to God, appealing to
His tender pity. The really devout man has a horror of evil, but
he has a still greater love of that which is good; he is more set on
doing what is right, than avoiding what is wrong. Generous,
large-hearted, he is not afraid of danger in serving God, and
would rather run the risk of doing His will imperfectly than not
strive to serve Him lest he fail in the attempt.

JEAN NICOLAS GROU

FEBRUARY 10

We have waited for Him, and He will save us: this is the Lord; we have waited for Him, we will be glad in His salvation.

—*Isaiah 25:9*

———————— ⌘ ————————

BLEST are the humble souls that wait
   With sweet submission to His will;
Harmonious all their passions move,
   And in the midst of storms are still.

P. DODDRIDGE

———————— ⌘ ————————

Do not be discouraged at your faults; bear with yourself in correcting them, as you would with your neighbour. Lay aside this ardour of mind, which exhausts your body, and leads you to commit errors. Accustom yourself gradually to carry prayer into all your daily occupations. Speak, move, work, in peace, as if you were in prayer, as indeed you ought to be. Do everything without excitement, by the spirit of grace. As soon as you perceive your natural impetuosity gliding in, retire quietly within. . . . listen to the leadings of grace, then say and do nothing but what the Holy Spirit shall put in your heart. You will find that you will become more tranquil, that your words will be fewer and more effectual, and that, with less effort, you will accomplish more good.

FÉNELON

FEBRUARY 11

I have finished the work which Thou gavest me to do.
—John 17:4

She hath done what she could.
—Mark 14:8

HE who God's will has borne and done,
   And his own restless longings stilled;
What else he does, or has foregone,
   His mission he has well fulfilled.

FROM THE GERMAN

Cheered by the presence of God, I will do at each moment, without anxiety, according to the strength which He shall give me, the work that His Providence assigns me. I will leave the rest without concern; it is not my affair. I ought to consider the duty to which I am called each day, as the work that God has given me to do, and to apply myself to it in a manner worthy of His glory, that is to say, with exactness and in peace. I must neglect nothing; I must be violent about nothing.

FÉNELON

It is thy duty oftentimes to do what thou wouldst not; thy duty, too, to leave undone what thou wouldst do.

THOMAS À KEMPIS

FEBRUARY 12

Blessed be the Lord, who daily loadeth us with benefits.
—Psalm 68:19

Nor trust in uncertain riches, but in the living God, who giveth us richly all things to enjoy.
—1 Timothy 6:17

SOURCE of my life's refreshing springs,
   Whose presence in my heart sustains me,
Thy love ordains me pleasant things,
   Thy mercy orders all that pains me.
A. L. WARING

And to be true, and speak my soul, when I survey the occurrences of my life, and call into account the finger of God, I can perceive nothing but an abyss and mass of mercies, either in general to mankind, or in particular to myself. Whether out of the prejudice of my affection, or an inverting [due to] His mercies, I know not; but those [circumstances] which others term crosses, afflictions, judgments, misfortunes, to me who inquire farther into them than their visible effects, they both appear, and have ever proved [to be], the secret and generous favours of His affection.

SIR T. BROWNE

FEBRUARY 13

The will of the Lord be done.
—Acts 21:14

Let Him do to me as seemeth good unto Him.
—2 Samuel 15:26

TO have, each day, the thing I wish,
　　Lord, that seems best to me;
But not to have the thing I wish,
　　Lord, that seems best to Thee.
Most truly, then, Thy will is done,
　　When mine, O Lord, is crossed,
'Tis good to see my plans o'erthrown,
　　My ways in Thine all lost.

H. BONAR

O Lord, Thou knowest what is best for us; let this or that be done, as Thou shalt please. Give what Thou wilt, and how much Thou wilt, and when Thou wilt. Deal with me as Thou thinkest good. Set me where Thou wilt, and deal with me in all things just as Thou wilt. Behold, I am Thy servant, prepared for all things: for I desire not to live unto myself, but unto Thee; and oh, that I could do it worthily and perfectly!

THOMAS À KEMPIS

Dare to look up to God, and say, 'Make use of me for the future as Thou wilt. I am of the same mind; I am one with Thee. I refuse nothing which seems good to Thee. Lead me whither Thou wilt, clothe me in whatever dress Thou wilt. Is it Thy will that I should be in a public or a private condition, dwell here, or be banished, be poor or rich? Under all these circumstances, I will testify unto Thee before men.'

EPICTETUS

FEBRUARY 14

I would have you without carefulness.
—1 Corinthians 7:32

———— ❧❧ ————

O LORD, how happy should we be
If we could cast our care on Thee,
   If we from self could rest;
And feel at heart that One above,
In perfect wisdom, perfect love,
   Is working for the best.

J. ANSTICE

———— ❧❧ ————

Cast *all* thy care on God. See that all thy cares be such as thou canst cast on God, and then hold none back. Never brood over thyself; never stop short in thyself; but cast thy whole self, even this very care which distresseth thee, upon God. Be not anxious about little things, if thou wouldst learn to trust God with thine all. Act upon faith in little things; commit thy daily cares and anxieties to Him; and He will strengthen thy faith for any greater trials. Rather, give thy whole self into God's hands, and so trust Him to take care of thee in all lesser things, as being His, for His own sake, whose thou art.

E. B. PUSEY

FEBRUARY 15

If ye fulfil the royal law according to the Scripture, Thou shalt love thy neighbour as thyself, ye do well.
—James 2:8

COME, children, let us go!
　We travel hand in hand;
Each in his brother finds his joy
　In this wild stranger land.
The strong be quick to raise
　The weaker when they fall;
Let love and peace and patience bloom
　In ready help for all.

G. TERSTEEGEN

It is a sad weakness in us, after all, that the thought of a man's death hallows him anew to us; as if life were not sacred too,—as if it were comparatively a light thing to fail in love and reverence to the brother who has to climb the whole toilsome steep with us, and all our tears and tenderness were due to the one who is spared that hard journey.

GEORGE ELIOT

Would we codify the laws that should reign in households, and whose daily transgression annoys and mortifies us, and degrades our household life,—we must learn to adorn every day with sacrifices. Good manners are made up of petty sacrifices. Temperance, courage, love, are made up of the same jewels. Listen to every prompting of honour.

R. W. EMERSON

FEBRUARY 16

Serve Him with a perfect heart, and with a willing mind.
—1 Chronicles 28:9

AND if some things I do not ask,
    In my cup of blessing be,
I would have my spirit filled the more
    With grateful love to Thee,—
More careful,—not to serve Thee much,
    But to please Thee perfectly.

A. L. WARING

Little things come daily, hourly, within our reach, and they are not less calculated to set forward our growth in holiness, than are the greater occasions which occur but rarely. Moreover, fidelity in trifles, and an earnest seeking to please God in little matters, is a test of real devotion and love. Let your aim be to please our dear Lord perfectly in little things, and to attain a spirit of childlike simplicity and dependence. In proportion as self-love and self-confidence are weakened, and our will bowed to that of God, so will hindrances disappear, the internal troubles and contests which harassed the soul vanish, and it will be filled with peace and tranquility.

JEAN NICOLAS GROU

FEBRUARY 17

My brethren, count it all joy when ye fall into divers temptations [or 'trials'], knowing this, that the trying of your faith worketh patience.

—James 1:2, 3

❧~❧

FOR patience, when the rough winds blow!
　For patience, when our hopes are fading,—
When visible things all backward go,
　And nowhere seems the power of aiding!
God still enfolds thee with His viewless hand,
　And leads thee surely to the Fatherland.

N. L. FROTHINGHAM,
from the German

❧~❧

We have need of patience with ourselves and with others;—with those below, and those above us, and with our own equals; with those who love us and those who love us not; for the greatest things and for the least; against sudden inroads of trouble, and under our daily burdens; disappointments as to the weather, or the breaking of the heart; in the weariness of the body, or the wearing of the soul; in our own failure of duty, or others' failure toward us; in every-day wants, or in the aching of sickness or the decay of age; in disappointment, bereavement, losses, injuries, reproaches; in heaviness of the heart; or its sickness amid delayed hopes. In all these things, from childhood's little troubles to the martyr's sufferings, patience is the grace of God, whereby we endure evil for the love of God.

E. B. PUSEY

FEBRUARY 18

It is good for me that I have been afflicted, that I might learn Thy statutes.

—Psalm 119:71

But though He cause grief, yet will He have compassion, according to the multitude of His mercies.

—Lamentations 3:32

AND yet these days of dreariness are sent us from above;
They do not come in anger, but in faithfulness and love;
They come to teach us lessons which bright ones could not
    yield,
And to leave us blest and thankful when their purpose is
    fulfilled.

ANONYMOUS

Heed not distressing thoughts when they rise ever so strongly in thee; nay, though they have entered thee, fear them not, but be still awhile, not believing in the power which thou feelest they have over thee, and it will fall on a sudden. It is good for thy spirit, and greatly to thy advantage to be much and variously exercised by the Lord. Thou dost not know what the Lord hath already done, and what He is yet doing for thee by them.

I. PENINGTON

Why should I start at the plough of my Lord, that maketh deep furrows on my soul? I know He is no idle husbandman, He purposeth a crop.

S. RUTHERFORD

FEBRUARY 19

My meat is to do the will of Him that sent me, and to finish His work.

—John 4:34

    I AM glad to think
I am not bound to make the world go right;
But only to discover and to do,
With cheerful heart, the work that God appoints.
    I will trust in Him,
That He can hold His own; and I will take
His will, above the work He sendeth me,
To be my chiefest good.

J. INGELOW

Don't object that your duties are so insignificant; they are to be reckoned infinite significance, and alone important to you. Were it but the more perfect regulation of your apartments, the sorting-away of your clothes and trinkets, the arranging of your papers,—'Whatsoever thy hand findeth to do, *do it* with all thy might,' and all thy worth and constancy. Much more, if your duties are of evidently higher, wider scope; if you have brothers, sisters, a father, a mother, weigh earnestly what claim does lie upon you, on behalf of each, and consider it as the one thing needful, to pay *them* more and more honestly and nobly what you owe. What matter how miserable one is, if one can do that? That is the sure and steady disconnexion and extinction of whatsoever miseries one has in this world.

T. CARLYLE

FEBRUARY 20

Let us not therefore judge one another any more: but judge this rather, that no man put a stumblingblock, or an occasion to fall, in his brother's way.
—Romans 14:13

Them that were entering in, ye hindered.
—Luke 11:52

MY mind was ruffled with small cares to-day,
And I said pettish words, and did not keep
Long-suffering patience well, and now how deep
My trouble for this sin! in vain I weep
For foolish words I never can unsay.

H. S. SUTTON

A vexation arises, and our expressions of impatience hinder others from taking it patiently. Disappointment, ailment, or even weather depresses us; and our look or tone of depression hinders others from maintaining a cheerful and thankful spirit. We say an unkind thing, and another is hindered in learning the holy lessons of charity that thinketh no evil. We say a provoking thing, and our sister or brother is hindered in that day's effort to be meek. How sadly, too, we may hinder without word or act! For wrong feeling is more infectious than wrong doing; especially the various phases of ill temper,—gloominess, touchiness, discontent, irritability,—do we not know how catching these are?

F. R. HAVERGAL

FEBRUARY 21

If ye then, being evil, know how to give good gifts unto your children, how much more shall your Father which is in heaven give good gifts to them that ask Him.
—*Matthew 7:11*

FOR His great love has compassed
    Our nature, and our need
We know not; but He knoweth,
    And He will bless indeed.
    Therefore, O heavenly Father,
    Give what is best to me;
And take the wants unanswered,
    As offerings made to Thee.

ANONYMOUS

Whatsoever we ask which is not for our good, He will keep it back from us. And surely in this there is no less of love than in the granting what we desire as we ought. Will not the same love which prompts you to give a good, prompt you to keep back an evil thing? If, in our blindness, not knowing what to ask, we pray for things which would turn in our hands to sorrow and death, will not our Father, out of His very love, deny us? How awful would be our lot, if our wishes should straightway pass into realities; if we were endowed with a power to bring about all that we desire; if the inclinations of our will were followed by fulfillment of our hasty wishes, and sudden longings were always granted. One day we shall bless Him, not more for what He has granted than for what He has denied.

H. E. MANNING

FEBRUARY 22

Be careful for nothing; but in everything by prayer and sup-
plication with thanksgiving let your requests be made known
unto God.

—Philippians 4:6

WE tell Thee of our care,
Of the sore burden, pressing day by day,
And in the light and pity of Thy face,
   The burden melts away.
   We breathe our secret wish,
The importunate longing which no man may see;
We ask it humbly, or, more restful still,
   We leave it all to Thee.

SUSAN COOLIDGE

That prayer which does not succeed in moderating our wish,
in changing the passionate desire into still submission, the anxious, tumultuous expectation into silent surrender, is no true
prayer, and proves that we have not the spirit of true prayer.
That life is most holy in which there is least of petition and
desire, and most of waiting upon God; that in which petition
most often passes into thanksgiving. Pray till prayer makes you
forget your own wish, and leave it or merge it in God's will. The
Divine wisdom has given us prayer, not as a means whereby to
obtain the good things of earth, but as a means whereby we
learn to do without them; not as a means whereby we escape
evil, but as a means whereby we become strong to meet it.

F. W. ROBERTSON

FEBRUARY 23

Let the Lord do that which is good in His sight.
—1 Chronicles 19:13

Let Thy mercy, O Lord, be upon us, according as we hope in Thee.

—Psalm 33:22

I CANNOT feel
That all is well, when darkening clouds conceal
   The shining sun;
   But then, I know
He lives and loves; and say, since it is so,
   Thy will be done.

S. G. BROWNING

No felt evil or defect becomes divine until it is inevitable; and only when resistance to it is exhausted and hope has fled, does surrender cease to be premature. The hardness of our task lies *here;* that we have to strive against the grievous things of life, while hope remains, as if they were evil; and then, when the stroke has fallen, to accept them from the hand of God, and doubt not they are good. But to the loving, trusting heart all things are possible; and even this instant change, from over-strained will to sorrowful repose, from fullest resistance to complete surrender, is realized without convulsion.

MARTINEAU

FEBRUARY 24

*These things I have spoken unto you that in me ye might
have peace. In the world ye shall have tribulation: but be of
good cheer; I have overcome the world.*

—John 16:33

O THOU, the primal fount of life and peace,
   Who shedd'st Thy breathing quiet all around,
In me command that pain and conflict cease,
   And turn to music every jarring sound.

J. STERLING

Accustom yourself to unreasonableness and injustice. Abide in
peace in the presence of God, who sees all these evils more
clearly than you do, and who permits them. Be content with
doing with calmness the little which depends upon yourself, and
let all else be to you as if it were not.

FÉNELON

It is rare when injustice, or slights patiently borne, do not
leave the heart at the close of the day filled with marvellous joy
and peace.

GOLD DUST

FEBRUARY 25

*But now thus saith the Lord that created thee, O Jacob, and
He that formed thee, O Israel, Fear not; for I have redeemed
thee, I have called thee by thy name; thou art mine.*
—Isaiah 43:1

THOU art as much His care as if beside
   Nor man nor angel lived in heaven or earth;
Thus sunbeams pour alike their glorious tide,
   To light up worlds, or wake an insect's mirth.
             J. KEBLE

God beholds thee individually, whoever thou art. 'He calls
thee by thy name.' He sees thee, and understands thee. He
knows what is in thee, all thy own peculiar feelings and
thoughts, thy dispositions and likings, thy strength and thy weakness. He views thee in thy day of rejoicing and thy day of sorrow. He sympathizes in thy hopes and in thy temptations; He
interests himself in all thy anxieties and thy remembrances, in all
the risings and fallings of thy spirit. He compasses thee round,
and bears thee in His arms; He takes thee up and sets thee
down. Thou dost not love thyself better than He loves thee.
Thou canst not shrink from pain more than He dislikes thy bearing it; and if He puts it on thee, it is as thou wilt put it on thyself,
if thou art wise, for a greater good afterwards.

              J. H. NEWMAN

FEBRUARY 26

The Lord is nigh unto all them that call upon Him, to all that call upon Him in truth.

—Psalm 145:18

I sought the Lord, and He heard me, and delivered me from all my fears.

—Psalm 34:4

BE Thou, O Rock of Ages, nigh!
　So shall each murmuring thought be gone;
And grief and fear and care shall fly,
　As clouds before the mid-day sun.
　　　　　　C. WESLEY

Take courage, and turn your troubles, which are without remedy, into material or spiritual progress. Often turn to our Lord, who is watching you, poor frail little being as you are, amid your labours and distractions. He sends you help, and blesses your affliction. This thought should enable you to bear your troubles patiently and gently, for love of Him who only allows you to be tried for your own good. Raise your heart continually to God, seek His aid, and let the foundation stone of your consolation be your happiness in being His. All vexations and annoyances will be comparatively unimportant while you know that you have such a Friend, such a Stay, such a Refuge. May God be ever in your heart.

FRANCIS DE SALES

FEBRUARY 27

Trust in the Lord, and do good; so shalt thou dwell in the land, and verily thou shalt be fed.

—Psalm 37:3

BUILD a little fence of trust
    Around to-day;
Fill the space with loving work,
    And therein stay;
Look not through the sheltering bars
    Upon to-morrow,
God will help thee bear what comes,
    Of joy or sorrow.

MARY FRANCES BUTTS

Let us bow our souls and say, 'Behold the handmaid of the Lord!' Let us lift up our hearts and ask, 'Lord, what wouldst thou have me to do?' Then light from the opened heaven shall stream on our daily task, revealing the grains of gold, where yesterday all seemed dust. A hand shall sustain us and our daily burden, so that, smiling at yesterday's fears, we shall say, *'This is easy, this is light;'* every 'lion in the way,' as we come up to it, shall be seen chained, and leave open the gates of the Palace Beautiful. And to us, even to us, feeble and fluctuating as we are, ministries shall be assigned, and through our hands blessings shall be conveyed in which the spirits of just men made perfect might delight.

ELIZABETH CHARLES

FEBRUARY 28

*Beloved, let us love one another: for love is of God; and
every one that loveth is born of God, and knoweth God.*
—1 John 4:7

GIRT with the love of God on every side,
Breathing that love as heaven's own healing air,
I work or wait, still following my Guide,
Braving each foe, escaping every snare.

HORATIUS BONAR

The Spirit of Love, wherever it is, is its own blessing and happiness, because it is the truth and reality of God in the soul. Therefore [it] is in the same joy of life, and is the same good to itself everywhere and on every occasion. Would you know the blessing of all blessings? It is this God of love dwelling in your soul, and killing every root of bitterness, which is the pain and torment of every earthly, selfish love. For all wants are satisfied, all disorders of nature are removed, no life is any longer a burden, every day is a day of peace, everything you meet becomes a help to you, because everything you see or do is all done in the sweet, gentle element of Love.

WM. LAW

FEBRUARY 29

Unto you that fear my name shall the Sun of Righteousness arise with healing in his wings.
—Malachi 4:2

O send out Thy light and Thy truth; let them lead me.
—Psalm 43:3

OPEN our eyes, thou Sun of life and gladness,
   That we may see that glorious world of Thine!
It shines for us in vain, while drooping sadness
   Enfolds us here like mist; come, Power benign,
     Touch our chilled hearts with vernal smile,
     Our wintry course do Thou beguile.
Nor by the wayside ruins let us mourn,
Who have th' eternal towers for our appointed bourn.
              J. KEBLE

Because all those scattered rays of beauty and loveliness which we behold spread up and down over all the world, are only the emanations of that inexhausted light which is above. Therefore should we love them all in that, and climb up always by those sunbeams unto the eternal Father of lights. We should look upon Him, and take from Him the pattern of our lives, and always eyeing Him, should, as Hierocles speaks, 'polish and shape our souls into the clearest resemblance of Him;' and in all our behaviour in this world (that great temple of His) deport ourselves decently and reverently, with that humility, meekness, and modesty that becomes His house.

              DR. JOHN SMITH, D. 1652

MARCH 1

Take no thought for your life, what ye shall eat, or what ye shall drink, nor yet for your body, what ye shall put on.
                          Matthew 6:25

ONE there lives whose guardian eye
Guides our earthly destiny;
One there lives, who, Lord of all,
Keeps His children lest they fall;
Pass we, then, in love and praise
Trusting Him through all our days,
Free from doubt and faithless sorrow,—
God provideth for the morrow.

R. HEBER

It has been well said that no man ever sank under the burden of the day. It is when to-morrow's burden is added to the burden of to-day that the weight is more than a man can bear. Never load yourselves so, my friends. If you find yourselves so loaded, at least remember this: it is your own doing, not God's. He begs you to leave the future to Him, and mind the present.

G. MACDONALD

MARCH 2

But to do good and to communicate forget not: for with such sacrifices God is well pleased.
—Hebrews 13:16

For this is the message that ye heard from the beginning, that we should love one another.
—1 John 3:11

BE useful where thou livest, that they may
Both want and wish thy pleasing presence still.
   . . . Find out men's wants and will,
And meet them there. All worldly joys go less
To the one joy of doing kindness.
                    G. HERBERT

Let the weakest, let the humblest remember, that in his daily course he can, if he will, shed around him almost a heaven. Kindly words, sympathizing attentions, watchfulness against wounding men's sensitiveness,—these cost very little, but they are priceless in their value. Are they not almost the staple of our daily happiness? From hour to hour, from moment to moment, we are supported, blest, by small kindnesses.

                F. W. ROBERTSON

Small kindness, small courtesies, small considerations, habitually practiced in our social [interaction], give a greater charm to the character than the display of great talents and accomplishments.

                M. A. KELTY

MARCH 3

I made haste, and delayed not to keep Thy commandments.
—Psalm 119:60

Ye know not what shall be on the morrow.
—James 4:14

    NEVER delay
To do the duty which the hour brings,
Whether it be in great or smaller things;
    For who doth know
What he shall do the coming day?
ANONYMOUS

It is quite impossible that an idle, floating spirit can ever look up with clear eye to God; spreading its miserable anarchy before the symmetry of the creative Mind; in the midst of a disorderly being, that has neither centre nor circumference, kneeling beneath the glorious sky, that everywhere has both; and for a life that is *all* failure, turning to the Lord of the silent stars, of whose punctual thought it is, that 'not one faileth.' The heavens, with their everlasting faithfulness, look down on no sadder contradiction, than the sluggard and the slattern in their prayers.

J. MARTINEAU

MARCH 4

So when this corruptible shall have put on incorruption, and this mortal shall have put on immortality, then shall be brought to pass the saying that is written, Death is swallowed up in victory.

— *1 Corinthians 15:54*

BUT souls that of His own good life partake,
He loves as His own self; dear as His eye
They are to Him: He'll never them forsake. . . .
They live, they live in blest eternity.

HENRY MORE

Though every good man is not so logically subtile as to be able to fit mediums to demonstrate his own immortality, yet he sees it in a higher light: his soul, being purged and enlightened by true sanctity, is more capable of those divine irradiations, whereby it feels itself in conjunction with God. It knows that God will never forsake His own life which He hath quickened in it. He will never deny those ardent desires of a blissful fruition of Himself, which the lively sense of His own goodness hath excited within it. Those breathings and gaspings after an eternal participation of Him are but the energy of His own breath within us; if He had had any mind to destroy it, He would never have shown it such things as He hath done.

DR. JOHN SMITH

MARCH 5

*And every man that hath this hope in him purifieth himself,
even as He is pure.*

—1 John 3:3

NOW, Lord, what wait I for?
   On thee alone
My hope is all rested,—
   Lord, seal me Thine own!
Only Thine own to be,
Only to live to Thee.
   Thine, with each day begun,
Thine, with each set of sun,
Thine, till my work is done.

ANNA WARNER

Now, believe me, God hides some ideal in every human soul.
At some time in our life we feel a trembling, fearful longing to
do some good thing. Life finds its noblest spring of excellence in
this hidden impulse to do our best. There is a time when we are
not content to be such merchants or doctors or lawyers as we
see on the dead level or below it. The woman longs to glorify
her womanhood as sister, wife, or mother. . . . Here is God,—
God standing silently at the door all day long,—God whispering
to the soul, that to be pure and true is to succeed in life, and
whatever we get short of that will burn up like stubble, though
the whole world try to save it.

ROBERT COLLYER

MARCH 6

The shadow of a great rock in a weary land.
—Isaiah 32:2

In returning and rest shall ye be saved; in quietness and in
confidence shall be your strength.
—Isaiah 30:15

O SHADOW in a sultry land!
   We gather to Thy breast!
Whose love, enfolding light the night,
   Brings quietude and rest,
Glimpse of the fairer life to be,
   In foretaste here possessed.

              C. M. PACKARD

Strive to see God in all things without exception, and acquiesce in His will with absolute submission. Do everything for God, uniting yourself to Him by a mere upward glance, or by the overflowing of your heart towards Him. Never be in a hurry; do everything quietly and in a calm spirit. Do not lose your inward peace for anything whatsoever, even if your whole world seems upset. Commend all to God, and then lie still and be at rest in His bosom. Whatever happens, abide steadfast in a determination to cling simply to God, trusting to His eternal love for you; and if you find that you have wandered forth from this shelter, recall your heart quietly and simply. Maintain a holy simplicity of mind, and do not smother yourself with a host of cares, wishes, or longings, under any pretext.

              FRANCIS DE SALES

MARCH 7

There are diversities of operations, but it is the same God which worketh all in all.
> —*1 Corinthians 12:6*

I form the light, and create darkness; I make peace, and create evil; I the Lord do all these things.
> —*Isaiah 45:7*

'ALL is of God that is, and is to be;
And God is good.' Let this suffice us still,
Resting in childlike trust upon His will,
Who moves to His great ends, unthwarted by the ill.

> J. G. WHITTIER

This then, is of faith, that everything, the very least, or what seemed to us great, every change in the seasons, everything that touches us in mind, body, or estate, whether brought about through this outward senseless nature, or by the will of man, good or bad, is overruled to each of us by the all-holy and all-loving will of God. Whatever befalls us, however it befalls us, we must receive as the will of God. If it befalls us through man's negligence, or ill-will, or anger, still it is, in every circumstance, to *us* the will of God. For if the least thing could happen to us without God's permission, it would be something out of God's control. God's providence or His love would not be what they are. Almighty God Himself would not be the same God; not the God whom we believe, adore, and love.

> E. B. PUSEY

MARCH 8

Study to show thyself approved unto God, a workman that needeth not to be ashamed.
                                        —2 Timothy 2:15

And let us not be weary in well-doing; for in due season we shall reap if we faint not.
                                        —Galatians 6:9

THE task Thy wisdom hath assigned,
   Oh, let me cheerfully fulfil;
In all my works Thy presence find,
   And prove Thine acceptable will.
                                        C. WESLEY

'What is my next duty? What is the thing that lies nearest to me?' 'That belongs to your every-day history. No one can answer that question but yourself. Your next duty is just to determine what your next duty is. Is there nothing you neglect? Is there nothing you know you ought not to do? You would know your duty, if you thought in earnest about it, and were not ambitious of great things.' 'Ah, then,' responded she, 'I suppose it is something very commonplace, which will make life more dreary than ever. That cannot help me.' 'It will, if it be as dreary as reading the newspapers to an old deaf aunt. It will soon lead you to something more. Your duty will begin to comfort you at once, [and] will at length open the unknown fountain of life in your heart.'

G. MACDONALD

MARCH 9

*Thou shalt rejoice before the Lord thy God, in all that thou
puttest thine hands unto.*

—Deuteronomy 12:18

Be ye thankful.

—Colossians 3:15

———————————— ∼⚬∼ ————————————

THOU that hast given so much to me,
Give one thing more, a grateful heart.
Not thankful when it pleaseth me,
As if thy blessings had spare days;
But such a heart, whose pulse may be
Thy praise.

G. HERBERT

———————————— ∼⚬∼ ————————————

If any one would tell you the shortest, surest way to all
happiness and all perfection, he must tell you to make it a rule
to yourself to thank and praise God for everything that happens
to you. For it is certain that whatever seeming calamity happens
to you, if you thank and praise God for it, you turn it into a
blessing. Could you, therefore, work miracles, you could not do
more for yourself than by this thankful spirit; for it heals with a
word speaking, and turns all that it touches into happiness.

WM. LAW

MARCH 10

When thou passest through the waters, I will be with thee; and through the rivers, they shall not overflow thee: when thou walkest through the fire, thou shalt not be burned; neither shall the flame kindle upon thee.
—Isaiah 43:2

I am with thee to deliver thee.
—Jeremiah 1:8

WHEN through the deep waters I call thee to go,
The rivers of sorrow shall not overflow;
For I will be with thee thy troubles to bless,
And sanctify to thee thy deepest distress.
ANONYMOUS

Turn it as thou wilt, thou must give thyself to suffer what is appointed thee. But if we did that, God would bear us up at all times in all our sorrows and troubles, and God would lay His shoulder under our burdens, and help us to bear them. For if, with cheerful courage, we submitted ourselves to God, no suffering would be unbearable.

J. TAULER

Learn to be as the angel, who could descend among the miseries of Bethesda without losing his heavenly purity or his perfect happiness. Gain healing from troubled waters. Make up your mind to the prospect of sustaining a certain measure of pain and trouble in your passage through life. By the blessing of God this will prepare you for it; it will make you thoughtful and resigned without interfering with your cheerfulness.

J. H. NEWMAN

MARCH 11

Cast thy burden upon the Lord, and He shall sustain thee;
He shall never suffer the righteous to be moved.
                                    —Psalm 55:22

NOW our wants and burdens leaving,
  To His care, who cares for all,
Cease we fearing, cease we grieving,
  At His touch our burdens fall.

S. LONGFELLOW

The circumstances of her life she could not alter, but she took them to the Lord, and handed them over into His management; and then she believed that He took it, and she left all the responsibility and the worry and anxiety with Him. As often as the anxieties returned she took them back; and the result was that, although the circumstances remained unchanged, her soul was kept in perfect peace in the midst of them. And the secret she found so effectual in her outward affairs, she found to be still more effectual in her inward ones, which were in truth even more utterly unmanageable. She abandoned her whole self to the Lord, with all that she was and all that she had. Believing that He took that which she had committed to Him, she ceased to fret and worry, and her life became all sunshine in the gladness of belonging to Him.

H. W. S.

MARCH 12

The Lord bless thee, and keep thee; the Lord make His face shine upon thee, and be gracious unto thee; the Lord lift up His countenance upon thee, and give thee peace.
—*Numbers 6:24-26*

O LOVE, how cheering is Thy ray!
  All pain before Thy presence flies;
Care, anguish, sorrow, melt away,
  Where'er Thy healing beams arise.
O Father, nothing may I see
Nothing desire, or seek, but Thee.

P. GERHARDT

There is a faith in God, and a clear perception of His will and designs, and a providence, and glory, which gives to its possessor a confidence and patience and sweet composure, under every varied and troubling aspect of events, such as no man can realize who has not felt its influences in his own heart. There is a communion with God, in which the soul feels the presence of the unseen One, in the profound depths of its being, with a vivid distinctness and a holy reverence, such as no words can describe. There is a state of union with God, I do not say often reached, yet it has been attained in this world, in which all the past and present and future seem reconciled, and eternity is won and enjoyed; and God and man, earth and heaven, with all their mysteries, are apprehended in truth as they lie in the mind of the Infinite.

SAMUEL D. ROBBINS

MARCH 13

He that abideth in me, and I in him, bringeth forth much fruit.
—John 15:5

Let the beauty of the Lord our God be upon us.
—Psalm 90:17

AS some rare perfume in a vase of clay
   Pervades it with a fragrance not its own,
So, then Thou dwellest in a moral soul,
   All Heaven's own sweetness seems around it thrown.

H. B. STOWE

Some glances of real beauty may be seen in their faces, who dwell in true meekness. There is a harmony in the sound of that voice to which Divine love gives utterance, and some appearance of right order in their temper and conduct whose passions are regulated.

JOHN WOOLMAN

I believe that no Divine truth can truly dwell in any heart, without an external testimony in manner, bearing, and appearance, that must reach the witness within the heart of the beholder, and bear an unmistakable, though silent, evidence to the eternal principle from which it emanates.

M. A. SCHIMMELPENNINCK

MARCH 14

*I have called upon Thee, for Thou wilt hear me, O God:
incline Thine ear unto me, and hear my speech.*
                                    —Psalm 17:6

*Ye people, pour out your heart before Him: God is a refuge
for us.*
                                    —Psalm 62:8

———————————

WHATE'ER the care which breaks thy rest,
Whate'er the wish that swells thy breast;
Spread before God that wish, that care,
   And change anxiety to prayer.
                   ANONYMOUS

———————————

Trouble and perplexity drive us to prayer, and prayer driveth
away trouble and perplexity.

                   P. MELANCHTHON

Whatsoever it is that presses thee, go tell thy Father; put over
the matter into His hand, and so thou shalt be freed from that
dividing, perplexing care that the world is full of. When thou art
either to do or suffer anything, when thou art about any purpose
or business, go tell God of it, and acquaint Him with it; yea, burden Him with it, and thou hast done for matter of caring; no
more care, but quiet, sweet diligence in thy duty, and dependence on Him for the carriage of thy matters. Roll thy cares, and
thyself with them, as one burden, all on thy God.

                  R. LEIGHTON

MARCH 15

Hear me, O Lord, for thy loving-kindness is good: turn unto me according to the multitude of Thy tender mercies.
— *Psalm 69:16*

Let, I pray Thee, Thy merciful kindness be for my comfort, according to Thy word unto Thy servant.
— *Psalm 119:76*

LOVE divine has seen and counted
    Every tear it caused to fall;
And the storm which Love appointed
    Was its choicest gift of all.

ANONYMOUS

O that thou couldst dwell in the knowledge and sense of this! even, that the Lord beholds thy sufferings with an eye of pity; and is able, not only to uphold thee under them, but also to do thee good by them. Therefore, grieve not at thy lot, be not discontented, look not out at the hardness of thy condition. But, when the storm and matters of vexation are sharp, look up to Him who can give meekness and patience, can lift up thy head over all, and cause thy life to grow, and be a gainer by all. If the Lord God help thee proportionably to thy condition of affliction and distress, thou wilt have no cause to complain, but to bless His Name.

I. PENINGTON

MARCH 16

Whether therefore ye eat, or drink, or whatsoever ye do, do all to the glory of God.

—1 Corinthians 10:31

With good will doing service, as to the Lord and not unto men.

—Ephesians 6:7

A SERVANT, with this clause,
　Makes drudgery divine:
Who sweeps a room, as for Thy laws,
　Makes that and th' action fine.

G. HERBERT

Surely the truth must be, that whatsoever in our daily life is lawful and right for us to be engaged in, is in itself a part of our obedience to God; a part, that is, of our very religion. Whensoever we hear people complaining of obstructions and hindrances put by the duties of life in the way of devoting themselves to God, we may be sure they are under some false view or other. They do not look upon their daily work as the task God has set them, and as obedience due to Him. We may go farther; and say, not only that the duties of life, be they never so toilsome and distracting, are no obstructions to a life of any degree of inward holiness; but that they are even direct means, when rightly used, to promote our sanctification.

H. E. MANNING

MARCH 17

Where hast thou gleaned today?
                    —Ruth 2:19

WHAT have I learnt where'er I've been,
From all I've heard, from all I've seen?
What know I more that's worth the knowing?
What have I done that's worth the doing?
What have I sought that I should shun?
What duties have I left undone?

                    PYTHAGORAS

All of this world will soon have passed away. But God will remain, and thou, whatever thou hast become, good or bad. Thy deeds now are the seed-corn of eternity. Each single act, in each several day, good or bad, is a portion of that seed. Each day adds some line, making thee more or less like Him, more or less capable of His love.

E. B. PUSEY

MARCH 18

❧

MAKE us of one heart and mind;
Courteous, pitiful, and kind;
Lowly, meek, in thought and word,
Altogether like our Lord.

C. WESLEY

❧

A little thought will show you how vastly your own happiness depends on the way other people bear themselves toward you. The looks and tones at your breakfast-table, the conduct of your fellow-workers or employers, the faithful or unreliable men you deal with, what people say to you on the street, the way your cook and housemaid do their work, the letters you get, the friends or foes you meet,—these things make up very much of the pleasure or misery of your day. Turn the idea around, and remember that just so much are you adding to the pleasure or the misery of other people's days. And this is the half of the matter which you can control. Whether any particular day shall bring to you more of happiness or of suffering is largely beyond your power to determine. Whether each day of your life shall *give* happiness or suffering rests with yourself.

GEORGE S. MERRIAM

MARCH 19

Showing all good fidelity, that they may adorn the doctrine of God our Saviour in all things.
$$—Titus\ 2:10$$

IF on our daily course our mind
Be set to hallow all we find,
New treasures still, of countless price,
God will provide for sacrifice.

J. KEBLE

If content and thankfulness, if the patient bearing of evil, be duties to God, they are the duties of every day, and in every circumstance of our life. If we are to follow Christ, it must be in our common way of spending every day.

WM. LAW

He who is faithful over a few things is a lord of cities. It does not matter whether you preach in Westminster Abbey, or teach a ragged class, so you be faithful. The faithfulness is all.

G. MACDONALD

I would have you invoke God often through the day, asking Him to kindle a love for your vocation within you, and saying with St. Paul, ' "Lord, what wouldst Thou have me to do?" Wouldst Thou have me serve Thee in the lowest ministries of Thy house? too happy if I may but serve Thee anyhow.' And when any special thing goes against you, ask 'Wouldst Thou have me do it? Then, unworthy though I be, I will do it gladly.'

FRANCIS DE SALES

MARCH 20

Thou shalt worship the Lord thy God, and Him only shalt thou serve.
> *—Matthew 4:10*

Blessed are they that keep His testimonies, and that seek Him with the whole heart.
> *—Psalm 119:2*

THE comfort of a mind at rest
From every care Thou hast not blest;
A heart from all the world set free,
To worship and to wait on Thee.

A. L. WARING

Resign every forbidden joy; restrain every wish that is not referred to His will; banish all eager desires, all anxiety. Desire only the will of God; seek Him alone, and you will find peace.

FÉNELON

'I've been a great deal happier since I have given up thinking about what is easy and pleasant, and being discontented because I couldn't have my own will. Our life is determined for us; and it makes the mind very free when we give up wishing, and only think of bearing what is laid upon us, and doing what is given us to do.'

GEORGE ELIOT

MARCH 21

Your heavenly Father knoweth that ye have need of all these things.

—Matthew 6:32

ALL as God wills, who wisely heeds
    To give or to withhold;
And knoweth more of all my needs
    Than all my prayers have told.

J. G. WHITTIER

Lord, I know not what I ought to ask of Thee; Thou only knowest what we need; Thou lovest me better than I know how to love myself. O Father! give to Thy child that which he himself knows not how to ask. I dare not ask either for crosses or consolations; I simply present myself before Thee; I open my heart to Thee. Behold my needs which I know not myself; see, and do according to Thy tender mercy. Smite, or heal; depress me, or raise me up; I adore all Thy purposes without knowing them. I am silent; I offer myself in sacrifice; I yield myself to Thee; I would have no other desire than to accomplish Thy will. Teach me to pray; pray Thyself in me.

FÉNELON

MARCH 22

Who can understand his errors? cleanse thou me from secret faults.

—Psalm 19:12

ONE finger's-breadth at hand will mar
A world of light in heaven afar,
A mote eclipse a glorious star,
   An eyelid hide the sky.

J. KEBLE

A single sin, however apparently trifling, however hidden in some obscure corner of our consciousness,—a sin *which we do not intend to renounce,*—is enough to render real prayer impracticable. A course of action not wholly upright and honourable, feelings not entirely kind and loving, habits not spotlessly chaste and temperate,—any of these are impassable obstacles. If we know of a kind act which we might, but do not intend to, perform,—if we be aware that our moral health requires the abandonment of some pleasure which yet we do not intend to abandon, here is cause enough for the loss of all spiritual power.

F. P. COBBE

It is astonishing how soon the whole conscience begins to unravel, if a single stitch drops; one little sin indulged makes a hole you could put your head through.

CHARLES BUXTON

MARCH 23

Beloved, thou doest faithfully whatsoever thou doest.
—3 John 5

And this also we wish, even your perfection.
—2 Corinthians 13:9

IN all the little things of life,
   Thyself, Lord, may I see;
In little and in great alike
   Reveal Thy love to me.

So shall my undivided life
   To Thee, my God, be given;
And all this earthly course below
   Be one dear path to heaven.

H. BONAR

In order to mould thee into entire conformity to His will, He must have thee pliable in His hands, and this pliability is more quickly reached by yielding in the little things than even by the greater. Thy one great desire is to follow Him fully. Canst thou not say then a continual 'yes' to all His sweet commands, whether small or great, and trust Him to lead thee by the shortest road to thy fullest blessedness?

H. W. S.

With meekness, humility, and diligence, apply yourself to the duties of your condition. They are the seemingly little things which make no noise that do the business.

HENRY MORE

MARCH 24

I will both lay me down in peace, and sleep; for Thou, Lord, only makest me dwell in safety.
                                        —Psalm 4:8

He giveth His beloved sleep.
                                        —Psalm 127:2

HE guides our feet, He guards our way,
His morning smiles bless all the day;
He spreads the evening veil, and keeps
The silent hours while Israel sleeps.

                              I. WATTS

We sleep in peace in the arms of God, when we yield ourselves up to His providence, in a delightful consciousness of His tender mercies. No more restless uncertainties, no more anxious desires, no more impatience at the place we are in, for it is God who has put us there, and who holds us in His arms. Can we be unsafe where He has placed us?

                    FÉNELON

One evening when Luther saw a little bird perched on a tree, to roost there for the night, he said, 'This little bird has had its supper, and now is getting ready to go to sleep here, quite secure and content, never troubling itself what its food will be, or where its lodging on the morrow. Like David, it "abides under the shadow of the Almighty." It sits on its little twig content, and lets God take care.'

MARCH 25

I will hear what God the LORD will speak: for He will speak peace unto His people.

—*Psalm 85:8*

THERE is a voice, 'a still, small voice' of love,
  Heard from above;
But not amidst the din of earthly sounds,
  Which here confounds;
By those withdrawn apart it best is heard,
And peace, sweet peace, breathes in each gentle word.

ANONYMOUS

He speaketh, but it is with us to hearken or no. It is much, yea, it is everything, not to turn away the ear, to be willing to hearken, not to drown His voice. 'The secret of the Lord is with them that fear Him.' It is a secret, hushed voice, a gentle [dialogue] of heart to heart, a still, small voice, whispering to the inner ear. How should we hear it, if we fill our ears and our hearts with the din of this world, its empty tumult, its excitement, its fretting vanities, or cares, or passions, or anxieties, or show, or rivalries, and its whirl of emptinesses?

E. B. PUSEY

MARCH 26

Are they not all ministering spirits?
                    —*Hebrews 1:14*

MAY I reach
That purest heaven, be to other souls
The cup of strength in some great agony,
Enkindle generous ardour, feed pure love,
Be the sweet presence of a good diffused,
And in diffusion ever more intense!
So shall I join the choir invisible
Whose music is the gladness of the world.

GEORGE ELIOT

Certainly, in our own little sphere, it is not the most active
people to whom we owe the most. Among the common people
whom we know, it is not necessarily those who are busiest, not
those who, meteor-like, are ever on the rush after some visible
charge and work. It is the lives, like the stars, which simply pour
down on us the calm light of their bright and faithful being, up to
which we look and out of which we gather the deepest calm and
courage. It seems to me that there is reassurance here for many
of us who seem to have no chance for active usefulness. We can
do nothing for our fellow-men. But still it is good to know that
we can be something for them; to know (and this we may know
surely) that no man or woman of the humblest sort can really be
strong, gentle, pure, and good, without the world being better
for it, without somebody being helped and comforted by the
very existence of that goodness.

PHILLIPS BROOKS

MARCH 27

*If we love one another, God dwelleth in us, and His love is
perfect in us.*
                              —1 John 4:12

*And he that keepeth His commandments dwelleth in Him,
and He in him. And hereby we know that He abideth in us, by
the Spirit which He hath given us.*
                              —1 John 3:24

ABIDE in me; o'ershadow by Thy love
Each half-formed purpose and dark thought of sin;
Quench, ere it rise, each selfish, low desire,
And keep my soul as Thine, calm and divine.
                              H. B. STOWE

The Spirit of Love [given by Christ] must work the works, and
speak the tones, of Love. It cannot exist and give no sign, or a
false sign. It cannot be a spirit of Love, and mantle into irritable
and selfish impatience. It cannot be a spirit of Love, and at the
same time make self the prominent object. It cannot rejoice to
lend itself to the happiness of others, and at the same time be
seeking its own. It cannot be generous, and envious. It cannot be
sympathizing, and unseemly; self-forgetful, and vain-glorious. It
cannot delight in the rectitude and purity of other hearts, as the
spiritual elements of their peace, and yet unnecessarily suspect
them.

                              J. H. THOM

MARCH 28

Giving thanks always for all things unto God.
—Ephesians 5:20

FOR blessings of the fruitful season,
   For work and rest, for friends and home,
For the great gifts of thought and reason,—
   To praise and bless Thee, Lord, we come.

Yes, and for weeping and for wailing,
   For bitter hail and blighting frost,
For high hopes on the low earth trailing,
   For sweet joys missed, for pure aims crossed.

                E. SCUDDER

   Notwithstanding all that I have suffered, notwithstanding all
the pain and weariness and anxiety and sorrow that necessarily
enter into life, and the inward errings that are worse than all, I
would end my record with a devout thanksgiving to the great
Author of my being. For more and more am I unwilling to make
my gratitude to Him what is commonly called 'a thanksgiving for
mercies,'—for any benefits or blessings that are peculiar to
myself, or my friends, or indeed to any man. Instead of this, I
would have it to be gratitude for *all* that belongs to my life and
being,—for joy and sorrow, for health and sickness, for success
and disappointment, for virtue and for temptation, for life and
death; because I believe that all is meant for good.

                ORVILLE DEWEY

MARCH 29

There shall no evil befall thee.
—Psalm 91:10

Whoso hearkeneth unto Me shall dwell safely, and shall be quiet from fear of evil.
—Proverbs 1:33

I ASK not, 'Take away this weight of care;'
No, for that love I pray that all can bear,
   And for the faith that whatsoe'er befall
Must needs be good, and for my profit prove,
Since from my Father's heart most rich in love,
   And from His bounteous hands it cometh all.
                C. J. P. SPITTA

Be like the promontory, against which the waves continually break; but it stands firm, and tames the fury of the water around it. Unhappy am I, because this has happened to me? Not so, but happy am I, though this has happened to me, because I continue free from pain, neither crushed by the present, nor fearing the future. Will then this which has happened prevent thee from being just, magnanimous, temperate, prudent, secure against inconsiderate opinions and falsehood? Remember, too, on every occasion which leads thee to vexation to apply this principle: that this is not a misfortune, but that to bear it nobly is good fortune.

MARCUS ANTONINUS

MARCH 30

Thou shalt guide me with Thy counsel, and afterward receive me to glory.
—Psalm 73:24

There remaineth therefore a rest to the people of God.
—Hebrews 4:9

GUIDE us through life; and when at last
   We enter into rest,
Thy tender arms about us cast,
   And fold us to Thy breast.

H. F. LYTE

Go forth to meet the solemnities and to conquer the trials of existence, believing in [the] Shepherd of your souls. Then faith in Him will support you in duty, and duty firmly done will strengthen faith. [Then] at last, when all is over here, and the noise and strife of the earthly battle fades upon your dying ear, you will hear, instead, the deep and musical sound of the ocean of eternity, and see the lights of heaven shining on its waters still and fair in their radiant rest. [Then] your faith will raise the song of conquest, and in its retrospect of the life which has ended, and its forward glance upon the life to come, take up the poetic inspiration of the Hebrew king. 'Surely goodness and mercy have followed me all the days of my life, and I will dwell in the house of the Lord forever.'

STOPFORD A. BROOKE

MARCH 31

Thou shalt be in league with the stones of the field, and the beasts of the field shall be at peace with thee. And thou shalt know that thy tabernacle shall be in peace.
—Job 5:23, 24

LOVE had he found in huts where poor men lie;
His daily teachers had been woods and rills,
The silence that is in the starry sky,
The sleep that is among the lonely hills.
W. WORDSWORTH

That spirit which suffices quiet hearts, which seems to come forth to such from every dry knoll of sere grass, from every pine-stump, and half-embedded stone, on which the dull March sun shines, comes forth to the poor and hungry, and to such as are of simple taste. If thou fill thy brain with Boston and New York, with fashion and covetousness, and wilt stimulate thy jaded senses with wine and French coffee, thou shalt find no radiance of wisdom in the lonely waste of the pine-woods.

R. W. EMERSON

APRIL 1

*He that hath my commandments, and keepeth them, he it is
that loveth me: and he that loveth me shall be loved of my
Father, and I will love him, and will manifest myself to him.*
—*John 14:21*

❦

HE prayeth best who loveth best
   All things both great and small
For the dear God who loveth us,
   He made and loveth all.

                S. T. COLERIDGE

❦

. . . . Love alone was the beginning of nature and creature,
nothing but Love encompasses the whole universe of things,
the governing Hand that overrules all, the watchful Eye that sees
through all, is nothing but omnipotent and omniscient Love.
[This Love uses] an infinity of wisdom to save every misguided
creature from the miserable works of his own hands, and to
make happiness and glory the perpetual inheritance of all the
creation. [This] is a reflection that must be quite ravishing to
every intelligent creature that is sensible of it.

             WM. LAW

APRIL 2

Know ye not that ye are the temple of God, and that the Spirit of God dwelleth in you?

—1 Corinthians 3:16

FATHER! replenish with Thy grace
  This longing heart of mine;
Make it Thy quiet dwelling-place,
  Thy sacred inmost shrine!

ANGELUS SILESIUS

Not man's manifold labours, but his manifold cares, hinder the presence of God. . . . Whatsoever thou doest, hush thyself to thine own feverish vanities, and busy thoughts, and cares; in silence seek thy Father's face, and the light of His countenance will stream down upon thee. He will make a secret cell in thine heart, and when thou enterest there, there shalt thou find Him. And if thou hast found Him there, all around shall reflect Him, all shall speak to Him, and He will speak through all. Outwardly thou mayest be doing the work of thy calling; inwardly, if thou commend thy work to God, thou mayest be with Him in the third Heaven.

E. B. PUSEY

APRIL 3

LORD, for the erring thought
Not into evil wrought;
Lord, for the wicked will
Betrayed and baffled still,
For the heart from itself kept,
Our Thanksgiving accept.

W. D. HOWELLS

What an amazing, what a blessed disproportion between the evil we do, and the evil we are capable of doing, and seem sometimes on the very verge of doing! If my soul has grown tares, when it was full of the seeds of nightshade, how happy ought I to be! And that the tares have not wholly strangled the wheat, what a wonder it is! We ought to thank God daily for the sins we have not committed.

F. W. FABER

We give thanks often with a tearful, doubtful voice, for our spiritual mercies *positive;* but what an almost infinite field there is for mercies negative! We cannot even imagine all that God has suffered us *not* to do, *not* to be.

F. R. HAVERGAL

You are surprised at your imperfections—why? I should infer from that, that your self-knowledge is small. Surely, you might rather be astonished that you do not fall into more frequent and more grievous faults, and thank God for His upholding grace.

JEAN NICOLAS GROU

APRIL 4

Well done, good and faithful servant: thou hast been faithful over a few things, I will make thee ruler over many things: enter thou into the joy of thy Lord.
—*Matthew 25:23*

O FATHER! help us to resign
  Our hearts, our strength, our wills to Thee;
Then even lowliest work of Thine
  Most noble, blest, and sweet will be.
                    H. M. KIMBALL

Nothing is too little to be ordered by our Father; nothing too little in which to see His hand; nothing, which touches our souls, too little to accept from Him; nothing too little to be done to Him.

E. B. PUSEY

A soul occupied with great ideas best performs small duties. The divinest views of life penetrate most clearly into the meanest emergencies. . . . A heavenly spirit taking up its abode with us can alone sustain well the daily toils, and tranquilly pass the humiliations of our condition.

J. MARTINEAU

Whoso neglects a thing which he suspects he ought to do, because it seems to him too small a thing, is deceiving himself; it is not too little, but too great for him, that he doeth it not.

E. B. PUSEY

APRIL 5

Yet I have left me seven thousand in Israel, all the knees which have not bowed unto Baal, and every mouth which hath not kissed him.

—1 Kings 19:18

BACK then, complainer; loathe thy life no more,
Nor deem thyself upon a desert shore,
   Because the rocks the nearer prospect close.
Yet in fallen Israel are there hearts and eyes
That day by day in prayer like thine arise:
   Thou know'st them not, but their Creator knows.

J. KEBLE

He went down to the great school with a glimmering of another lesson in his heart,—the lesson that he who has conquered his own coward spirit has conquered the whole outward world. [Another] one which the old prophet learnt in the cave in Mount Horeb, [came] when he hid his face, and the still, small voice asked, 'What doest thou here, Elijah?'. . . We may fancy ourselves alone on the side of good, [but] the King and Lord of men is nowhere without His witnesses, for in every society, however seemingly corrupt and godless, there are those who have not bowed the knee to Baal.

THOMAS HUGHES

So, then, Elijah's life had been no failure, after all. Seven thousand at least in Israel had been braced and encouraged by his example, and silently blessed him, perhaps, for the courage which they felt. In God's world, for those who are in earnest there is no failure. No work truly done, no word earnestly spoken, no sacrifice freely made, was ever made in vain.

F. W. ROBERTSON

APRIL 6

In the multitude of my thoughts within me Thy comforts delight my soul.
> —*Psalm 94:19*

Perplexed, but not in despair; cast down, but not destroyed.
> —*2 Corinthians 4:8, 9*

DISCOURAGED in the work of life,
   Disheartened by its load,
Shamed by its failures or its fears,
   I sink beside the road;—
But let me only think of Thee,
   And then new heart springs up in me.
> S. LONGFELLOW

Discouragement is an inclination to give up all attempts after the devout life, in consequence of the difficulties by which it is beset, and our already numerous failures in it. We lose heart; and partly in ill-temper, partly in real doubt of our own ability to persevere, we first grow querulous and peevish with God, and then relax in our efforts to mortify ourselves and to please Him. It is a sort of shadow of despair, and will lead us into numberless venial sins the first half-hour we give way to it.

> F. W. FABER

Never let us be discouraged with ourselves. It is not when we are conscious of our faults that we are the most wicked; on the contrary, we are less so. We see by a brighter light; and let us remember, for our consolation, that we never perceive our sins till we begin to cure them.

> FÉNELON

APRIL 7

That ye may prove what is that good, and acceptable, and perfect will of God.

—Romans 12:2

THOU knowest what is best;
   And who but Thee, O God, hath power to know?
In Thy great will my trusting heart shall rest;
   Beneath that will my humble head shall bow.

T. C. UPHAM

To those who are His, all things are not only easy to be borne, but even to be gladly chosen. Their will is united to that will which moves heaven and earth, which gives laws to angels, and rules the courses of the world. It is a wonderful gift of God to man, of which we that know so little must needs speak little. To be at the centre of that motion, where is everlasting rest; to be sheltered in the peace of God; even now to dwell in heaven, where all hearts are stayed, and all hopes fulfilled. 'Thou shalt keep him in perfect peace whose mind is stayed on Thee.'

H. E. MANNING

Study to follow His will in all, to have no will but His. This is thy duty, and thy wisdom. Nothing is gained by spurning and struggling but to hurt and vex thyself; but by complying all is gained—sweet peace. It is the very secret, the mystery of solid peace within, to resign all to His will, to be disposed of at His pleasure, without the least contrary thought.

R. LEIGHTON

APRIL 8

The Lord is my Shepherd; I shall not want.
            —Psalm 23:1

They that seek the Lord shall not want any good thing.
            —Psalm 34:10

―――――――――⁕―――――――――

GOD, who the universe doth hold
    In his fold,
Is my shepherd kind and heedful.
Is my shepherd, and doth keep
    Me, his sheep,
Still supplied with all things needful.

                    F. DAVISON

―――――――――⁕―――――――――

Who is it that is your shepherd? The Lord! Oh, my friends,
what a wonderful announcement! The Lord God of heaven and
earth, the almighty Creator of all things, He who holds the universe in His hand as though it were a very little thing,—HE is
your shepherd, and has charged Himself with the care and keeping of you, as a shepherd is charged with the care and keeping
of his sheep. If your hearts could really take in this thought, you
would never have a fear or a care again; for with such a shepherd, how could it be possible for you ever to want any good
thing?

                    H. W. S.

APRIL 9

Watch and pray, that ye enter not into temptation.
—Matthew 26:41

I WANT a sober mind,
   A self-renouncing will,
That tramples down and casts behind
   The baits of pleasing ill;
A spirit still prepared,
   And armed with jealous care,
Forever standing on its guard,
   And watching unto prayer.

C. WESLEY

When you say, 'Lead us not into temptation,' you must in good earnest mean to avoid in your daily conduct those temptations which you have already suffered from. When you say, 'Deliver us from evil,' you must mean to struggle against that evil in your heart, which you are conscious of, and which you pray to be forgiven. . . . To watch and pray are surely in our power, and by these means we are certain of getting strength. You feel your weakness; you fear to be overcome by temptation: then keep out of the way of it. This is watching. Avoid [those who are] likely to mislead you; flee from the very shadow of evil; you cannot be too careful; better be a little too strict than a little too easy,—it is the safer side. Abstain from reading books which are dangerous to you. Turn from bad thoughts when they arise.

J. H. NEWMAN

APRIL 10

Whatsoever ye do, do it heartily, as to the Lord, and not unto men.

—Colossians 3:23

Not with eye-service, as men-pleasers; but in singleness of heart, fearing God.

—Colossians 3:22

TEACH me, my God and King,
　In all things Thee to see,
And what I do in anything,
　To do it as for Thee.

G. HERBERT

There is no action so slight nor so mean but it may be done to a great purpose, and ennobled therefore. Nor is any purpose so great but that slight actions may help it, and may be so done as to help it much, most especially, that chief of all purposes—the pleasing of God.

J. RUSKIN

Every duty, even the least duty, involves the whole principle of obedience. And little duties make the will *dutiful,* that is, supple and prompt to obey. Little obediences lead into great. The daily round of duty is full of probation and of discipline; it trains the will, heart, and conscience. We need not to be prophets or apostles. The commonest life may be full of perfection. The duties of home are a discipline for the ministries of heaven.

H. E. MANNING

APRIL 11

Wherefore, beloved . . . be diligent that ye may be found of Him in peace, without spot, and blameless.
                    —2 Peter 3:14

HIS conscience knows no secret stings,
    While grace and joy combine
To form a life whose holy springs
    Are hidden and divine.

I. WATTS

Even the smallest discontent of conscience may render turbid the whole temper of the mind. But only produce the effort that restores its peace, and over the whole atmosphere a breath of unexpected purity is spread. Doubt and irritability pass away as clouds. The withered sympathies of earth and home open their leaves and live; and through the clearest blue the deep is seen of the heaven where God resides.

J. MARTINEAU

The state of mind which is described as meekness, or quietness of spirit, is characterized in a high degree by inward harmony. There is not, as formerly, that inward jarring of thought contending with thought, and conscience asserting rights which it could not maintain.

T. C. UPHAM

APRIL 12

Be perfect, be of good comfort, be of one mind, live in peace; and the God of love and peace shall be with you.
                                    —2 Corinthians 13:11

He that loveth not his brother whom he hath seen, how can he love God whom he hath not seen?
                                    —1 John 4:20

LORD! subdue our selfish will;
   Each to each our tempers suit,
By Thy modulating skill,
   Heart to heart, as lute to lute.
                                    C. WESLEY

It requires far more of the constraining love of Christ to love our cousins and neighbours as members of the heavenly family, than to feel the heart warm to our suffering brethren in Tuscany or Madeira. To love the whole Church is one thing; to love—that is, to delight in the graces and veil the defects—of the person who misunderstood me and opposed my plans yesterday, whose peculiar infirmities grate on my most sensitive feelings, or whose natural faults are precisely those from which my natural character most revolts, is quite another.

ELIZABETH CHARLES

APRIL 13

*In all these things we are more than conquerors through
Him that loved us.*

—*Romans 8:37*

THUS my soul before her God
   Lieth still nor speaketh more,
Conqueror thus o'er pain and wrong,
   That once smote her to the core;
Like a silent ocean, bright
With her God's great praise and light.

WINKLER, 1713

My mind is forever closed against embarrassment and perplexity, against uncertainty, doubt, and anxiety; my heart against grief and desire. Calm and unmoved, I look down on all things, for I know that I cannot explain a single event, nor comprehend its connexion with that which alone concerns me. In His world all things prosper; this satisfies me, and in this belief I stand fast as a rock.

J. G. FICHTE

APRIL 14

All things are yours; whether Paul, or Apollos, or Cephas, or the world, or life, or death, or things present, or things to come; all are yours.

—1 Corinthians 3:21, 22

As having nothing, and yet possessing all things.

—2 Corinthians 6:10

OLD friends, old scenes, will lovelier be,
As more of Heaven in each we see:
Some softening gleam of love and prayer
Shall dawn on every cross and care.

J. KEBLE

Out of love and hatred, out of earnings, and borrowings, and lendings, and losses; out of sickness and pain; out of wooing and worshipping; out of travelling, and voting, and watching, and caring; out of disgrace and contempt, comes our tuition in the serene and beautiful laws. Let him not slur his lesson; let him learn it by heart. Let him endeavor exactly, bravely, and cheerfully, to solve the problem of that life which is set before *him*. And this, by punctual action, and not by promises or dreams. Believing, as in God, in the presence and favour of the grandest influences, let him . . . learn how to receive and use it, by fidelity also to the lower observances.

R. W. EMERSON

APRIL 15

We know that all things work together for good to them that love God.

—*Romans 8:28*

As for you, ye thought evil against me; but God meant it unto good.

—*Genesis 50:20*

ILL that He blesses is our good,
    And unblest good is ill;
And all is right that seems most wrong,
    If it be His sweet Will.

F. W. FABER

To those who know [Him], all things work together for good, and all things seem to be, as they are to them, good. The goods which God gives seem 'very good,' and God Himself in them, because they know that they deserve them not. The evils which God allows and overrules seem also 'very good,' because they see in them His loving hand, put forth to heal them of what shuts out God from the soul. They love God intensely, in that He is so good to them in each, and every, the least good, because it is more than they deserve: how much more in the greatest! They love God for every, and each, the very greatest of what seem evils, knowing them to be, from His love, real goods. For He by whom 'all the hairs of our head are numbered,' and who 'knoweth whereof we are made,' directs everything which befalls us in life, in perfect wisdom and love, to the well-being of our souls.

E. B. PUSEY

APRIL 16

*The very God of peace sanctify you wholly, and I pray God
your whole spirit, and soul, and body, be preserved blameless.
Faithful is He that calleth you, who also will do it.*
—1 Thessalonians 5:23, 24

———————————— ❧ ————————————

BE still, my soul!—the Lord is on thy side;
   Bear patiently the cross of grief and pain;
Leave to thy God to order and provide,—
   In every change He faithful will remain.

HYMNS FROM THE
LAND OF LUTHER

———————————— ❧ ————————————

It was no relief from temporal evils that the Apostle promised.
. . . No; the mercy of God might send them to the stake, or the
lions; it was still His mercy, if it but kept them 'unspotted from
the world.' It might expose them to insult, calumny, and wrong;
they received it still as mercy, if it 'established them in every
good work and work.' O brethren! how many of *you* are content
with *such* faithfulness as this on the part of your heavenly
Father? Is this, indeed, the tone and tenor of your prayers?

WM. ARCHER BUTLER

APRIL 17

Blessed is that man that maketh the Lord his trust.
—Psalm 40:4

That we may lead a quiet and peaceable life.
—1 Timothy 2:2

JUST to let thy Father do
   What He will;
Just to know that He is true,
   And be still;
Just to trust Him, this is all!
   Then, the day will surely be
Peaceful, whatsoe'er befall,
   Bright and blessed, calm and free.

                    F. R. HAVERGAL

Every morning compose your soul for a tranquil day, and all through it be careful often to recall your resolution, and bring yourself back to it, so to say. If something discomposes you, do not be upset, or troubled; but having discovered the fact, humble yourself gently before God, and try to bring your mind into a quiet attitude. Say to yourself, 'Well, I have made a false step; now I must go more carefully and watchfully.' Do this each time, however frequently you fall. When you are at peace use it profitably, making constant acts of meekness, and seeking to be calm even in the most trifling things. Above all, do not be discouraged; be patient; wait; strive to attain a calm, gentle spirit.

                    FRANCIS DE SALES

APRIL 18

What doth the Lord thy God require of thee, but to fear the Lord thy God, to walk in all His ways, and to love Him, and to serve the Lord thy God with all thy heart and with all thy soul?
—Deuteronomy 10:12

WHAT asks our Father of His children save
    Justice and mercy and humility,
    A reasonable service of good deeds,
    Pure living, tenderness to human needs,
Reverence, and trust, and prayer for light to see
    The master's footprints in our daily ways?
    No knotted scourge, nor sacrificial knife,
    But the calm beauty of an ordered life
Whose every breathing is unworded praise.

J. G. WHITTIER

Give up yourself to God without reserve; in singleness of heart, meeting everything that every day brings forth, as something that comes from God, and is to be received and gone through by you, in such an heavenly use of it, as you would suppose the holy Jesus would have done, in such occurrences. This is an attainable degree of perfection.

WM. LAW

We ought to measure our actual lot, and to fulfil it; to be with all our strength that which our lot requires and allows. What is beyond it, is no calling of ours. How much peace, quiet, confidence, and strength, would people attain, if they would go by this plain rule.

H. E. MANNING

APRIL 19

The hand of our God is upon all them for good that seek Him.
                                    —*Ezra 8:22*

Into Thy hand I commit my spirit.
                                    —*Psalm 31:5*

THOU layest Thy hand on the fluttering heart,
  And sayest, 'Be still!'
The silence and shadow are only a part
  Of Thy sweet will;
Thy presence is with me, and where Thou art
  I fear no ill.

                            F. R. HAVERGAL

Be still and cool in thy own mind and spirit from thy own thoughts, and then thou wilt feel the principle of God; turn thy mind to the Lord God, from whom life comes. [By this] thou mayest receive His strength, and power to allay all blustering storms and tempests. That is it which works up into patience, into innocency, into soberness, into stillness, into stayedness, into quietness, up to God with His power. . . . Therefore be still awhile from thy own thoughts, searching, seeking, desires, and imaginations, and be stayed in the principle of God in thee, that it may raise thy mind up to God, and stay it upon God. [Thus] thou wilt find strength from Him, and find Him to be a God at hand, a present help in the time of trouble and need.

                            GEORGE FOX

APRIL 20

I waited patiently for the Lord; and He inclined unto me, and heard my cry.

—Psalm 40:1

Tribulation worketh patience; and patience experience; and experience, hope.

—Romans 5:3, 4

———————————— ✦ ————————————

LORD, we have wandered forth through doubt and sorrow,
    And Thou hast made each step an onward one;
And we will ever trust each unknown morrow,—
    Thou wilt sustain us till its work is done.
                    S. JOHNSON

———————————— ✦ ————————————

It is possible, when the future is dim, when our depressed faculties can form no bright ideas of the perfection and happiness of a better world,—it is possible still to cling to the conviction of God's merciful purpose towards His creatures, of His parental goodness even in suffering. Still [we can] feel that the path of duty, though trodden with a heavy heart, leads to peace; still to be true to conscience; still to do our work, to resist temptation, to be useful, though with diminished energy, to give up our wills when we cannot rejoice under God's mysterious providence. In this patient, though uncheered obedience, we become prepared for light. The soul gathers force.

WM. E. CHANNING

APRIL 21

Whom having not seen, ye love; in whom, though now ye see Him not, ye rejoice with joy unspeakable, and full of glory.
—*1 Peter 1:8*

If ye love me, keep my commandments.
—*John 14:15*

———— ❧ ————

BLEST be Thy love, dear Lord,
   That taught us this sweet way,
Only to love Thee for Thyself,
   And for that love obey.

J. AUSTIN

———— ❧ ————

To love God is to love His character. For instance, God is Purity. And to be pure in thought and look, to turn away from unhallowed books and conversation, to abhor the moments in which we have not been pure, is to love God. God is Love; and to love men till private attachments have expanded into a philanthropy which embraces all,—at last even the evil and enemies with compassion,—that is to love God. God is Truth. To be true, to hate every form of falsehood, to live a brave, true, real life,—that is to love God. God is Infinite; and to love the boundless reaching on from grace to grace, adding charity to faith, and rising upwards ever to see the Ideal still above us, and to die with it unattained, aiming insatiably to be perfect even as the Father is perfect,—that is to love God.

F. W. ROBERTSON

APRIL 22

Enter thou into the joy of thy Lord.
                    —Matthew 25:23

Serving the Lord; rejoicing in hope.
                    —Romans 12:11, 12

IF our love were but more simple,
  We should take Him at His word;
And our lives would be all sunshine
  In the sweetness of our Lord.
                    F. W. FABER

What would it be to love absolutely a Being absolutely love-ly,—to be able to give our whole existence, every thought, every act, every desire, to that adored One,—to know that He accepts it all, and loves us in return as God alone can love? . . . This happiness grows forever. The larger our natures become, the wider our scope of thought, the stronger our will, the more fervent our affections, the deeper must be the rapture of such God-granted prayer. Every sacrifice *resolved on* opens wide the gate; every sacrifice *accomplished* is a step towards the paradise within. Soon it will be no transitory glimpse, no rapture of a day, to be followed by clouds and coldness. Let us but labour, and pray, and wait, and the intervals of human frailty shall grow shorter and less dark, the days of our delight in God longer and brighter, till at last life shall be nought but His love; our eyes shall never grow dim, His smile never turn away.

                    F. B. COBBE

APRIL 23

These were the potters, and those that dwelt among plants and hedges: there they dwelt with the king for his work.
—1 Chronicles 4:23

A LOWLIER task on them is laid,
  With love to make the labour light;
And there their beauty they must shed
  On quiet homes, and lost to sight.
Changed are their visions high and fair,
Yet, calm and still, they labour there.

HYMNS OF THE AGES

Anywhere and everywhere we may dwell 'with the King for His work.' We may be in a very unlikely or unfavourable place for this; it may be in a literal country life, with little enough to be seen of the 'goings' of the King around us; it may be among hedges of all sorts, hindrances in all directions; it may be, furthermore, with our hands full of all manner of pottery for our daily task. No matter! The King who placed us 'there' will come and dwell there with us. The hedges are all right, or He would soon do away with them . . . what seems to hinder our way may be for its very protection. As for the pottery, why, that is exactly what He has seen fit to put into our hands, and therefore it is, for the present, 'His work.'

F. R. HAVERGAL

APRIL 24

Bear ye one another's burdens, and so fulfil the law of Christ.

—Galatians 6:2

IS thy cruse of comfort wasting?
   Rise and share it with another,
And through all the years of famine,
   It shall serve thee and thy brother.
Is thy burden hard and heavy?
   Do thy steps drag heavily?
Help to bear thy brother's burden;
   God will bear both it and thee.

ELIZABETH CHARLES

However perplexed you may at any hour become about some question of truth, one refuge and resource is always at hand: you can do something for some one besides yourself. When your own burden is heaviest, you can always lighten a little some other burden. At the times when you cannot see God, there is still open to you this sacred possibility, to *show* God; for it is the love and kindness of human hearts through which the divine reality comes home to men, whether they name it or not. Let this thought, then, stay with you; there may be times when you cannot find help, but there is no time when you cannot give help.

GEORGE S. MERRIAM

APRIL 25

Surely, I have behaved and quieted myself, as a child that is weaned of his mother; my soul is even as a weaned child.
                    —*Psalm 131:2*

QUIET, Lord, my froward heart,
Make me teachable and mild,
Upright, simple, free from art,
Make me as a weaned child;
From distrust and envy free,
Pleased with all that pleaseth Thee.

                    J. NEWTON

Oh! look not after great things: small breathings, small desires after the Lord, if true and pure, are sweet beginnings of life. Take heed of despising 'the day of small things,' by looking after some great visitation, proportionable to thy distress, according to thy eye. Nay, thou must become a child; thou must lose thy own will quite by degrees. Thou must wait for life to be measured out by the Father, and be content with what proportion, and at what time, He shall please to measure.

I. PENINGTON

'When Israel was a child, then I loved him' (Hosea 11:1). Aim to be ever this little child, contented with what the Father gives of pleasure or of play; and when restrained from pleasure or from play, and led for a season into the chamber of sorrow, rest quiet on His bosom, and be patient, and smile, as one who is nestled in a sweet and secure asylum.

ANONYMOUS

APRIL 26

If we hope for what we see not, then do we with patience wait for it.

—Romans 8:25

One day is with the Lord as a thousand years, and a thousand years as one day.

—2 Peter 3:8

LORD! who Thy thousand years dost wait
   To work the thousandth part
Of Thy vast plan, for us create
   With zeal a patient heart.

J. H. NEWMAN

I believe that if we can only see before-hand what it is that our heavenly Father means us to be,—the *soul* beauty and perfection and glory, the glorious and lovely spiritual body that this soul is to dwell in through all eternity,—if we can have a glimpse of *this,* we should not grudge all the trouble and pains He is taking with us now, to bring us up to that ideal, which is His thought of us. We know that it is God's way to work slowly, so we must not be surprised if He takes a great many years of discipline to turn a mortal being into [His likeness].

ANNIE KEARY

APRIL 27

Speak ye every man the truth to his neighbour.
—Zechariah 8:16

For our rejoicing is this, the testimony of our conscience,
that in simplicity and godly sincerity . . . we have had our con-
versation in the world.

—2 Corinthians 1:12

APPEAR I always what I am?
   And am I what I am pretending?
   Know I what way my course is bending?
And sound my word and thought the same?
                ANONYMOUS

Am I acting in simplicity, from a germ of the Divine life with-in, or am I shaping my path to obtain some immediate result of expediency? Am I endeavouring to compass effects, amidst a tan-gled web of foreign influences I cannot calculate; or am I seek-ing simply to do what is right, and leaving the consequences to the good providence of God?

M. A. SCHIMMELPENNINCK

Let it not be in any man's power to say truly of thee that thou art not simple, or that thou art not good; but let him be a liar whoever shall think anything of this kind about thee; and this is altogether in thy power. For who is he that shall hinder thee from being good and simple?

MARCUS ANTONINUS

APRIL 28

The Lord is thy keeper; the Lord is thy shade upon thy right hand.

—Psalm 121:5

Great peace have they which love Thy law; and nothing shall offend them.

—Psalm 119:165

I REST beneath the Almighty's shade,
   My griefs expire, my troubles cease;
Thou, Lord, on whom my soul is stayed,
   Wilt keep me still in perfect peace.

            C. WESLEY

One great sign of the practical recognition of the 'divine moment,' and of our finding God's habitation in it, is constant calmness and peace of mind. Events and things come with the moment; but God comes with them too. So that if He comes in the sunshine, we find rest and joy; and if He comes in the storm, we know He is King of the storms, and our hearts are not troubled. God Himself, though possessing a heart filled with the tenderest feelings, is, nevertheless, an everlasting tranquility; and when we enter into His holy tabernacle, our souls necessarily enter into the tabernacle of rest.

T. C. UPHAM

My soul was not only brought into harmony with itself and with God, but with God's providences. In the exercise of faith and love, I endured and performed whatever came in God's providence, in submission, and thankfulness, and silence.

MADAME GUYON

APRIL 29

I will arise and go to my Father.
                    —Luke 15:18

———————— ∽ ————————

OH MY God, my Father! hear,
    And help me to believe;
Weak and weary I draw near;
    Thy child, O God, receive.
I so oft have gone astray;
    To the perfect Guide I flee;
Thou wilt turn me not away,
    Thy love is pledged to me.

                    HYMNS OF THE SPIRIT

———————— ∽ ————————

O child, hast thou fallen? arise, and go, with childlike trust, to thy Father, like the prodigal son, and humbly say, with heart and mouth, 'Father, I have sinned against heaven, and before Thee, and am no more worthy to be called Thy son; make me as one of Thy hired servants.' And what will thy heavenly Father do but what that father did in the parable? Assuredly He will not change His essence, which is love, for the sake of thy misdoings. Is it not His own precious treasure, and a small thing with Him to forgive thee thy trespasses, if thou believe in Him? for His hand is not shortened that it cannot make thee fit to be saved.

JOHN TAULER

APRIL 30

Speak unto the children of Israel, that they go forward.
—Exodus 14:15

No man, having put his hand to the plough, and looking back, is fit for the kingdom of God.
—Luke 9:62

BE trustful, be steadfast, whatever betide thee,
   Only one thing do thou ask of the Lord,—
Grace to go forward wherever He guide thee,
   Simply believing the truth of His word.

ANONYMOUS

The soul ceases to weary itself with planning and foreseeing, giving itself up to God's Holy Spirit within, and to the teachings of His providence without. . . . He is not forever fretting as to his progress, or looking back to see how far he is getting on; rather he goes steadily and quietly on, and makes all the more progress because it is unconscious. So he never gets troubled and discouraged; if he falls he humbles himself, but gets up at once, and goes on with renewed earnestness.

JEAN NICOLAS GROU

MAY 1

I will bless the Lord at all times: His praise shall continually be in my mouth.

—*Psalm 34:1*

I will praise Thee, O Lord, with my whole heart; I will show forth all Thy marvellous works.

—*Psalm 9:1*

THRICE blest will all our blessings be,
When we can look through them to Thee;
When each glad heart its tribute pays
Of love and gratitude and praise.

M. J. COTTERILL

That which befits us . . . is cheerfulness, and courage, and the endeavour to realize our aspirations. Shall not the heart which has received so much, trust the Power by which it lives? May it not quit our leadings, and listen to the [God who] has guided it so gently, and taught it so much, secure that the future will be worthy of the past?

R. W. EMERSON

I have experienced that the habit of taking out of the hand of our Lord every little blessing and brightness on our path, confirms us, in an especial manner, in communion with His love.

M. A. SCHIMMELPENNINCK

MAY 2

The ornament of a meek and quiet spirit, which is in the sight of God of great price.

—*1 Peter 3:4*

To present you holy, and unblameable, and unreproveable in His sight.

—*Colossians 1:22*

THY sinless mind in us reveal,
  Thy spirit's plenitude impart!
Till all my spotless life shall tell
  The abundance of a loving heart.

C. WESLEY

Holiness appeared to me to be of a sweet, pleasant, charming, serene, calm nature. It seemed to me, it brought an inexpressible purity, brightness, peacefulness, and ravishment to the soul; and that it made the soul like a field or garden of God, with all manner of pleasant flowers, that is all pleasant, delightful, and undisturbed; enjoying a sweet calm, and the gently vivifying beams of the sun. The soul of a true Christian appeared like such a little white flower, as we see in the spring of the year, low and humble on the ground, opening its bosom to receive the pleasant beams of the sun's glory; rejoicing, as it were, in a calm rapture; diffusing around a sweet fragrancy; standing peacefully and lovingly in the midst of other flowers round about, all in like manner opening their bosoms to drink in the light of the sun.

JONATHAN EDWARDS

MAY 3

The Lord is good, a strong-hold in the day of trouble; and He knoweth them that trust in Him.
—Nahum 1:7

LEAVE God to order all thy ways,
　And hope in Him whate'er betide.
Thou'lt find Him in the evil days
　Thy all-sufficient strength and guide;
Who trusts in God's unchanging love,
Builds on the rock that nought can move.

G. NEUMARCK

Our whole trouble in our lot in this world rises from the disagreement of our mind therewith. Let the mind be brought to the lot, and the whole tumult is instantly hushed; let it be kept in that disposition, and the man shall stand at ease, in his affliction, like a rock unmoved with waters beating upon it.

T. BOSTON

How does our will become sanctified? By conforming itself unreservedly to that of God. We will all that He wills, and will nothing that He does not will; we attach our feeble will to that all-powerful will which performs everything. Thus, nothing can ever come to pass against [this] will; for nothing can happen save that which God wills, and we find in His good pleasure an inexhaustible source of peace and consolation.

FÉNELON

MAY 4

Who through faith subdued kingdoms, wrought righteousness, obtained promises, stopped the mouths of lions, out of weakness were made strong.

— *Hebrews 11:33, 34*

SHE met the hosts of Sorrow with a look
    That altered not beneath the frown they wore,
And soon the lowering brood were tamed, and took,
    Meekly, her gentle rule, and frowned no more.
Her soft hand put aside the assaults of wrath,
    And calmly broke in twain
    The fiery shafts of pain,
And rent the nets of passion from her path.
    By that victorious hand despair was slain;
With love she vanquished hate, and overcame
    Evil with good, in her great Master's name.

W. C. BRYANT

As to what may befall us outwardly, in this confused state of things, shall we not trust our tender Father, and rest satisfied in His will? Shall anything hurt us? Can tribulation, distress, persecution, famine, nakedness, peril, or sword, come between the love of the Father to the child, or the child's rest, content, and delight in His love? And doth not the love, the rest, the peace, and joy felt, swallow up all the bitterness and sorrow of the outward condition?

I. PENINGTON

MAY 5

If thou hast run with the footmen, and they have wearied thee, then how canst thou contend with horses? and if in the land of peace wherein thou trustedst, they wearied thee, then how wilt thou do in the swelling of Jordan?
    —Jeremiah 12:5

HOW couldst thou hang upon the cross,
To whom a weary hour is loss?
Or how the thorns and scourging brook,
Who shrinkest from a scornful look?
                    J. KEBLE

A heart unloving among kindred has no love towards God's saints and angels. If we have a cold heart towards a servant or a friend, why should we wonder if we have no fervour towards God? If we are cold in our private prayers, we should be earthly and dull in the most devout religious order; if we cannot bear the vexations of a companion, how should we bear the contradiction of sinners? If a little pain overcomes us, how could we endure a cross? If we have no tender, cheerful, affectionate love to those with whom our daily hours are spent, how should we feel the pulse and ardour of love to the unknown and the evil, the ungrateful and repulsive?

                    H. E. MANNING

MAY 6

Be kindly affectioned one to another with brotherly love.
—Romans 12:10

In her tongue is the law of kindness.
—Proverbs 31:26

SINCE trifles make the sum of human things,
And half our misery from our foibles springs;
Since life's best joys consist in peace and ease,
And though but few can serve, yet all can please;
Oh, let the ungentle spirit learn from hence,
A small unkindness is a great offence.

HANNAH MORE

All usefulness and all comfort may be prevented by an unkind, a sour, crabbed temper of mind,—a man that can bear with no difference of opinion or temperament. A spirit of fault-finding; an unsatisfied temper; a constant irritability; little inequalities in the look, the temper, or the manner; a brow cloudy and dissatisfied—your husband or your wife cannot tell why—will more than neutralize all the good you can do, and render life anything but a blessing.

ALBERT BARNES

You have not fulfilled every duty, unless you have fulfilled that of being pleasant.

CHARLES BUXTON

MAY 7

He healeth the broken in heart, and bindeth up their wounds. He telleth the number of the stars; He calleth them all by their names.

—Psalm 147:3, 4

TEACH me your mood, O patient stars!
   Who climb every night the ancient sky,
Leaving on space no shade, no scars,
   No trace of age, no fear to die.

               R. W. EMERSON

I looked up to the heavens once more, and the quietness of the stars seemed to reproach me. 'We are safe up here,' they seemed to say; 'we shine, fearless and confident, for the God who gave the primrose its rough leaves to hide it from the blast of uneven spring, hangs us in the awful hollow of space. We cannot fall out of His safety. Lift up your eyes on high, and behold! Who hath created these things—that bringeth out their host by number? He calleth them all by names. By the greatness of His might, for that He is strong in power, not one faileth. Why sayest thou, O Jacob! and speakest, O Israel! my way is hid from the Lord, and my judgment is passed over from my God?'

             G. MACDONALD

MAY 8

*This is the day which the Lord hath made; we will rejoice
and be glad in it.*
                              —Psalm 118:24

Why stand ye here all the day idle?
                              —Matthew 20:6

───────────────── ❧ ─────────────────

SO here hath been dawning another blue day;
Think, wilt thou let it slip useless away?
Out of eternity this new day is born;
Into eternity at night will return.

                    T. CARLYLE

───────────────── ❧ ─────────────────

Small cares, some deficiencies in the mere arrangement and
ordering of our lives, daily fret our hearts, and cross the clearness of our faculties. These entanglements hang around us, and
leave us no free soul able to give itself up, in power and gladness, to the true work of life. . . . [We need] much more of the
practised and vigorous mind, ready at every call, and thoroughly
furnished unto all good works.

                    J. H. THOM

True, we can never be at peace till we have performed the
highest duty of all,—till we have arisen, and gone to our Father.
But the performance of smaller duties, yes, even of the smallest,
will do more to give us temporary repose, will act more as
healthful anodynes, than the greatest joys that can come to us
from any other quarter.

                    G. MACDONALD

MAY 9

The Lord gave, and the Lord hath taken away; blessed be the name of the Lord.

—Job 1:21

WHAT Thou hast given, Thou canst take,
And when thou wilt new gifts can make.
 All flows from Thee alone;
When Thou didst give it, it was Thine;
When Thou retook'st it, 'twas not mine.
 Thy will in all be done.

JOHN AUSTIN

We are ready to praise when all shines fair. But when life is overcast, when all things seem to be against us, when we are in fear for some cherished happiness, or in the depths of sorrow, or in the solitude of a life which has no visible support, or in a season of sickness, and with the shadow of death approaching, —then [it is harder] to praise God; then to say, This fear, loneliness, affliction, pain, and trembling awe are as sure token of love, as life, health, joy, and the gifts of home. 'The Lord gave, and the Lord hath taken away;' on either side it is He, and all is love alike; 'blessed be the name of the Lord,'—this is the true sacrifice of praise. What can come amiss to a soul which is so in accord with God? What can make so much as one jarring tone in all its harmony? In all the changes of this fitful life, it ever dwells in praise.

H. E. MANNING

MAY 10

The Lord redeemeth the soul of His servants; and none of them that trust in Him shall be desolate.
—Psalm 34:22

Though He slay me, yet will I trust in Him.
—Job 13:15

I PRAISE Thee while my days go on;
I love Thee while my days go on:
Through dark and dearth, through fire and frost,
With emptied arms and treasure lost,
I thank Thee while my days go on.

E. B. BROWNING

The sickness of the last week was fine medicine; pain [had to either] disintegrate the spirit, or [become] spiritual. I rose,—I felt that I had given to God [a great amount],—[I] had promised Him in youth that to be a blot on this fair world, at His command, would be acceptable. [I would] constantly offer myself to continue the obscurest and loneliest thing ever heard of, with one proviso,—His agency. Yes, [I will] love Thee, and all Thou dost, [even] while Thou sheddest frost and darkness on every path of mine.

MARY MOODY EMERSON

MAY 11

Shall we receive good at the hand of God, and shall we not receive evil?

—Job 2:10

Thou hast dealt well with Thy servant, O Lord, according to Thy word.

—Psalm 119:65

WHATSOE'ER our lot may be,
  Calmly in this thought we'll rest,—
Could we see as Thou dost see,
  We should choose it as the best.

WM. GASKELL

It is a proverbial saying, that every one makes his own destiny. This is usually interpreted, that every one, by his wise or unwise conduct, prepares good or evil for himself. But we may also understand it, that whatever it be that he receives from the hand of Providence, he may accommodate himself to it; [and thus] he will find his lot good for him, however much [it] may seem to others to be wanting.

WM. VON HUMBOLDT

What God may hereafter require of you, you must not give yourself the least trouble about. Everything He gives you to do, you must do as well as ever you can, and that is the best possible preparation for what He may want you to do next. If people would but do what they have to do, they would always find themselves ready for what came next.

G. MACDONALD

MAY 12

Fear none of those things which thou shalt suffer: . . . ye shall have tribulation ten days: be thou faithful unto death, and I will give thee a crown of life.
—Revelation 2:10

———— ⧢ ————

THEN, O my soul, be ne'er afraid,
On Him who thee and all things made
   Do thou all calmly rest;
Whate'er may come, where'er we go,
Our Father in the heavens must know
   In all things what is best.

               PAUL FLEMMING

———— ⧢ ————

Guide me, O Lord, in all the changes and varieties of the world; that in all things that shall happen, I may have an evenness and tranquillity of spirit; that my soul may be wholly resigned to Thy divine will and pleasure, never murmuring at Thy gentle chastisements and fatherly correction. Amen.

               JEREMY TAYLOR

Thou art never at any time nearer to God than when under tribulation; which He permits for the purification and beautifying of thy soul.

               M. MOLINOS

Prize inward exercises, griefs, and troubles; and let faith and patience have their perfect work in them.

               I. PENINGTON

MAY 13

I pray not that Thou shouldest take them out of the world, but that Thou shouldest keep them from the evil.
—John 17:15

IN busy mart and crowded street,
No less than in the still retreat,
Thou, Lord, art near, our souls to bless,
With all a Father's tenderness.

I. WILLIAMS

A constant anticipation of evils which perhaps never will come, a foreboding which takes away life and energy from the present, will simply hinder and cloud the soul, and make it timid and sad. If troublous thoughts as to the future will press, darkening a bright present, or hurrying on coming clouds, the safest thing is to offer them continually as they arise to God, offering too the future which they contemplate, and asking for grace to concentrate our energies on the immediate duties surrounding us. Many have dreaded troubles which they thought must come; and while they went on ever expecting to make the turn in their path which was to open out fully the evil, lo! they found that they had reached the journey's end, and were at the haven where they would be. Even for others it is not wise to indulge in over-much looking forward in fearfulness. Come what may to the dearest ones we have on earth, God and His upholding grace will be there, and He cares for them more than even we can do. An earnest commendation to His love will avail them more than all our fretting.

H. L. SIDNEY LEAR

MAY 14

*And what doth the Lord require of thee, but to do justly, and
to love mercy, and to walk humbly with thy God?*
               —Micah 6:8

*Put on therefore . . . kindness, humbleness of mind, meek-
ness, long-suffering.*

                              —Colossians 3:12

PLANT in us an humble mind,
Patient, pitiful, and kind;
Meek and lowly let us be,
Full of goodness, full of Thee.
                              C. WESLEY

There is no true and constant gentleness without humility.
While we are so fond of ourselves, we are easily offended with
others. Let us be persuaded that nothing is due to us, and then
nothing will disturb us. Let us often think of our own infirmities,
and we shall become indulgent towards those of others.

                    FÉNELON

Endeavour to be patient in bearing with the defects and infirmities of others, of what sort soever they be; for that thyself also
hast many failings which must be borne with by others. If thou
canst not make thyself such an one as thou wouldest, how canst
thou expect to have another in all things to thy liking?

                THOMAS À KEMPIS

MAY 15

My presence shall go with thee, and I will give thee rest.
—Exodus 33:14

Thou wilt show me the path of life: in Thy presence is fulness of joy; at Thy right hand there are pleasures for evermore.
—Psalm 16:11

THY presence fills my mind with peace,
  Brightens the thoughts so dark erewhile,
Bids cares and sad forebodings cease,
  Makes all things smile.

CHARLOTTE ELLIOTT

How shall we rest in God? By giving ourselves wholly to Him. If you give yourself by halves, you cannot find full rest; there will ever be a lurking disquiet in that half which is withheld. Martyrs, confessors, and saints have tested this rest, and 'counted themselves blessed in that they endured.' A countless host of God's faithful servants have drunk deeply of it under the daily burden of a weary life,—dull, commonplace, painful, or desolate. All that God has been to them He is ready to be to you. [When] the heart [is] fairly given to God, with a clear conscience, a fitting rule of life, and a steadfast purpose of obedience, you will find a wonderful sense of rest coming over you.

JEAN NICOLAS GROU

MAY 16

Finally, my brethren, be strong in the Lord, and in the power of His might.
>   *—Ephesians 6:10*

No man can serve two masters.
>   *—Matthew 6:24*

OH, there are heavenly heights to reach
　　In many a fearful place,
Where the poor timid heir of God
　　Lies blindly on his face;
Lies languishing for grace divine
　　That he shall never see
Till he go forward at thy sign,
　　And trust himself to Thee.

>   A. L. WARING

Reservations lie latent in the mind concerning some unhallowed sentiments or habits in the present, some possibly impending temptations in the future; and thus do we cheat ourselves of inward and outward joys together. We give up many an indulgence for conscience' sake, but stop short at that point of entire faithfulness wherein conscience could reward us. If we would but give ourselves wholly to God,—give up, for the present and the future, every act, and, above all, every thought and feeling, to be all purified to the uttermost, and rendered the best, noblest, holiest we can conceive,—then would sacrifice bear with it a peace rendering itself, I truly believe, far *easier* than before.

>   F. P. COBBE

MAY 17

Wherefore comfort yourselves together, and edify one another, even as also ye do.
> —*1 Thessalonians 5:11*

Thou shalt love thy neighbour as thyself.
> —*Matthew 19:19*

SO others shall
Take patience, labour, to their heart and hand,
From thy hand, and thy heart, and thy brave cheer,
And God's grace fructify through thee to all.
The least flower with a brimming cup may stand,
And share its dewdrop with another near.

E. B. BROWNING

What is meant by "our neighbour" we cannot doubt; it is every one with whom we are brought into contact. First of all, he is literally our neighbour who is next to us in our own family and household; husband to wife, wife to husband, parent to child, brother to sister, master to servant, servant to master. Then it is he who is close to us in our own neighbourhood, in our own town, in our own parish, in our own street. With these all true charity begins. . . . But, besides these, as our Lord teaches, it is every one who is thrown across our path by the changes and chances of life; he or she, whosoever it be, whom we have any means of helping,—the unfortunate stranger whom we may meet in travelling, the deserted friend whom no one else cares to look after.

A. P. STANLEY

MAY 18

We know that we have passed from death unto life, because we love the brethren.
—1 John 3:14

He that loveth not knoweth not God; for God is love.
—1 John 4:8

MUTUAL love the token be,
Lord, that we belong to Thee:
Love, Thine image, love impart;
Stamp it on our face and heart;
Only love to us be given;
Lord, we ask no other heaven.

C. WESLEY

Oh, how many times can most of us remember when we would gladly have made any compromise in our consciences, would gladly have made the most costly sacrifices to God, if He would only have excused us from this duty of loving, of which our nature seemed utterly incapable. It is far easier to feel kindly, to act kindly, toward those with whom we are seldom brought into contact, whose tempers and prejudices do not rub against ours, whose interests do not clash with ours, than to keep up an habitual, steady, self-sacrificing love towards those whose weaknesses and faults are always forcing themselves upon us, and are stirring up our own. A man may pass good muster as a philanthropist who makes but a poor master to his servants, or father to his children.

F. D. MAURICE

MAY 19

Rest in the Lord, and wait patiently for Him.
                                    —Psalm 37:7

Trust in Him at all times.
                                    —Psalm 62:8

DOST thou ask when comes His hour?
    Then, when it shall aid thee best.
Trust His faithfulness and power,
    Trust in Him, and quiet rest.
                                    ANONYMOUS

I had found [communion with God] to consist, not only in the silencing of the outward man, but in the silencing also of every thought, and in the concentration of the soul and all its powers into a simple, quiet watching and waiting for the food which its heavenly Father might see fit either to give or to withhold. In no case could it be sent empty away; for, if comfort, light, or joy were withheld, the act of humble waiting at the gate of heavenly wisdom could not but work patience in it, and thus render it, by humility and obedience, more 'meet to be a partaker of the inheritance of the saints in light,' and also more blessed in itself.

M. A. KELTY

'Rest in the Lord; wait patiently for Him.' In Hebrew, 'be silent to God, and let Him mould thee.' Keep still, and He will mould thee to the right shape.

MARTIN LUTHER

MAY 20

To be spiritually minded is life and peace.
—Romans 8:6

STILLED now be every anxious care;
See God's great goodness everywhere;
Leave all to Him in perfect rest:
He will do all things for the best.

FROM THE GERMAN

We should all [aim] for a calmer spirit, that we may the better serve God in praying to Him and praising Him; and serve one another in love, that we may be fitted to do and receive good; that we may make our passage to heaven more easy and cheerful, without drooping and hanging the wing. So much as we are quiet and cheerful upon good ground, so much we live, and are, as it were, in heaven.

R. SIBBES

Possess yourself as much as you possibly can in peace; not by any effort, but by letting all things fall to the ground which trouble or excite you. This is no work, but is, as it were, a setting down a fluid to settle that has become turbid through agitation.

MADAME GUYON

MAY 21

*The beloved of the Lord shall dwell in safety by Him; and
the Lord shall cover him all the day long.*
—*Deuteronomy 33:12*

WHATE'ER events betide,
   Thy will they all perform;
Safe in Thy breast my head I hide,
   Nor fear the coming storm.

H. F. LYTE

I have seemed to see a need of everything God gives me, and
want nothing that He denies me. There is no dispensation,
though afflictive, but either in it, or after it, I find that I could
not be without it. Whether it be taken from or not given me,
sooner or later God quiets me in Himself without it. I cast all my
concerns on the Lord, and live securely on the care and wisdom
of my heavenly Father. My ways, you know, are in a sense,
hedged up with thorns, and grow darker and darker daily; but
yet I distrust not my good God in the least, and live more quietly
in the absence of all by faith, than I should do, I am persuaded,
if I possessed them.

ANONYMOUS, 1810

MAY 22

*He that dwelleth in the secret place of the Most High shall
abide under the shadow of the Almighty.*
—Psalm 91:1

THEY who on the Lord rely,
Safely dwell though danger's nigh;
Lo! His sheltering wings are spread
O'er each faithful servant's head.
When they wake, or when they sleep,
Angel guards their vigils keep;
Death and danger may be near,
Faith and love have nought to fear.

HARRIET AUBER

'There shall no evil befall thee, neither shall any plague come
nigh thy dwelling,' is a promise to the fullest extent verified in
the case of all 'who dwell in the secret place of the Most High.'
To them sorrows are not 'evils,' sicknesses are not 'plagues;' the
shadow of the Almighty extending far around those who abide
under it, alters the character of all things which come within its
influence.

ANONYMOUS

It is faith's work to claim and challenge loving-kindness out of
all the roughest strokes of God.

S. RUTHERFORD

MAY 23

Be content with such things as ye have.
—Hebrews 13:5

I have learned, in whatsoever state I am, therewith to be content.

—Philippians 4:11

NO longer forward or behind
   I look in hope or fear;
But, grateful, take the good I find,
   The best of now and here.

J. G. WHITTIER

If we wished to gain contentment, we might try such rules as these:

1. Allow thyself to complain of nothing, not even of the weather.

2. Never picture thyself to thyself under any circumstances in which thou art not.

3. Never compare thine own lot with that of another.

4. Never allow thyself to dwell on the wish that this or that had been, or were, otherwise than it was, or is. God Almighty loves thee better and more wisely than thou dost thyself.

5. Never dwell on the morrow. Remember that it is God's, not thine. The heaviest part of sorrow often is to look forward to it. 'The Lord will provide.'

E. B. PUSEY

MAY 24

Now no chastening for the present seemeth to be joyous, but grievous: nevertheless afterward it yieldeth the peaceable fruit of righteousness unto them which are exercised thereby.
                                        —*Hebrews 12:11*

I CANNOT say,
Beneath the pressures of life's cares to-day,
    I joy in these;
    But I can say
That I had rather walk this rugged way,
    If Him it please.

                        S. G. BROWNING

The particular annoyance which befell you this morning; the vexatious words which met your ear and 'grieved' your spirit; the disappointment which was His appointment for to-day; the slight but hindering ailment; the presence of some one who is 'a grief of mind' to you,—whatever this day seemeth not joyous, but grievous, is linked in 'the good pleasure of His goodness' with a corresponding afterward of 'peaceable fruit,' the very seed from which, if you only do not choke it, this shall spring and ripen.

                        F. R. HAVERGAL

MAY 25

O my Father, if it be possible, let this cup pass from me; nevertheless not as I will, but as Thou wilt.
—Matthew 26:39

O LORD my God, do Thou Thy holy will,—
    I will lie still.
I will not stir, lest I forsake Thine arm,
    And break the charm
Which lulls me, clinging to my Father's breast,
    In perfect rest.

J. KEBLE

Resignation to the will of God is the whole of piety. It includes in it all that is good, and is a source of the most settled quiet and composure of mind. Our resignation to the will of God may be said to be perfect, when our will is lost and resolved up into His; when we rest in His will as our end, as being itself most just, and right, and good. Such [a love for] what is just and right and good, such a loyalty of heart of the Governor of the universe, shall prevail over all sinister indirect desires of our own.

JOSEPH BUTLER

There are no disappointments to those whose wills are buried in the will of God.

F. W. FABER

Lord, Thy will be done in father, mother, child, in everything and everywhere; without a reserve, without a BUT, an IF, or a limit.

FRANCIS DE SALES

MAY 26

The Lord heareth your murmurings, which ye murmur against Him.

—Exodus 16:8

———————————— ✦ ————————————

WITHOUT murmur, uncomplaining,
   In His hand,
Leave whatever things thou canst not
   Understand.

K. R. HAGENBACH

———————————— ✦ ————————————

One great characteristic of holiness is never to be exacting—never to complain. Each complaint drags us down a degree, in our upward course. If you would discern in whom God's spirit dwells, watch that person, and notice whether you ever hear him murmur.

GOLD DUST

When we wish things to be otherwise than they are, we lose sight of the great practical parts of the life of godliness. We wish, and wish—when, if we have done all that lies on us, we [ought to] fall quietly into the hands of God. Such wishing cuts the very sinews of our privileges and consolations. You are leaving me for a time; and you say that you wish you could leave me better, or leave me with some assistance. But if it is right for you to go, it is right for me to meet what lies on me, without a wish that I had less to meet, or were better able to meet it.

R. CECIL

MAY 27

He that is faithful in that which is least is faithful also in much.

—*Luke 16:10*

The Lord preserveth the faithful.

—*Psalm 31:23*

THE trivial round, the common task,
Would furnish all we ought to ask;
Room to deny ourselves; a road
To bring us, daily, nearer God.

J. KEBLE

Exactness in little duties is a wonderful source of cheerfulness.

F. W. FABER

The unremitting retention of simple and high sentiments in obscure duties is hardening the character of that temper which will work with honour, if need be, in the tumult or on the scaffold.

R. W. EMERSON

We are too fond of our own will. We want to be doing what we fancy mighty things; but the great point is, to do small things, when called to them, in a right spirit.

R. CECIL

It is not on great occasions only that we are required to be faithful to the will of God. O*ccasions constantly occur, and we should be surprised to perceive how much our spiritual advancement depends on small obediences.

MADAME SWETCHINE

MAY 28

Strengthened with all might, according to His glorious
power, unto all patience and long-suffering with joyfulness.
—Colossians 1:11

GOD doth not need
Either man's works or His own gifts; who best
Bear His mild yoke, they serve Him best; His state
Is kingly; thousands at His bidding speed,
And post o'er land and ocean without rest;
They also serve who only stand and wait.

J. MILTON

We cannot always be doing a great work, but we can always
be doing something that belongs to our condition. To be silent,
to suffer, to pray when we cannot act, is acceptable to God. A
disappointment, a contradiction, a harsh word, an annoyance,
a wrong received and endured as in His presence, is worth
more than a long prayer. We do not lose time if we bear loss
with gentleness and patience, provided the loss was inevitable,
and was not caused by our own fault.

FÉNELON

MAY 29

Be not slothful, but followers of them who through faith and patience inherit the promises.

—*Hebrews 6:12*

WHERE now with pain thou treadest, trod
The whitest of the saints of God!
To show thee where their feet were set,
The light which led them shineth yet.

J. G. WHITTIER

Let us learn from this communion of saints to live in hope.
Those who are now at rest were once like ourselves. They
were once weak, faulty, sinful; they had their burdens and
hindrances, their slumbering and weariness, their failures and
their falls. But now they have overcome. Their life was once
homely and commonplace. Their day ran out as ours. Morning
and noon and night came and went to them as to us. Their life,
too, was as lonely and sad as yours. Little fretful circumstances
and frequent disturbing changes wasted away their hours as
yours. There is nothing in your life that was not in theirs; there
was nothing in theirs but may be also in your own. They have
overcome, each one, and one by one; each in his turn, when the
day came, and God called him to the trial. And so shall you like-
wise.

H. E. MANNING

MAY 30

Zebulun and Naphtali were a people that jeoparded their lives unto the death in the high places of the field.
—Judges 5:18

THOUGH Love repine, and Reason chafe,
  There came a voice without reply,—
'Tis man's perdition to be safe,
  When for the truth he ought to die.
                    R. W. EMERSON

Some say that the age of chivalry is past. The age of chivalry is never past, so long as there is a wrong left unredressed on earth, or a man or woman left to say, 'I will redress that wrong, or spend my life in the attempt.' The age of chivalry is never past, so long as we have faith enough to say, 'God will help me redress that wrong; or, if not me, He will help those that come after me, for His eternal Will is to overcome evil with good.'

C. KINGSLEY

Whatever God tells us to do, He also helps us to do.

DORA GREENWELL

MAY 31

Let all those that put their trust in Thee rejoice: . . . let them also that love Thy name be joyful in Thee.
—Psalm 5:11

He maketh me to lie down in green pastures.
—Psalm 23:2

I CAN hear these violets chorus
   To the sky's benediction above;
And we all are together lying
   On the bosom of Infinite Love.

Oh, the peace at the heart of Nature!
   Oh, the light that is not of day!
Why seek it afar forever,
   When it cannot be lifted away?

                  W. C. GANNETT

What inexpressible joy for me, to look up through the apple-blossom and the fluttering leaves, and to see God's love there; to listen to the thrush that has built his nest among them, and to feel God's love, who cares for the birds, in every note that swells his little throat; to look beyond to the bright blue depths of the sky, and feel they are a canopy of blessing,—the roof of the house of my Father. If clouds pass over it, it is the unchangeable light they veil. Even when the day itself passes, I shall see that the night itself only unveils new worlds of light. [I] know that if I could unwrap fold after fold of God's universe, I should only unfold more and more blessing, and see deeper and deeper into the love which is at the heart of all.

                  ELIZABETH CHARLES

JUNE 1

One thing have I desired of the Lord, that will I seek after;
that I may dwell in the house of the Lord all the days of my
life, to behold the beauty of the Lord, and to enquire in His
temple.

—*Psalm 27:4*

THY beauty, O my Father! All is Thine;
   But there is beauty in Thyself, from whence
The beauty Thou hast made doth ever flow
   In streams of never-failing affluence.

Thou art the Temple! and though I am lame,—
   Lame from my birth, and shall be till I die,—
I enter through the gate called Beautiful,
   And am alone with Thee, O Thou Most High!

J. W. CHADWICK

Consider that all which appears beautiful outwardly, is solely derived from the invisible Spirit which is the source of that external beauty, and say joyfully, 'Behold, these are streamlets from the uncreated Foundation; behold, these are drops from the infinite Ocean of all good! Oh! how does my inmost heart rejoice at the thought of that eternal, infinite Beauty, which is the source and origin of all created beauty!'

L. SCUPOLI

JUNE 2

We all, with open face, beholding as in a glass the glory of the Lord, are changed into the same image, from glory to glory, even as by the Spirit of the Lord.
—2 Corinthians 3:18

———————————— ⟡ ————————————

THEN every tempting form of sin,
   Shamed in Thy presence, disappears,
And all the glowing, raptured soul
   The likeness it contemplates wears.

P. DODDRIDGE

———————————— ⟡ ————————————

Then does a good man become the tabernacle of God, wherein the divine Shechinah does rest, and which the divine glory fills, when the frame of his mind and life is wholly according to that idea and pattern which he receives from the mount. We best glorify Him when we grow most like to Him. We act most for His glory when a true spirit of sanctity, justice, meekness, etc., runs through all our actions; when we so live in the world as becomes those that converse with the great Mind and Wisdom of the whole world, with that Almighty Spirit that made, supports, and governs all things, with that Being from whence all good flows, and in which there is no spot, stain, or shadow of evil. Being [thus] captivated and overcome by the sense of the Divine loveliness and goodness, [we] endeavour to be like Him, and conform ourselves, as much as may be, to Him.

DR. JOHN SMITH

JUNE 3

The righteous shall be glad in the Lord, and shall trust in Him.

—*Psalm 64:10*

Whoso trusteth in the Lord, happy is he.
—*Proverbs 16:20*

THE heart that trusts forever sings,
And feels as light as it had wings,
A well of peace within it springs,—
   Come good or ill,
Whate'er to-day, to-morrow brings,
   It is His will.

I. WILLIAMS

He will weave no longer a spotted life of shreds and patches, but he will live with a divine unity. He will cease from what is base and frivolous in his life, and be content with all places, and with any service he can render. He will calmly front the morrow, in the negligency of that trust which carries God with it, and so hath already the whole future in the bottom of the heart.

R. W. EMERSON

He who believes in God is not careful for the morrow, but labours joyfully and with a great heart. 'For He giveth His beloved, as in sleep.' They must work and watch, yet never be careful or anxious, but commit all to Him, and live in serene tranquillity; with a quiet heart, as one who sleeps safely and quietly.

MARTIN LUTHER

JUNE 4

Therefore, my beloved brethren, be ye stedfast, unmoveable, always abounding in the work of the Lord, forasmuch as ye know that your labour is not in vain in the Lord.
— *1 Corinthians 15:58*

SAY not, 'Twas all in vain,
  The anguish and the darkness and the strife;
Love thrown upon the waters comes again
  In quenchless yearnings for a nobler life.
ANNA SHIPTON

Did you ever hear of a man who had striven all his life faithfully and singly toward an object and in no measure obtained it? If a man constantly aspires, is he not elevated? Did ever a man try heroism, magnanimity, truth, sincerity, and find that there was no advantage in them,—that it was a vain endeavour?

H. D. THOREAU

Do right, and God's recompense to you will be the power of doing more right. Give, and God's reward to you will be the spirit of giving more: a blessed spirit, for it is the Spirit of God himself, whose Life is the blessedness of giving. Love, and God will pay you with the capacity of more love; for love is Heaven—love is God within you.

F. W. ROBERTSON

JUNE 5

Speak, Lord: for Thy servant heareth.
—1 Samuel 3:9

THOUGH heralded with nought of fear
  Or outward sign or show:
Though only to the inward ear
  It whispers soft and low;
Though dropping, as the manna fell,
  Unseen, yet from above,
Noiseless as dew-fall, heed it well,—
  Thy Father's call of love.

J. G. WHITTIER

This is one result of the attitude into which we are put by humility, by disinterestedness, by purity, by calmness—that we have the opportunity, the disengagement, the silence in which we may watch what is the will of God concerning us. If we think no more of ourselves than we ought to think, if we seek not our own but others' welfare, if we are prepared to take all things as God's dealings with us, then we may have a chance of catching from time to time what God has to tell us. In the Mussulman devotions one constant gesture is to put the hands to the ears, as if to listen for the messages from the other world. This is the attitude, the posture which our minds assume, if we have a standing-place above and beyond the stir and confusion and dissipation of this mortal world.

A. P. STANLEY

JUNE 6

Him that overcometh will I make a pillar in the temple of my God.
> —*Revelation 3:12*

In whom ye also are builded together for an habitation of God through the Spirit.
> —*Ephesians 2:22*

❧

NONE the place ordained refuseth,
    They are one, and they are all,
Living stones, the Builder chooseth
    For the courses of his wall.

JEAN INGELOW

❧

Slowly, through all the universe, that temple of God is being built. Wherever a soul, by free-willed obedience, catches the fire of God's likeness, it is set into the growing walls, a living stone. When, in your hard fight, in your tiresome drudgery, or in your terrible temptation, you catch the purpose of your being and give yourself to God, and so give Him the chance to give Himself to you, your life, a living stone, is taken up and set into that growing wall. . . . Wherever souls are being tried and ripened, in whatever commonplace and homely ways;—there God is hewing out the pillars for His temple. Oh, if the stone can only have some vision of the temple of which it is to lie a part forever, what patience must fill it as it feels the blows of the hammer, and knows that success for it is simply to let itself be wrought into what shape the Master wills.

PHILLIPS BROOKS

JUNE 7

Ye are the children of light, and the children of the day.
—1 Thessalonians 5:5

Light is sown for the righteous, and gladness for the upright
in heart.

—Psalm 97:11

SERENE will be our days and bright,
   And happy will our nature be,
When love is an unerring light,
   And joy its own security.

W. WORDSWORTH

Nothing can produce so great a serenity of life as a mind
free from guilt, and kept untainted, not only from actions, but
purposes that are wicked. By this means the soul will be not
only unpolluted, but not disturbed. The fountain will run clear
and unsullied, and the streams that flow from it will be just and
honest deeds, ecstasies of satisfaction, a brisk energy of spirit,
which makes a man an enthusiast in his joy, and [gives] a tena-
cious memory, sweeter than hope. For as shrubs which are cut
down with the morning dew upon them do for a long time after
retain their fragrance, so the good actions of a wise man perfume his mind, and leave a rich scent behind them.

PLUTARCH

JUNE 8

Who hath despised the day of small things?
—Zechariah 4:10

LITTLE things
   On little wings
Bear little souls to heaven.

ANONYMOUS

An occasional effort, even of an ordinary holiness, may accomplish great acts of sacrifice. . . . Constant discipline in unnoticed ways, and the spirit's silent unselfishness, becoming the hidden habit of the life, give to it its true saintly beauty, and this is the result of care and lowly love in little things. Perfection is attained most readily by this constancy of religious faithfulness in all minor details of life, consecrating the daily efforts of self-forgetting love.

T. T. CARTER

Love's secret is to be always doing things for God, and not to mind because they are such very little ones.

F. W. FABER

There may be living and habitual conversation in heaven, under the aspect of the most simple, ordinary life. Let us always remember that holiness does not consist in doing uncommon things, but in doing everything with purity of heart.

H. E. MANNING

JUNE 9

He that is slow to anger is better than the mighty; and he
that ruleth his spirit than he that taketh a city.
                    —*Proverbs 16:32*

PURGE from our hearts the stains so deep and foul,
  Of wrath and pride and care;
Send Thine own holy calm upon the soul,
  And bid it settle there!

ANONYMOUS

Let this truth be present to thee in the excitement of anger,—
that to be moved by passion is not manly, but that mildness and
gentleness, as they are more agreeable to human nature, so also
are they more manly. . . . For in the same degree in which a
man's mind is nearer to freedom from all passion, in the same
degree also it is nearer to strength.

MARCUS ANTONINUS

It is no great matter to associate with the good and gentle, for
this is naturally pleasing to all, and every one willingly enjoyeth
peace, and loveth those best that agree with him. But to be able
to live peaceably with hard and perverse persons, or with the
disorderly, or with such as go contrary to us, is a great grace, and
a most commendable and manly thing.

THOMAS À KEMPIS

JUNE 10

Who is among you that feareth the Lord, that obeyeth the voice of His servant, that walketh in darkness, and hath no light? let him trust in the name of the Lord, and stay upon his God.
                                        —Isaiah 1:10

The Lord my God will enlighten my darkness.
                                        —Psalm 18:28

————————— ❧ —————————

WHEN we in darkness walk,
    Nor feel the heavenly flame,
Then is the time to trust our God,
    And rest upon His name.
                                        A. M. TOPLADY

————————— ❧ —————————

He has an especial tenderness of love towards thee for that thou art in the dark and hast no light, and His heart is glad when thou dost arise and say, 'I will go to my Father.' For He sees thee through all the gloom through which thou canst not see Him. Say to Him, 'My God, I am very dull and low and hard; but Thou art wise and high and tender, and Thou art my God. I am Thy child. Forsake me not.' Then fold the arms of thy faith, and wait in quietness until light goes up in the darkness. Fold the arms of thy Faith, I say, but not of thy Action. Think of something that thou oughtest to do, and go and do it, if it be but the sweeping of a room, or the preparing of a meal, or a visit to a friend. Heed not thy feelings: do thy work.

                        G. MACDONALD

JUNE 11

In the day when I cried Thou answeredst me and strength-
enedst me with strength in my soul.

—*Psalm 138:3*

IT is not that I feel less weak, but Thou
Wilt be my strength; it is not that I see
Less sin; but more of pardoning love with Thee,
   And all-sufficient grace, Enough! And now
All fluttering thought is stilled; I only rest,
And feel that Thou art near, and know that I am blest.

F. R. HAVERGAL

Even though you cannot believe, yet be not dismayed [by
this]. But do sink into, or at least pant after the hidden measure
of life—which is not in that which distresses, disturbs and fills
you with thoughts, fears, troubles, anguish, darknesses, terrors,
and the like; no, no! [Instead, desire] that which inclines to
patience, to stillness, to hope, to waiting, to silence before the
Father.

I. PENINGTON

We have only to be patient, to pray, and to do His will, according to our present light and strength, and the growth of the soul
will go on. The plant grows in the mist and under clouds as truly
as under sunshine. So does the heavenly principle within.

W. E. CHANNING

JUNE 12

Have not I commanded thee? Be strong and of a good courage; be not afraid, neither be thou dismayed: for the Lord thy God is with thee whithersoever thou goest.
                    —Joshua 1:9

ONE holy Church, one army strong,
　　One steadfast high intent,
One working band, one harvest-song,
　　One King omnipotent.

                    S. JOHNSON

We listened to a man whom we felt to be, with all his heart and soul and strength, striving against whatever was mean and unmanly and unrighteous in our little world. It was not the cold clear voice of one giving advice, and warning from serene heights to those who were struggling and sinning below, but the warm loving voice of one who was fighting for us and by our sides, and calling on us to help him and ourselves and one another. And so, wearily and little by little, but surely and steadily on the whole, was brought home to the young boy, for the first time, the meaning of his life—that it was no fool's or sluggard's paradise into which he had wandered by chance, but a battlefield ordained from on old, where there are no spectators, but the youngest must take his side, and the stakes are life and death.

                    THOMAS HUGHES

JUNE 13

If we walk in the light as He is in the light, we have fellow-ship one with another.
—1 John 1:7

God is not unrighteous to forget your work and labour of love, which ye have showed toward His name, in that ye have ministered to the saints, and do minister.
—Hebrews 6:10

WHEREVER in the world I am,
  In whatsoe'er estate,
I have a fellowship with hearts,
  To keep and cultivate,
And a work of lowly love to do
  For the Lord on whom I wait.

A. L. WARING

We do not always perceive that even the writing of a note of congratulation, the fabrication of something intended as an offering of affection, our necessary [interaction] with characters which have no congeniality with our own, or hours apparently trifled away in the domestic circle, may be made by us the performance of a most sacred and blessed work—even the carrying out, after our feeble measure, of the design of God for the increase of happiness.

ANNA, OR PASSAGES FROM HOME LIFE

Definite work is not always that which is cut and squared for us, but that which comes as a claim upon the conscience, whether it's nursing in a hospital, or hemming a handkerchief.

ELIZABETH M. SEWELL

JUNE 14

The Lord shall give thee rest from thy sorrow, and from thy fear, and from the hard bondage wherein thou wast made to serve.

—Isaiah 14:3

TO-DAY, beneath Thy chastening eye,
I crave alone for peace and rest;
Submissive in Thy hand to lie,
   And feel that it is best.

J. G. WHITTIER

O Lord, who art as the Shadow of a great Rock in a weary land, who beholdest Thy weak creatures weary of labour, weary of pleasure, weary of hope deferred, weary of self; in Thine abundant compassion, and unutterable tenderness, bring us, I pray Thee, unto Thy rest. Amen.

CHRISTINA G. ROSSETTI

Grant to me, above all things that can be desired, to rest in Thee, and in Thee to have my heart at peace. Thou art the true peace of the heart, Thou its only rest. Out of Thee all things are hard and restless. In this very peace, that is, in Thee, the One Chief Eternal Good, I will sleep and rest. Amen.

THOMAS À KEMPIS

Thou hast made us for Thyself, O Lord; and our heart is restless until it rests in Thee.

ST. AUGUSTINE

JUNE 15

God is our refuge and strength, a very present help in trou-
ble. Therefore will not we fear, though the earth be removed,
and though the mountains be carried into the midst of the
sea.

—Psalm 46:1, 2

THOUGH waves and storms go o'er my head,
    Though strength and health and friends be gone,
Though joys be withered all, and dead,
    Though every comfort be withdrawn,
On this my steadfast soul relies,—
    Father! Thy mercy never dies.

                    JOHANN A. RÖTHE

Your external circumstances may change, toil may take the
place of rest, sickness of health, trials may thicken within and
without. Externally, you are the prey of such circumstances. But if
your heart is stayed on God, no changes or chances can touch it,
and all that may befall you will but draw you closer to Him. Whatever the present moment may bring, your knowledge that it is His
will, and that your future heavenly life will be influenced by it,
will make all not only tolerable, but welcome to you. No vicissi-
tudes can affect you greatly, [since you] know that He who holds
you in His powerful hand cannot change, but abideth forever.

               JEAN NICOLAS GROU

JUNE 16

Now unto Him that is able to do exceeding abundantly above all that we ask or think, according to the power that worketh in us, unto Him be glory, throughout all ages, world without end. Amen.

—*Ephesians 3:20, 21*

❧

WE would not meagre gifts down-call
When Thou dost yearn to yield us all;
But for this life, this little hour,
Ask all Thy love and care and power.

J. INGELOW

❧

God so loveth us that He would make all things [serve] us [as] messengers of His love. Do for His sake deeds of love, and He will give thee His love. Still thyself, thy own cares, thy own thoughts for Him, and He will speak to thy heart. Ask for Himself, and He will give thee Himself. Truly, a secret hidden thing is the love of God, known only to them who seek it. [Whatever] man can have of it here is how slight a foretaste of that endless ocean of His love!

E. B. PUSEY

JUNE 17

Consider the lilies of the field, how they grow.
—Matthew 6:28

———————— ⚭ ————————

THEY do not toil:
Content with their allotted task
They do but grow; they do not ask
A richer lot, a higher sphere,
But in their loveliness appear,
And grow, and smile, and do their best,
And unto God they leave the rest.

MARIANNE FARNINGHAM

———————— ⚭ ————————

Interpose no barrier to His mighty life-giving power, working in you all the good pleasure of His will. Yield yourself up utterly to His sweet control. Put your growing into His hands as completely as you have put all your other affairs. Suffer Him to manage it as He will. Do not concern yourself about it, nor even think of it. Trust Him absolutely and always. Accept each moment's dispensation as it comes to you from His dear hands, as being the needed sunshine or dew for that moment's growth. Say a continual 'yes' to your Father's will.

H. W. S.

Thine own self-will and anxiety, thy hurry and labour, disturb thy peace and prevent Me from working in thee. Look at the little flowers, in the serene summer days; they quietly open their petals, and the sun shines into them with his gentle influences. So will I do for thee, if thou wilt yield thyself to Me.

G. TERSTEEGEN

JUNE 18

Wherefore, if God so clothe the grass of the field, which to-day is, and tomorrow is cast into the oven, shall He not much more clothe you, O ye of little faith?
—*Matthew 6:30*

I trust in the mercy of God for ever and ever.
—*Psalm 52:8*

CALMLY we look behind us, on joys and sorrows past,
We know that all is mercy now, and shall be well at last;
Calmly we look before us,—we fear no future ill,
Enough for safety and for peace, if Thou art with us still.

JANE BORTHWICK

Neither go back in fear and misgiving to the past, nor in anxiety and forecasting to the future. [Instead,] lie quiet under His hand, having no will but His.

H. E. MANNING

I saw a delicate flower [that] had grown up two feet high, between the horses' path and the wheeltrack. An inch more to right or left [would have] sealed its fate, or an inch higher. Yet it lived to flourish as much as if it had a thousand acres of untrodden space around it, and never knew the danger it incurred. It did not borrow trouble, nor invite an evil fate by apprehending it.

HENRY D. THOREAU

JUNE 19

The Lord shall preserve thee from all evil; He shall preserve thy soul.

—*Psalm 121:7*

UNDER Thy wings, my God, I rest,
    Under Thy shadow safely lie;
By Thy own strength in peace possessed,
    While dreaded evils pass me by.

A. L. WARING

A heart rejoicing in God delights in all His will, and is surely provided with the most firm joy in all estates. If nothing can come to pass beside or against His will, then that soul cannot be vexed which delights in Him and hath no will but His, but follows Him in all times, in all estates: not only when He shines bright on them, but when they are clouded. That flower which follows the sun doth so even in dark and cloudy days: when [the sun] doth not shine forth, yet it follows the hidden course and motion of it. So the soul that moves after God keeps that course when He hides His face. [It] is content, yea, even glad at His will in all estates, conditions or events.

R. LEIGHTON

Let God do with me what He will, anything He will. Whatever it be, it will be either heaven itself or some beginning of it.

WM. MOUNTFORD

JUNE 20

Be merciful unto me, O God, be merciful unto me: for my soul trusteth in Thee: yea, in the shadow of Thy wings will I make my refuge, until these calamities be overpast.
—Psalm 57:1

MY God! in whom are all the springs
    Of boundless love and grace unknown,
Hide me beneath Thy spreading wings,
    Till the dark cloud is overblown.

I. WATTS

The whole benefit of trial consists in silence, patience, rest, and resignation. In this condition divine strength is found for the hard warfare, because God Himself fights for the soul.

M. MOLINOS

In vain will you let your mind run out after help in times of trouble; it is like putting to sea in a storm. Sit still, and *feel after* your principles. If you find none that furnish you with somewhat of a stay and prop, and which point you to quietness and silent submission, depend upon it you have never yet learned Truth from the Spirit of Truth, whatever notions thereof you may have picked up from [various] descriptions of it.

M. A. KELTY

JUNE 21

Thou calledst in trouble, and I delivered thee.
—Psalm 81:7

Be strong, and of good courage; dread not, nor be dismayed.
—1 Chronicles 22:13

THOU canst calm the troubled mind,
   Thou its dread canst still;
Teach me to be all resigned
   To my Father's will.

HEINRICH PUCHTA

Though this patient, meek resignation is to be exercised with regard to all outward things and occurrences of life, yet it chiefly respects our own inward state, the troubles, perplexities, weaknesses, and disorders of our own souls. To stand turned to a patient, meek, humble resignation to God—when your own impatience, wrath, pride, and irresignation attack you—is a higher and more beneficial performance of this duty, than when you stand turned to meekness and patience [as you are being] attacked by the pride, or wrath, or disorderly passions of other people.

WM. LAW

JUNE 22

There hath no temptation taken you, but such as is common to man: but God is faithful, who will not suffer you to be tempted above what ye are able; but will with the temptation also make a way to escape, that ye may be able to bear it.
— *1 Corinthians 10:13, 14*

NOT so, not so, no load of woe
   Need bring despairing frown;
For while we bear it, we can bear;
   Past that, we lay it down.

SARAH WILLIAMS

The thought may help us in regard to all the temptations of our life, even the most hidden and solitary. It may help us to do battle with our despondency and sadness, with our restlessness and resentment, with the perverting and corrupting misery of ambition. We must be watchful and uncompromising, if self-consecration is to do its work. One sin alone indulged, condoned, domesticated, may spoil it all. [It] may cripple all our hope of helpfulness, [it] may baffle the willingness of God to use us in His work for others. "For their sakes I consecrate myself." This, then, is our constant hope: that God will so cleanse and purify our hearts that they may not hinder the transmission to others of that light and truth which issue from His Presence. For that hope we would cast out all that defiles and darkens us. We would freely give ourselves to Christ, that He may enter in and rule and animate us, so that [in spite of] all our unworthiness, something of His brightness and peace may be made known to men.

FRANCIS PAGET

JUNE 23

Why art thou cast down, O my soul? and why art thou dis-
quieted within me? hope thou in God; for I shall yet praise
Him, who is the health of my countenance, and my God.
                                              —Psalm 42:11

AH! why by passing clouds oppressed,
Should vexing thoughts distract thy breast?
Turn thou to Him in every pain,
Whom never suppliant sought in vain;
Thy strength in joy's ecstatic day,
Thy hope, when joy has passed away.

                                    H. F. LYTE

Beware of letting your care degenerate [into] anxiety and
unrest. Tossed as you are amid the winds and waves of sundry
troubles, keep your eyes fixed on the Lord. Say, 'Oh, my God, I
look to Thee alone; be Thou my guide, my pilot;' and then be
comforted. When the shore is gained, who will [remember] the
toil and the storm? We shall steer safely through every storm, so
long as our heart is right, our intention fervent, our courage
steadfast, and our trust fixed on God. If at times we are somewhat stunned by the tempest, never fear; let us take breath, and
go on afresh. Do not be disconcerted by the fits of vexation and
uneasiness which are sometimes produced by the multiplicity of
your domestic worries. No indeed, dearest child, all these are
but opportunities of strengthening yourself in the loving, forbearing graces which our dear Lord sets before us.

                          FRANCIS DE SALES

JUNE 24

Even so, Father, for it seemed good in Thy sight.
—Matthew 11:26

LET nothing make thee sad or fretful,
   Or too regretful;
      Be still;
What God hath ordered must be right,
Then find in it thine own delight,
      My will.

P. FLEMMING

    If we listen to our self-love, we shall estimate our lot less by what it is, than by what it is not. [We] shall dwell on its hindrances, and be blind to its possibilities. Comparing it only with imaginary lives, [we] shall indulge in flattering dreams of what we should do, if we had but power; and give, if we had but wealth; and be, if we had no temptations. We shall be forever querulously pleading our difficulties and privations as excuses for our unloving temper and unfruitful life. Fancying ourselves injured beings, [we would be] virtually frowning at the dear Providence that loves us, and chafing with a self-torture which invites no pity. [But] if we yield ourselves unto God, and sincerely accept our lot as assigned by Him, we shall count up its contents, and disregard its omissions. Be it as feeble as a cripple's and as narrow as a child's, [we] shall find in it resources of good surpassing our best economy, and sacred claims that may keep awake our highest will.

J. MARTINEAU

JUNE 25

My times are in Thy hand.
—Psalm 31:15

Every purpose of the Lord shall be performed.
—Jeremiah 51:29

———————————— ❧ ————————————

I AM so glad! It is such rest to know
That Thou hast ordered and appointed all,
And wilt yet order and appoint my lot.
For though so much I cannot understand,
And would not choose, has been, and yet may be,
Thou choosest, Thou performest, THOU my Lord;
This is enough for me.

F. R. HAVERGAL

———————————— ❧ ————————————

'We mustn't be in a hurry to fix and choose our own lot. We must wait and be guided. We are led on, like the little children, by a way that we know not. It is a vain thought to flee from the work that God appoints us, for the sake of finding a greater blessing to our own souls—as if we could choose for ourselves where we shall find the fulness of the Divine Presence, instead of seeking it where alone it is to be found, in loving obedience.'

GEORGE ELIOT

Everywhere and at all times, it is in thy power piously to acquiesce in thy present condition, and to behave justly to those who are about thee.

MARCUS ANTONINUS

JUNE 26

And when ye stand praying, forgive, if ye have aught against any; that your Father who is in heaven may forgive you your trespasses. But if ye do not forgive, neither will your Father who is in heaven forgive your trespasses.
—Mark 11:25, 26

'TIS not enough to weep my sins,
    'Tis but one step to heaven;—
When I am kind to others,—then
    I know myself forgiven.

F. W. FABER

Every relation to mankind, of hate or scorn or neglect, is full of vexation and torment. There is nothing to do with men but to love them: to contemplate their virtues with admiration, their faults with pity and forbearance, and their injuries with forgiveness. Task all the ingenuity of your mind to devise some other thing, but you never can find it. To hate your adversary will not help you. To kill him will not help you. Nothing within the compass of the universe can help you, but to love him. But let that love flow out upon all around you, and what could harm you? How many a knot of mystery and misunderstanding would be untied by one word spoken in simple and confiding truth of heart! How many a solitary place would be made glad if love were there, and how many a dark dwelling would be filled with light!

ORVILLE DEWEY

JUNE 27

The kingdom of God is within you.
                    —Luke 17:21

OH, take this heart that I would give
    Forever to be all Thine own;
I to myself no more would live,—
    Come, Lord, be Thou my King alone.

                    G. TERSTEEGEN

Herein is the work assigned to the individual soul: to have life
in itself, to make our sphere, whatever it is, sufficient for a reign
of God within ourselves, for a true and full reign of our Father's
abounding spirit. [We must be] thankful, unutterably thankful, if
with the place and the companionship assigned to us we are
permitted to build an earthly tabernacle of grace, goodness and
holy love, a home like a temple. But, should this be denied us,
[let us] resolve for our own souls that God shall reign there, and
that for ourselves at least we will not, by sin or disobedience or
impious distrust, break with our own wills or filial connexion
with our Father. Whether joyful or sorrowing, struggling with
the perplexity and foulness of circumstance, or in an atmosphere of peace; whether in dear fellowship or alone, our desire
and prayer shall be that God may have in us a realm where His
will is law, and where obedience and submission spring, not
from calculating prudence or ungodly fear, but from communion
of spirit, every humble aspiration, and ever-loving trust.

                    J. H. THOM

JUNE 28

The Lord preserveth the simple.
—Psalm 116:6

———————— ❧ ————————

THY home is with the humble, Lord!
    The simple are Thy rest;
Thy lodging is in childlike hearts;
    Thou makest there Thy nest.

                    F. W. FABER

———————— ❧ ————————

This deliverance of the soul from all useless, selfish and unquiet cares, brings to it an unspeakable peace and freedom. This is true simplicity. This state of entire resignation and perpetual acquiescence produces true liberty; and this liberty brings perfect simplicity. The soul which knows no self-seeking, no interested ends, is thoroughly candid. It goes straight forward without hindrance. Its path opens daily more and more to 'perfect day,' in proportion as its self-renunciation and its self-forgetfulness increase. And its peace, amid whatever troubles beset it, will be as boundless as the depths of the sea.

                    FÉNELON

JUNE 29

*Let not him that girdeth on his harness boast himself as he
that putteth it off.*

—1 Kings 20:11

Put on the whole armour of God.

—Ephesians 6:11

WAS I not girded for the battle-field?
Bore I not helm of pride and glittering sword?
Behold the fragments of my broken shield,
And lend to me Thy heavenly armor, Lord!

ANONYMOUS

Oh, be at least able to say in that day,—Lord I am no hero. I
have been careless, cowardly, sometimes all but mutinous. Pun-
ishment I have deserved, I deny it not. But a traitor I have never
been. A deserter I have never been. I have tried to fight on Thy
side in Thy battle against evil. I have tried to do the duty which
lay nearest me, and to leave whatever Thou didst commit to my
charge a little better than I found it. I have not been good, but I
have at least tried to be good. Take the will for the deed, good
Lord. Strike not my unworthy name off the role-call of the noble
and victorious army, which is the blessed company of all faithful
people. Let me, too, be found written in the Book of Life, even
though I stand the lowest and last upon its list. Amen.

C. KINGSLEY

JUNE 30

And the work of righteousness shall be peace; and the effect
of righteousness, quietness and assurance forever.
—Isaiah 32:17

THE heart that ministers for Thee
   In Thy own work will rest;
And the subject spirit of a child
   Can serve Thy children best.

                A. L. WARING

It matters not where or what we are, if we are His servants.
They are happy who have a wide field and great strength to
fulfil His missions of compassion. They, too, are blessed who, in
sheltered homes and narrow ways of duty, wait upon Him in
lowly services of love. Wise or simple, gifted or slender in
knowledge, in the world's gaze or in hidden paths, high or
low, encompassed by affections and joys of home, or lonely
and content in God alone, what matters, if they bear the seal of
the living God?

           H. E. MANNING

JULY 1

In the morning, then ye shall see the glory of the Lord.
                    —Exodus 16:7

Serving the Lord; rejoicing in hope.
                    —Romans 12:11, 12

EVERY day is a fresh beginning,
  Every morn is the world made new.
You who are weary of sorrow and sinning,
Here is a beautiful hope for you;
  A hope for me and a hope for you.
                    SUSAN COOLIDGE

Be patient with every one, but above all with yourself. I mean, do not be disturbed because of your imperfections, and always rise up bravely from a fall. I am glad that you make a daily new beginning. There is no better means of progress in the spiritual life than to be continually beginning afresh, and never to think that we have done enough.

                    FRANCIS DE SALES

Because perseverance is so difficult, even when supported by the grace of God, thence is the value of new beginnings. For new beginnings are the life of perseverance.

                    E. B. PUSEY

JULY 2

Herein do I exercise myself, to have always a conscience void of offence toward God, and toward men.
—Acts 24:16

I will instruct thee and teach thee in the way which thou shalt go; I will guide thee with mine eye.
—Psalm 32:8

OH, KEEP thy conscience sensitive;
    No inward token miss;
And go where grace entices thee;—
    Perfection lies in this.

F. W. FABER

We need only obey. There is guidance for each of us, and by lowly listening we shall hear the right word.

R. W. EMERSON

The heights of Christian perfection can only be reached by faithfully each moment following the Guide who is to lead you there. He reveals your way to you one step at a time, in the little things of your daily lives, asking only on your part that you yield yourselves up to His guidance. If then, in anything you feel doubtful or troubled, be sure that it is the voice of your Lord, and surrender it at once to His bidding, rejoicing with a great joy that He has begun thus to lead and guide you.

H. W. S.

JULY 3

He shall redeem Israel from all his iniquities.
—Psalm 130:8

BE it according to Thy word;
　　Redeem me from all sin;
My heart would now receive Thee, Lord,
　　Come in, my Lord, come in!

　　　　　　　　　C. WESLEY

When you wake, or as soon as you are dressed, offer up your whole self to God, soul and body, thoughts and purposes and desires, to be for that day what He wills. Think of the occasions of the sin likely to befall you, and go, as a child, to your Father which is in heaven, and tell Him in childlike, simple words, your trials. Use simple words such as these—'You know, good Lord, that I am tempted to—[*then name the temptations and the ways in which you sin, as well as you know them*]. But, good Lord, for love of You, I would this day keep wholly from all [*naming the sin*] and be very [*naming the opposite grace*]. I will not, by Your grace, do one [sinful] act, or speak one [sinful] word, or give one [sinful] look, or harbour one [sinful] thought in my soul. If You allow any of these temptations to come upon me this day, I desire to think, speak, and do only what You will. Lord, without You I can do nothing; with You I can do all.'

E. B. PUSEY

JULY 4

Remember, O Lord, Thy tender mercies, and Thy loving-kindnesses; for they have been ever of old.
                                    —Psalm 25:6

MY Father! see
I trust the faithfulness displayed of old,
I trust the love that never can grow cold—
    I trust in Thee.

CHRISTIAN INTELLIGENCER

Be not so much discouraged in the sight of what is yet to be done, as comforted in His goodwill towards thee. 'Tis true, He hath chastened thee with rods and sore afflictions, but did He ever take away His loving-kindness from thee? Or did His faithfulness ever fail in the sorest, blackest, thickest, darkest night that ever befell thee?

I. PENINGTON

We call Him the *'God of our fathers,'* and we feel that there is some stability at centre, while we can tell our cares to One listening at our right hand, by whom their [cares were] remembered and removed.

J. MARTINEAU

JULY 5

He stayeth his rough wind in the day of the east wind.
—*Isaiah 27:8*

A bruised reed shall He not break.
—*Isaiah 42:3*

———— ✖ ————

ALL my life I still have found,
   And I will forget it never;
Every sorrow hath its bound,
   And no cross endures forever.
All things else have but their day,
God's love only lasts for aye.

               P. GERHARDT

———— ✖ ————

We never have more than we can bear. The present hour we are always able to endure. As our day, so is our strength. If the trials of many years were gathered into one, they would overwhelm us. Therefore, in pity to our little strength, He sends first one, then another, then removes both, and lays on a third, heavier, perhaps, than either; but all is so wisely measured to our strength that the bruised reed is never broken. We do not enough look at our trials in this continuous and successive view. Each one is sent to teach us something, and altogether they have a lesson which is beyond the power of any to teach alone.

               H. E. MANNING

JULY 6

I the Lord have called thee in righteousness, and will hold thine hand, and will keep thee.
—*Isaiah 42:6*

O keep my soul, and deliver me: for I put my trust in Thee.
—*Psalm 25:20*

I DO not ask my cross to understand,
    My ways to see;
Better in darkness just to feel Thy hand,
    And follow Thee.

ADELAIDE A. PROCTER

O Lord, if only my will may remain right and firm towards Thee, do with me whatsoever it shall please Thee. For it cannot be anything but good, whatsoever Thou shalt do with me. If it be Thy will I should be in darkness, be Thou blessed. And, if it be Thy will I should be in light, be Thou again blessed. If Thou vouchsafe to comfort me, be Thou blessed; and, if Thou wilt have me afflicted, be Thou equally blessed. O Lord! for Thy sake I will cheerfully suffer whatever shall come to me with Thy permission.

THOMAS À KEMPIS

My soul could not incline itself on the one side or the other, since another will had taken the place of its own. [It could] only nourish itself with the daily providences of God.

MADAME GUYON

JULY 7

The Lord is my light and my salvation; whom shall I fear?
The Lord is the strength of my life; of whom shall I be afraid?
—Psalm 27:1

THOU hidden Source of calm repose,
　　Thou all-sufficient Love divine,
My Help and Refuge from my foes,
　　Secure I am while Thou art mine.
And lo! from sin, and grief, and shame,
I hide me, Father, in Thy name.

C. WESLEY

Whatever troubles come on you, of mind, body, or estate, from within or from without, from chance or from intent, from friends or foes—whatever your trouble be, though you be lonely, O children of a heavenly Father, be not afraid!

J. H. NEWMAN

Whatsoever befalleth thee, receive it not from the hand of any creature, but from Him alone. [Then] render back all to Him, seeking in all things His pleasure and honour, the purifying and subduing of thyself. What can harm thee, when all must first touch God, within whom thou hast enclosed thyself?

R. LEIGHTON

How God rejoices over a soul, which, surrounded on all sides by suffering and misery, does that upon earth which the angels do in heaven—namely, loves, adores, and praises God!

G. TERSTEEGEN

JULY 8

Be ye kind one to another.
> *—Ephesians 4:32*

SHE doeth little kindnesses
   Which most leave undone or despise;
For nought which sets one heart at ease,
And giveth happiness or peace,
   Is low-esteemed in her eyes.
> J. R. LOWELL

What was the secret of such a one's power? What had she done? Absolutely nothing—but radiant smiles, beaming good-humour, the tact of [understanding] what every one felt and every one wanted. [She was] told that she had got out of herself and learned to think of others. At one time it showed itself in deprecating the quarrel, which lowering brows and raised tones already showed to be impending, by sweet words. At another [time it could be seen] by smoothing an invalid's pillow; at another, by soothing a sobbing child; at another by humouring and softening a father who had returned weary and ill-tempered from the irritating cares of business. None but she saw those things. None but a lovely heart *could* see them. That was the secret of her heavenly power. The one who will be found in trial capable of great acts of love, is ever the one who is always doing considerate small ones.

> F. W. ROBERTSON

JULY 9

Love is of God; and every one that loveth is born of God, and knoweth God.
—1 John 4:7

Forbearing one another, and forgiving one another, if any man have a quarrel (or 'complaint') against any.
—Colossians 3:13

OH, might we all our lineage prove,
Give and forgive, do good and love;
By soft endearments, in kind strife,
Lightening the load of daily life.

J. KEBLE

We may, if we choose, make the worst of one another. Every one has his weak points. Every one has his faults. We may make the worst of these; we may fix our attention constantly upon these. But we may also make the best of one another. We may forgive, even as we hope to be forgiven. We may put ourselves in the place of others, and ask what we should wish to be done to us, and thought of us, were we in their place. By loving whatever is lovable in those around us, love will flow back from them to us, and life will become a pleasure instead of a pain. Earth will become like heaven, and we shall become worthy followers of Him whose name is Love.

A. P. STANLEY

JULY 10

The Lord will perfect that which concerneth me: Thy mercy, O Lord, endureth forever; forsake not the works of Thine own hands.

—Psalm 138:8

AS God leads me, will I go,—
    Nor choose my way;
Let Him choose the joy or woe
    Of every day:
They cannot hurt my soul,
Because in His control:
I leave to Him the whole,—
    His children may.

L. GEDICKE

Why is it that we are so busy with the future? It is not *our* province. Is there not a criminal interference with *Him* to whom it belongs, in our feverish, anxious attempts to dispose of it, filling it up with shadows of good and evil shaped by our own wild imaginations? To do God's will as fast as it is made known to us, to inquire hourly—I had almost said each moment—what He requires of us, and to leave ourselves, our friends, and every interest at His control, with a cheerful trust that the path which He marks out leads to our perfection and to Himself,—this is at once our duty and happiness. Why will we not walk in the plain, simple way?

WILLIAM E. CHANNING

JULY 11

When He giveth quietness, who then can make trouble?
—Job 34:29

None of these things move me.
—Acts 20:24

I'VE many a cross to take up now,
 And many left behind;
But present troubles move me not,
 Nor shake my quiet mind.
And what may be to-morrow's cross
 I never seek to find;
My Father says, 'Leave that to me,
 And keep a quiet mind.'

ANONYMOUS

Let us then think only of the present, and not even permit our minds to wander with curiosity into the future. This future is not yet ours; perhaps it never will be. It is exposing ourselves to temptation to wish to anticipate God, and to prepare ourselves for things which He may not destine for us. If such things should come to pass, He will give us light and strength according to the need. Why should we desire to meet difficulties prematurely, when we have neither strength nor light as yet provided for them? Let us give heed to the present, whose duties are pressing. It is fidelity to the present which prepares us for fidelity in the future.

FÉNELON

Every hour comes with some little light regarding God's will fastened upon its back.

F. W. FABER

JULY 12

Be strong, and of good courage, fear not, nor be afraid . . .
for the Lord thy God, He it is that doth go with thee; He will
not fail thee, nor forsake thee.

—Deuteronomy 31:6

THE timid it concerns to ask their way,
And fear what foe in caves and swamps can stray;
To make no step until the event is known,
And ills to come as evils past bemoan.
No so the wise; no coward watch he keeps
To spy what danger on his pathway creeps;
Go where he will, the wise man is at home,
His hearth the earth,—his hall the azure dome;
Where his clear spirit leads him, there's his road,
By God's own light illumined and foreshowed.

R. W. EMERSON

Though I sympathize, I do not share in the least the feeling of being disheartened and cast down. It is not things of this sort that depress me, or ever will. The contrary things, praise, openings, the feeling of the greatness of my work, and my inability in relation to it, these things oppress and cast me down. But little hindrances, the closing up of accustomed or expected avenues, and the presence of difficulties to be overcome,—I'm not going to be cast down by trifles such as these.

JAMES HINTON

JULY 13

And the Lord shall guide thee continually, and satisfy thy soul in drought.

—Isaiah 58:11

⁓

WHEREVER He may guide me,
   No want shall turn me back;
My Shepherd is beside me,
   And nothing can I lack.
His wisdom ever waketh,
   His sight is never dim,—
He knows the way He taketh,
   And I will walk with Him.

A. L. WARING

⁓

Abandon yourself to His care and guidance, as a sheep in the care of a shepherd, and trust Him utterly. No matter though you may seem to yourself to be in the very midst of a desert, with nothing green about you, inwardly or outwardly. You may think you will have to make a long journey before you can get into the green pastures. Our Shepherd will turn that very place where you are into green pastures, for He has power to make the desert rejoice and blossom as a rose.

H. W. S.

JULY 14

Be not conformed to this world; but be ye transformed by the renewing of your mind.

—*Romans 12:2*

FATHER, let our faithful mind
Rest, on Thee alone inclined;
Every anxious thought repress,
Keep our souls in perfect peace.

C. WESLEY

Retirement from anxieties of every kind; entering into no disputes; avoiding all frivolous talk; and simplifying everything we engage in, whether in a way of doing or suffering; denying the imagination its false activities, and the intellect its false searchings after what it cannot obtain,—these seem to be some of the steps that lead to obedience to the holy precept in our text.

JAMES P. GREAVES

Retire inwardly. Wait to feel somewhat of God's Spirit, discovering and drawing away from that which is contrary to His holy nature, and leading into that which is acceptable to Him. As the mind is joined to this, some true light and life is received.

I. PENINGTON

Act faithfully to your convictions. When you have been unfaithful, bear with yourself, and always resume your little task with calm simplicity. Suppress, as much as you possibly can, all recurrence to yourself, and you will suppress much vanity. Accustom yourself to such calmness, and [cultivate] an indifference to events.

MADAME GUYON

JULY 15

Lift up your heads, O ye gates; even lift them up, ye everlasting doors; and the King of glory shall come in.
—Psalm 24:9

Ye are the temple of the living God.
—2 Corinthians 6:16

FLING wide the portals of your heart,
Make it a temple set apart
From earthly use for Heaven's employ,
Adorned with prayer, and love, and joy.
So shall your Sovereign enter in,
And new and nobler life begin.

WEISSEL

Thou art to know that thy soul is the centre, habitation, and kingdom of God. Therefore, [so that] the sovereign King may rest on that throne of thy soul, thou oughtest to take pains to keep it clean, quiet, and peaceable,—clean from guilt and defects; quiet from fears; and peaceable in temptations and tribulations. Thou oughtest always, then, to keep thine heart in peace, that thou mayest keep pure that temple of God. With a right and pure intention thou art to work, pray, obey, and suffer (without being in the least moved) whatever it pleases the Lord to send unto thee.

M. MOLINOS

JULY 16

Oh how great is Thy goodness, which Thou hast laid up for them that fear Thee; which Thou hast wrought for them that trust in Thee.

—Psalm 31:19

I will sing unto the Lord, because He hath dealt bountifully with me.

—Psalm 13:6

THY calmness bends serene above
   My restlessness to still;
Around me flows Thy quickening life,
   To nerve my faltering will;
Thy presence fills my solitude;
Thy providence turns all to good.

S. LONGFELLOW

With a heart devoted to God and full of God, no longer seek Him in the heavens above or the earth beneath, or in the things under the earth. [Instead,] recognize Him as the great fact of the universe, separate from no place or part, but revealed in all places and in all things and events, *moment by moment*. As eternity alone will exhaust this momentary revelation, which has sometimes been called the ETERNAL Now, thou shalt thus find God ever present and ever new. Thy soul shall adore Him and feed upon Him in the things and events which each new moment brings. Thou shalt never be absent from Him, and He shall never be absent from thee.

T. C. UPHAM

JULY 17

For I reckon that the sufferings of this present time are not worthy to be compared with the glory which shall be revealed in us.

—*Romans 8:18*

The power of an endless life.

—*Hebrews 7:16*

BELIEV'ST thou in eternal things?
   Thou knowest, in thy inmost heart,
Thou art not clay; thy soul hath wings,
   And what thou seest is but part.
Make this thy med'cine for the smart
   Of every day's distress; be dumb,
In each new loss thou truly art
   Tasting the power of things that come.

T. W. PARSONS

Every contradiction of our will, every little ailment, every petty disappointment, will, if we take it patiently, become a blessing. So, walking on earth, we may be in heaven. The ill-tempers of others, the slights and rudeness of the world, ill-health, the daily accidents with which God has mercifully strewed our paths, instead of ruffling or disturbing our peace, may cause His peace to be shed abroad in our hearts abundantly.

E. B. PUSEY

JULY 18

A new commandment I give unto you, That ye love one another; as I have loved you, that ye also love one another.
—John 13:34

And the Lord make you to increase and abound in love, one toward another, and toward all men.
— 1 Thessalonians 3:12

LET love through all my conduct shine,
An image fair, though faint, of Thine;
Thus let me His disciple prove,
Who come to manifest Thy love.

ANONYMOUS

We should arrive at a fullness of love extending to the whole creation, a desire to impart, to pour out in full and copious streams the love and goodness we bear to all around us.

J. P. GREAVES

How shall we become lovely? By loving Him who is ever lovely.

ST. AUGUSTINE

The soul within had so often lighted up her countenance with its own full happiness and joy, that something of a permanent radiance remained upon it.

ANNA, OR PASSAGES
FROM HOME LIFE

JULY 19

The Lord is good to all; and His tender mercies are over all His works.

—*Psalm 145:9*

For every beast of the forest is Mine, and the cattle upon a thousand hills.

—*Psalm 50:10*

MAKER of earth and sea and sky,
　　Creation's sovereign Lord and King,
Who hung the starry worlds on high,
　　And formed alike the sparrow's wing;
Bless the dumb creatures of Thy care,
And listen to their voiceless prayer.

ANONYMOUS

I believe [that] where the love of God is verily perfected, and the true spirit of government watchfully attended to, a tenderness towards all creatures made subject to us will be experienced. [We will be concerned] that we do not lessen that sweetness of life in the animal creation, which the great Creator intends for them under our government. . . . To say we love God as unseen, and at the same time exercise cruelty, [is] a contradiction in itself.

JOHN WOOLMAN

I would give nothing for that man's religion whose very dog and cat are not the better for it.

ROWLAND HILL

JULY 20

Then I said, I have laboured in vain, I have spent my strength for nought, and in vain.

—*Isaiah 49:4*

BECAUSE I spent the strength Thou gavest me
In struggle which Thou never didst ordain,
And have but dregs of life to offer Thee—
　　O Lord, I do repent.

SARAH WILLIAMS

Mind, it is our best work that He wants, not the dregs of our exhaustion. I think He must prefer quality to quantity.

GEORGE MACDONALD

If the people about you are carrying on their business or their benevolence at a pace which drains the life out of you, resolutely take a slower pace. Be called a laggard, make less money, accomplish less work than they, but be what you were meant to be and can be. You have your natural limit of power as much as an engine,—ten-horse power, or twenty, or a hundred. You are fit to do certain kinds of work, and you need a certain kind and amount of fuel, and a certain kind of handling.

GEORGE S. MERRIAM

In your occupations, try to possess your soul in peace. It is not a good plan to be in haste to perform any action that it may be the sooner over. On the contrary, you should accustom yourself to do whatever you have to do with tranquillity, in order that you may retain the possession of yourself and of settled peace.

MADAME GUYON

JULY 21

For which cause we faint not; but, though our outward man perish, yet the inward man is renewed day by day.
—2 Corinthians 4:16

LET my soul beneath her load
Faint not through the o'erwearied flesh;
Let me hourly drink afresh
Love and peace from Thee, my God!
RICHTER

In my attempts to promote the comfort of my family, the quiet of my spirit has been disturbed. Some of this is doubtless owing to physical weakness. But, with every temptation there is a way of escape; there is *never* any *need* to sin. Another thing I have suffered loss from,—entering into the business of the day without seeking to have my spirit quieted and directed. So many things press upon me [that] this is sometimes neglected; shame to me that it should be so.

This is of great importance, to watch carefully,—now I am so weak—not to over-fatigue myself, because then I cannot contribute to the pleasure of others. A [calm] face and a gentle tone will make my family more happy than anything else I can do for them. Our own will gets sadly into the performance of our duties sometimes.

ELIZABETH T. KING, 1856

JULY 22

Whoso is wise, and will observe these things, even they shall understand the lovingkindness of the Lord.
—*Psalm 107:43*

WHAT channel needs our faith, except the eyes?
   God leaves no spot of earth unglorified;
Profuse and wasteful, lovelinesses rise;
   New beauties dawn before the old have died.

Trust thou thy joys in keeping of the Power
   Who holds these changing shadows in His hand;
Believe and live, and know that hour by hour
   Will ripple newer beauty to thy strand.
             T. W. HIGGINSON

I wondered over again for the hundredth time what could be the principle which, in the wildest, most lawless, fantastically chaotic, apparently capricious work of nature, always kept it beautiful. The beauty of holiness must be at the heart of it somehow, I thought. Because our God is so free from stain, so loving, so unselfish, so good, so altogether what He wants us to be, so holy—therefore all His works declare Him in beauty. His fingers can touch nothing but to mould it into loveliness. Even the play of His elements is in grace and tenderness of form.

             G. MACDONALD

JULY 23

Thou shalt love the Lord thy God with all thy heart, and with all thy soul, and with all thy strength, and with all thy mind.

—Luke 10:27

O GOD, what offering shall I give
    To Thee, the Lord of earth and skies?
My spirit, soul, and flesh receive,
    A holy, living sacrifice.

J. LANGE

To love God 'with all our heart,' is to know the spiritual passion of measureless gratitude for loving-kindness, and self-devotedness to goodness. To love Him 'with all our mind,' is to know the passion for Truth that is the enthusiasm of Science, the passion for Beauty that inspires the poet and the artist, when all truth and beauty are regarded as the self-revealings of God. To love Him 'with all our soul,' is to know the saint's rapture of devotion and gaze of penitential awe into the face of the All-holy, the saint's abhorrence of sin, and agony of desire to save a sinner's soul. To love Him 'with all our strength,' is the supreme spiritual passion that tests the rest—the passion for reality, for worship in spirit and in truth, for *being* what we adore, for *doing* what we know to be God's word; the loyalty that exacts the living sacrifice, the whole burnt-offering that is our reasonable service. In our coldest hours [this passion] keeps steadfast to what seemed good when we were aglow.

J. H. THOM

JULY 24

*Walk worthy of God, who hath called you unto His king-
dom and glory.*
>   *—1 Thessalonians 2:12*

Surely the Lord is in this place; and I knew it not.
>   *—Genesis 28:16*

THOU camest not to thy place by accident,
It is the very place God meant for thee;
And shouldst thou there small scope for action see,
Do not for this give room to discontent.
>   R. C. TRENCH

Accept the place the divine providence has found for you, the
society of your contemporaries, the connexion of events.

>   R. W. EMERSON

Adapt thyself to the things with which thy lot has been cast;
and love the men with whom it is thy portion to live, and that
with a sincere affection. . . . No longer be either dissatisfied
with thy present lot, or shrink from the future.

>   MARCUS ANTONINUS

I love best to have each thing in its season, doing without it at
all other times. I have never got over my surprise that I should
have been born into the most estimable place in all the world,
and in the very nick of time too.

>   H. D. THOREAU

JULY 25

He knoweth the way I take.
                                    —Job 23:10

*Man's goings are of the Lord; how can a man then under-
stand his own way?*
                                    —Proverbs 20:24

BE quiet, why this anxious heed
About thy tangled ways?
God knows them all, He giveth speed,
And He allows delays.

                    E. W.

We complain of the slow, dull life we are forced to lead, of
our humble sphere of action, of our low position in the scale of
society, of our having no room to make ourselves known, of our
wasted energies, of our years of patience. [In this way] we say
that we have no Father who is directing our life; we say that
God has forgotten us; we boldly judge what life is best for us;
and by our complaining we lose the use and profit of the quiet
years. O men of little faith! Because you are not sent out yet into
your labour, do you think God has ceased to remember you?
Because you are forced to be outwardly inactive, don't you think
you [should,] in your years of quiet, [be] 'about your Father's
business?' . . . It is a period given to us in which to mature ourselves for the work which God will give us to do.

                    STOPFORD A. BROOKE

JULY 26

They that trust in the Lord shall be as Mount Zion, which cannot be removed, but abideth for ever. As the mountains are round about Jerusalem, so the Lord is round about His people from henceforth even for ever.

—Psalm 125:1, 2

HOW on a rock they stand,
Who watch His eye, and hold His guiding hand!
Not half so fixed amid her vassal hills,
Rises the holy pile that Kedron's valley fills.

J. KEBLE

That is the way to be immovable in the midst of troubles, as a rock amidst the waves. When God is in the midst of a kingdom or city, He makes it firm as Mount Zion, that cannot be removed. When He is in the midst of a soul, though calamities throng about it on all hands, and roar like the billows of the sea, yet there is a constant calm within, such a peace as the world can neither give nor take away. What is it but want of lodging God in the soul, and that in His stead the world is in men's hearts, that makes them shake like leaves at every blast of danger?

R. LEIGHTON

JULY 27

He that received seed into the good ground is he that
heareth the word, and understandeth it; which also beareth
fruit, and bringeth forth, some an hundredfold, some sixty,
some thirty.

—*Matthew 13:23*

THEN bless thy secret growth, nor catch
   At noise, but thrive unseen and dumb;
Keep clean, bear fruit, earn life, and watch
   Till the white-winged reapers come.

H. VAUGHAN

He does not need to transplant us into a different field, but
[we should grow] right where we are, with just the circumstances that surround us. He makes His sun to shine and His
dew to fall upon us, and transforms the very things that before
were our greatest hindrances, into the chiefest and most blessed
means of our growth. . . . No difficulties in your case can baffle
Him. No dwarfing of your growth in years that are past, no
apparent dryness of your inward springs of life, no crookedness
or deformity in any of your past development, can in the least
mar the perfect work that He will accomplish. Put yourselves
absolutely into His hands, and let Him have His own way with
you.

H. W. S.

JULY 28

But I would not have you to be ignorant, brethren, concerning them which are asleep, that ye sorrow not, even as others which have no hope.

—1 Thessalonians 4:13

YET Love will dream, and Faith will trust
    (Since He who knows our need is just),
That somehow, somewhere, meet we must.
    Alas for him who never sees
    The stars shine through his cypress trees;
Who hath not learned in hours of faith,
    The truth to flesh and sense unknown,
That life is ever Lord of Death,
    And Love can never lose its own.

J. G. WHITTIER

While we poor wayfarers still toil, with hot and bleeding feet, along the highway and the dust of life, our companions have mounted the divergent path, to explore the more sacred streams, and visit the diviner vales, and wander amid the everlasting Alps of God's upper province of creation. [Thus] we keep up the courage of our hearts, refresh ourselves with the memories of love, and travel forward in the ways of duty, with less weary step, feeling ever for the hand of God, and listening for the voices of [those] whose happy welcome waits us. Death, in short, under the Christian aspect, is but God's method of colonization—the transition from his mother-country of our race to the fairer and newer world of our emigration.

J. MARTINEAU

JULY 29

But this I say, brethren, the time is short.
—1 Corinthians 7:29

I SOMETIMES feel the thread of life is slender,
And soon with me the labour will be wrought;
   Then grows my heart to other hearts more tender.
      The time is short.

D. M. CRAIK

Oh, my dear friends, you who are letting miserable misunderstandings run on from year to year, meaning to clear them up some day. You who are keeping wretched quarrels alive because you cannot quite make up your mind that now is the day to sacrifice your pride and kill them. You who are passing men sullenly upon the street, not speaking to them out of some silly spite, and yet know that it would fill you with shame and remorse if you heard that one of these men were dead tomorrow morning. You who are letting your neighbour starve, till you hear that he is dying of starvation; or letting your friend's heart ache for a word of appreciation or sympathy, which you mean to give him some day,—if you only could know and see and feel, all of a sudden, that 'the time is short,' how it would break the spell! How you would go instantly and do the thing which you might never have another chance to do.

PHILLIPS BROOKS

JULY 30

Remember not the sins of my youth, nor my transgressions; according to Thy mercy remember Thou me for Thy goodness' sake, O Lord.

—*Psalm 25:7*

WHEN on my aching, burdened heart
   My sins lie heavily,
My pardon speak, new peace impart,
   In love remember me.

T. HAWEIS

We need to know that our sins are forgiven. And how shall we know this? By feeling that we have peace with God,—by feeling that we are able so to trust in the divine compassion and infinite tenderness of our Father, as to arise and go to Him, whenever we commit sin, and say at once to Him, 'Father, I have sinned; forgive me.' To know that we are forgiven, it is only necessary to look at our Father's love till it sinks into our heart, to open our soul to Him till He shall pour His love into it; to wait on Him till we find peace, till our conscience no longer torments us, till the weight of responsibility ceases to be an oppressive burden to us, till we can feel that our sins, great as they are, cannot keep us away from our Heavenly Father.

J. F. CLARKE

JULY 31

*I have blotted out, as a thick cloud, thy transgressions, and,
as a cloud, thy sins: return unto Me, for I have redeemed thee.*
—Isaiah 44:22

*He will turn again, He will have compassion upon us; He
will subdue our iniquities; and Thou wilt cast all their sins
into the depths of the sea.*
—Micah 7:19

IF my shut eyes should dare their lids to part,
I know how they must quail beneath the blaze
Of thy Love's greatness. No; I dare not raise
One prayer, to look aloft, lest it should gaze
On such forgiveness as would break my heart.

H. S. SUTTON

O Lord God gracious and merciful, give us, I entreat Thee, a
humble trust in Thy mercy, and suffer not our heart to fail us.
Though our sins be seven, though our sins be seventy times
seven, though our sins be more in number than the hairs of our
head, yet give us grace in loving penitence to cast ourselves
down into the depth of Thy compassion. Let us fall into the
hand of the Lord. Amen.

C. G. ROSSETTI

AUGUST 1

Be not hasty in thy spirit to be angry; for anger resteth in the bosom of fools.
                              —Ecclesiastes 7:9

Let not the sun go down upon your wrath.
                              —Ephesians 4:26

QUENCH thou the fires of hate and strife,
    The wasting fever of the heart;
From perils guard our feeble life,
    And to our souls Thy peace impart.
                              J. H. NEWMAN, *Tr. from Latin*

When thou art offended or annoyed by others, suffer not thy thoughts to dwell thereon, or on anything relating to them. For example, 'they ought not to have treated thee so; who are they, or whom do they think themselves to be;' or the like. All this is the fuel and kindling of wrath, anger, and hatred.

L. SCUPOLI

Struggle diligently against your impatience, and strive to be amiable and gentle, in season and out of season, towards every one, however much they may vex and annoy you—and be sure that God will bless your efforts.

FRANCIS DE SALES

AUGUST 2

*Behold, God is my salvation; I will trust, and not be afraid:
for the Lord Jehovah is my strength and my song; He also is
become my salvation.*
                              —Isaiah 12:2

Why are ye so fearful? How is it that ye have no faith?
                              —Mark 4:40

———————————— ❧ ————————————

STILL heavy is thy heart?
   Still sink thy spirits down;
Cast off the weight, let fear depart,
   And every care be gone.
                              P. GERHARDT

———————————— ❧ ————————————

Go on in all simplicity. Do not be so anxious to win a quiet
mind, and it will be all the quieter. Do not examine so closely
into the progress of your soul. Do not crave so much to be perfect, but let your spiritual life be formed by your duties, and by
the actions which are called forth by circumstances. Do not take
too much thought for tomorrow. God, who has led you safely on
so far, will lead you on to the end. Be altogether at rest in the
loving holy confidence which you ought to have in His heavenly
Providence.

                    FRANCIS DE SALES

AUGUST 3

Thou hast made him exceeding glad with Thy countenance.
—Psalm 21:6

MY heart for gladness springs,
    It cannot more be sad,
For very joy it laughs and sings,
    Sees nought but sunshine glad.
P. GERHARDT

A new day rose upon me. It was as if another sun had risen into the sky. The heavens were indescribably brighter, and the earth fairer; and that day has gone on brightening to the present hour. I have known the other joys of life, I suppose, as much as most men. I have known art and beauty, music and gladness; I have known friendship and love and family ties. But it is certain that till we see GOD in the world—GOD in the bright and boundless universe—we never know the highest joy. It is far more than if one were translated to a world a thousand times fairer than this. That supreme and central Light of Infinite Love and Wisdom, shining over this world and all worlds, alone can show us how noble and beautiful, how fair and glorious they are.

ORVILLE DEWEY

When I look like this into the blue sky, it seems so deep, so peaceful, so full of a mysterious tenderness, that I could lie for centuries and wait for the dawning of the face of God out of the awful loving-kindness.

G. MACDONALD

AUGUST 4

*He satisfieth the longing soul, and filleth the hungry soul
with goodness.*
>—*Psalm 107:9*

That ye might be filled with all the fulness of God.
>—*Ephesians 3:19*

ENOUGH that He who made can fill the soul
  Here and hereafter till its deeps o'erflow;
Enough that love and tenderness control
  Our fate where'er in joy or doubt we go.
>ANONYMOUS

O God, the Life of the Faithful, the Bliss of the righteous, mercifully receive the prayers of Thy suppliants, that the souls which thirst for Thy promises may evermore be filled from Thy abundance. Amen.

>GELASIAN, A.D. 492

God makes every common thing serve, if thou wilt, to enlarge your capacity of bliss in His love. Not a prayer, not an act of faithfulness in your calling, not a self-denying or kind word or deed, done out of love for Himself; not a weariness or painfulness endured patiently; not a duty performed; not a temptation resisted; but it enlarges the whole soul for the endless capacity of the love of God.

>E. B. PUSEY

AUGUST 5

Thanks be unto God for His unspeakable gift.
—2 Corinthians 9:15

O GIVER of each perfect gift!
This day our daily bread supply;
While from the Spirit's tranquil depths
We drink unfailing draughts of joy.

LYRA CATHOLICA

The best way for a man rightly to enjoy himself is to maintain a universal, ready, and cheerful compliance with the divine and uncreated Will in all things. He knows that nothing can issue and flow forth from the fountain of goodness but that which is good. Therefore a good man is never offended with any piece of divine dispensation, nor hath he any reluctancy against that Will that dictates and determines all things by an eternal rule of goodness. He knows that there is an unbounded and almighty Love, that without any disdain or envy, freely communicates itself to everything He made. [This Love] always enfolds those in His everlasting arms who are made partakers of His own image, perpetually nourishing and cherishing them with the fresh and vital influences of His grace.

DR. JOHN SMITH

AUGUST 6

Bless the Lord, O my soul, and forget not all His benefits.
—Psalm 103:2

WISER it were to welcome and make ours
What'er of good, though small, the Present brings,—
Kind greetings, sunshine, songs of birds, and flowers,
With a child's pure delight in little things.
R. C. TRENCH

Into all our lives, in many simple, familiar, homely ways, God infuses this element of joy from the surprises of life, which unexpectedly brighten our days, and fill our eyes with light. He drops this added sweetness into His children's cup, and makes it to run over. The success we were not counting on, the blessing we were not trying after, the strain of music in the midst of drudgery, the beautiful morning picture or sunset glory thrown in as we pass to or from our daily business, the unsought word of encouragement or expression of sympathy, the sentence that meant for us more than the writer or speaker thought,—these and a hundred others that everyone's experience can supply are instances of what I mean. You may call it accident or chance—it often is. You may call it human goodness—it often is. But always, always call it God's love, for that is always in it. These are the overflowing riches of His grace. These are His free gifts.

S. LONGFELLOW

AUGUST 7

If thou canst believe, all things are possible to him that believeth.
> —*Mark 9:23*

Nothing shall be impossible unto you.
> —*Matthew 17:20*

SO nigh is grandeur to our dust,
   So near is God to man,
When Duty whispers low, *Thou must*,
The youth replies, *I can*.

R. W. EMERSON

Know that 'impossible,' where truth and mercy and the everlasting voice of nature order, has no place in the brave man's dictionary. That when all men have said 'Impossible,' and tumbled noisily elsewhither, and thou alone art left, then first thy time and possibility have come. It is for thee now: do thou that, and ask no man's counsel, but thy own only and God's. Brother, thou hast possibility in thee for much: the possibility for writing on the eternal skies the record of a heroic life.

T. CARLYLE

God does not demand impossibilities.

ST. AUGUSTINE

AUGUST 8

Stand fast therefore in the liberty wherewith Christ hath made us free, and be not entangled again with the yoke of bondage.

—*Galatians 5:1*

I believed, and therefore have I spoken.

—*2 Corinthians 4:13*

THEY are slaves who fear to speak
For the fallen and the weak;
They are slaves who will not choose
Hatred, scoffing, and abuse,
Rather than in silence shrink
From the truth they needs must think;
They are slaves who dare not be
In the right with two or three.

J. R. LOWELL

The real corrupters of society may be, not the corrupt, but those who have held back the righteous leaven, the salt that has lost its savour, the innocent who have not even the moral courage to show what they think of the effrontery of impurity. [The corruptors may be] the serious, who yet timidly succumb before some loud-voiced scoffer. [Theirs is] the heart trembling all over with religious sensibilities that yet suffers itself, through false shame, to be beaten down into outward and practical acquiescence by some rude and worldly nature.

J. H. THOM

AUGUST 9

The things which are impossible with men are possible with God.

—Luke 18:27

Unless the Lord had been my help, my soul had almost dwelt in silence.

—Psalm 94:17

WHEN obstacles and trials seem
  Like prison-walls to be,
I do the little I can do,
  And leave the rest to Thee.

F. W. FABER

The mind never puts forth greater power over itself than when, in great trials, it yields up calmly its desires, affections, and interests to God. There are seasons when to be *still* demands immeasurably higher strength than to act. Composure is often the highest result of power. [Consider that] it demands no power to calm the stormy elements of passion, to moderate the vehemence of desire, to throw off the load of dejection, to suppress every repining thought, when the dearest hopes are withered, and to turn the wounded spirit from dangerous reveries and wasting grief, to the quiet discharge of ordinary duties? Is there no power put forth when a man, stripped of his property, of the fruits of a life's labours, quells discontent and gloomy forebodings, and serenely and patiently returns to the tasks which Providence assigns?

WM. E. CHANNING

AUGUST 10

The cup which my Father has given me, shall I not drink it?
—John 18:11

EVERY sorrow, every smart,
That the Eternal Father's heart
Hath appointed me of yore,
Or hath yet for me in store,
As my life flows on, I'll take
Calmly, gladly, for His sake,
No more faithless murmurs make.

P. GERHARDT

The very least and the very greatest sorrows that God ever suffers to befall thee, proceed from the depths of His unspeakable love. Such great love were better for thee than the highest and best gifts besides that He has given thee, or ever could give thee, if thou could but see it in this light. So that if your little finger only aches, if you are cold, if you are hungry or thirsty, if others vex you by their words or deeds, or whatever happens to you that causes you distress or pain, it will all help to fit you for a noble and blessed state.

J. TAULER

AUGUST 11

The Lord thy God shall bless thee in all thy works, and in all that thou puttest thine hand unto.
                                        —Deuteronomy 15:10

MY place of lowly service, too,
   Beneath Thy sheltering wings I see;
For all the work I have to do
   Is done through sheltering rest in Thee.
                                        A. L. WARING

I think I find most help in trying to look on all interruptions and hindrances to work that one has planned out for oneself as discipline, trials sent by God to help one against getting selfish over one's work. Then one can feel that perhaps one's true work—one's work for God—consists in doing some trifling haphazard thing that has been thrown into one's day. It is not waste of time, as one is tempted to think. It is the most important part of the work of the day,—the part one can best offer to God. After such a hindrance, do not rush after the planned work; trust that the time to finish it will be given sometime, and keep a quiet heart about it.

ANNIE KEARY

AUGUST 12

Master, what shall I do to inherit eternal life?
—Luke 10:25

Whatsoever thy hand findeth to do, do it with thy might.
—Ecclesiastes 9:10

'WHAT shall I do to gain eternal life?'
   'Discharge aright
The simple dues with which each day is rife
   Yea, with thy might.'

F. VON SCHILLER

A man is relieved and happy when he has put his heart into his work, and done his best; but what he has said or done otherwise, shall give him no peace.

R. W. EMERSON

Be diligent, after thy power, to do deeds of love. Think nothing too little, nothing too low, to do lovingly for the sake of God. Bear with infirmities, ungentle tempers, and contradictions. Visit, if thou mayest, the sick, relieve the poor, forego thyself and thine own ways for love. He whom in them thou lovest, to whom in them thou ministerest, will own thy love, and will pour His own love into thee.

E. B. PUSEY

AUGUST 13

In your patience possess ye your souls.
—Luke 21:19

WHAT though thy way be dark, and earth
With ceaseless care do cark, till mirth
   To thee no sweet strain singeth;
Still hide thy life above, and still
Believe that God is love; fulfil
   Whatever lot ye bringeth.

ALBERT E. EVANS

The soul loses command of itself when it is impatient. Whereas, when it submits without a murmur it possesses itself in peace, and possesses God. To be impatient is to desire what we have not, or not to desire what we have. Peace does not dwell in outward things, but within the soul. We may preserve it in the midst of the bitterest pain, if our will remains firm and submissive. Peace in this life springs from acquiescence even in disagreeable things, not in an exemption from bearing them.

FÉNELON

The chief pang of most trials is not so much the actual suffering itself, as our own spirit of resistance to it.

JEAN NICOLAS GROU

AUGUST 14

I will lift up mine eyes unto the hills, from whence cometh my help.

—Psalm 121:1

My grace is sufficient for thee.

—2 Corinthians 12:9

———————— ❧ ————————

I LOOK to Thee in every need,
  And never look in vain;
I feel thy touch, Eternal Love,
  And all is well again:
The thought of Thee is mightier far
Than sin and pain and sorrow are.

S. LONGFELLOW

———————— ❧ ————————

How can you live sweetly amid the vexatious things, the irritating things, the multitude of little worries and frets, which lie all along your way, and which you cannot evade? You cannot at present change your surroundings. Whatever kind of life you are to live, must be lived amid precisely the experiences in which you are now moving. Here you must win your victories or suffer your defeats. No restlessness or discontent can change your lot. Others may have other circumstances surrounding them, but here are yours. You had better make up your mind to accept what you cannot alter. You *can* live a beautiful life in the midst of your present circumstances.

J. R. MILLER

AUGUST 15

God hath not given us the spirit of fear; but of power, and of love, and of a sound mind.
—2 Timothy 1:7

WE cast behind fear, sin, and death;
 With Thee we seek the things above;
Our inmost souls Thy spirit breathe,
 Of power, of calmness, and of love.

                    HYMNS OF THE SPIRIT

I must conclude with a more delightful subject,—my most dear and blessed sister: I never saw a more perfect instance of the spirit of power and of love, and of a sound mind. She showed intense love, almost to the annihilation of selfishness—a daily martyrdom for twenty years, during which she adhered to her early-formed resolution of never talking about herself. She was thoughtful about the very pins and ribands of my wife's dress, or about the making of a doll's cap for a child,—but of herself, save only as regarded her ripening in all goodness, wholly thoughtless. [She] enjoyed everything lovely, graceful, beautiful, high-minded, whether in God's works or man's, with the keenest relish. She inherited the earth to the very fullness of the promise, though never leaving her crib, nor changing her posture. And she has preserved [this attitude] through the very valley of the shadow of death, [free] from all fear or impatience, or from every cloud of impaired reason, which might mar the beauty of the glorious work of Christ's Spirit [in her].

                    THOMAS ARNOLD

AUGUST 16

Whatsoever a man soweth, that shall he also reap.
—Galatians 6:7

THE life above, when this is past,
   Is the ripe fruit of life below.

Sow love, and taste its fruitage pure;
   Sow peace, and reap its harvest bright
Sow sunbeams on the rock and moor,
   And find a harvest-home of light.

              H. BONAR

The dispositions, affections, and inclinations which shall issue hereafter in perfection, must be trained and nurtured in us throughout the whole course of this earthly life. We must bear in mind this plain truth, that the future perfection of the saints is not a translation from one state or disposition of soul into another, diverse from the former. [Instead, it is] the carrying out, the blossom and the fruitage of one and the same principle of spiritual life, which through [our] whole career on earth has been growing with an even strength, putting itself forth in the beginnings and promise of perfection, reaching upward with steadfast aspirations after perfect holiness.

            H. E. MANNING

AUGUST 17

O turn unto me, and have mercy upon me; Thy strength
unto Thy servant, and save the son of Thy handmaid.
—Psalm 86:16

THOU art my King—
My King henceforth alone;
And I, Thy servant, Lord, am all Thine own.
Give me Thy strength; oh! let Thy dwelling be
In this poor heart that pants, my Lord, for Thee!
G. TERSTEEGEN

When it is the one-ruling, never-ceasing desire of our hearts
that God may be the beginning and end, the reason and motive,
the rule and measure, of our doing or not doing, from morning
to night—then everywhere, whether speaking or silent, whether
inwardly or outwardly employed, we are equally offered up to
the eternal Spirit, we have our life in Him and from Him, and we
are united to Him by the Spirit of Prayer. [This] is the comfort,
the support, the strength and security of the soul, travelling by
the help of God through the vanity of time into the riches of
eternity. Let us have no thought or care but how to be wholly
His devoted instruments—everywhere, and in everything, His
adoring, joyful, and thankful servants.

WM. LAW

AUGUST 18

Beloved, if our heart condemn us not, then have we confidence toward God.

—1 John 3:21

O LORD, how happy is the time
　　When in Thy love I rest:
When from my weariness I climb
　　E'en to Thy tender breast.
The night of sorrow ended there,
　　Thy rays outshine the sun;
And in Thy pardon and Thy care
　　The heaven of heavens is won.

W. C. DESSLER

Nothing doth so much establish the mind amidst the rollings and turbulency of present things, as both a look above them, and a look beyond them. [Look] above them to the good and steady Hand by which they are ruled, and beyond them to the sweet and beautiful purpose to which, by that Hand, they shall be brought. . . . Study pure and holy walking, if you would have your confidence firm, and have boldness and joy in God. You will find that a little sin will shake your trust and disturb your peace more than the greatest sufferings. Yea, in those sufferings, your assurance and joy in God will grow and abound most if sin be kept out. So much sin as gets in, so much peace will go out.

R. LEIGHTON

AUGUST 19

Teach me Thy way, O Lord, and lead me in a plain path.
—Psalm 27:11

LEAD, kindly Light, amid the encircling gloom,
    Lead Thou me on;
The night is dark, and I am far from home,
    Lead Thou me on.
Keep Thou my feet; I do not ask to see
The distant scene, one step enough for me.

               J. H. NEWMAN

God only is holy. He alone knows how to lead His children in the paths of holiness. He knows every aspect of your soul, every thought of your heart, every secret of your character, its difficulties and hindrances. He knows how to mould you to His will, and lead you onwards to perfect sanctification. He knows exactly how each event, each trial, each temptation, will tell upon you, and he disposes all things accordingly. The consequences of this belief, if fully grasped, will influence your whole life. You will seek to give yourself up to God more and more unreservedly, asking nothing, refusing nothing, wishing nothing, but what He wills. [Instead of] seeking to bring things about for yourself, [you will] take all He sends joyfully, and believe the 'one step' set before you to be enough for you. You will be satisfied that even though there are clouds around, and your way seems dark, He is directing all, and that what seems a hindrance will prove a blessing, since He wills it.

               JEAN NICOLAS GROU

AUGUST 20

*Wait on the Lord: be of good courage, and He shall strength-
en thine heart: wait, I say, on the Lord.*
> *—Psalm 27:14*

*He giveth power to the faint; and to them that have no
might He increaseth strength.*
> *—Isaiah 40:29*

LEANING on Him, make with reverent meekness
   His own thy will,
And with strength from Him shall thy utter weakness
   Life's task fulfil.
> J. G. WHITTIER

Should we feel at times disheartened and discouraged, a confiding thought, a simple movement of heart towards God will
renew our powers. Whatever He may demand of us, He will give
us at the moment the strength and the courage that we need.

FÉNELON

We require a certain firmness in all circumstances of life, even
the happiest, and perhaps contradictions come in order to prove
and exercise this. If we can only determine so to use them, the
very effort brings back tranquillity to the soul, which always
enjoys having exercised its strength in conformity to duty.

WM. VON HUMBOLDT

AUGUST 21

We then that are strong ought to bear the infirmities of the weak, and not to please ourselves.
—Romans 15:1

The Lord God hath given me the tongue of the learned, that I should know how to speak a word in season to him that is weary.
—Isaiah 50:4

IF there be some weaker one,
Give me strength to help him on;
If a blinder soul there be,
Let me guide him nearer Thee.

J. G. WHITTIER

Ask Him to increase your powers of sympathy: to give you more quickness and depth of sympathy, in little things as well as great. Opportunities of doing a kindness are often lost from mere want of thought. Half a dozen lines of kindness may bring sunshine into the whole day of some sick person. Think of the pleasure you might give to someone who is shut in, and has fewer pleasures than you have, by sharing with her some little comfort or enjoyment that *you* have learnt to look upon as a necessary of life,—the pleasant drive, the new book, flowers from the country, etc. Try to put yourself in another's place. Ask, 'What should I like myself, if I were hardworked, or sick, or lonely?' Cultivate the *habit* of sympathy.

G. H. WILKINSON

AUGUST 22

I beseech you therefore, brethren, by the mercies of God, that ye present your bodies a living sacrifice, holy, acceptable unto God, which is your reasonable service.
—*Romans 12:1*

THOU hast my flesh, Thy hallowed shrine
   Devoted solely to Thy will;
Here let Thy light forever shine,
   This house still let Thy presence fill;
O Source of Life, live, dwell, and move
In me, till all my life be love!

JOACHIM LANGE

May it not be a comfort to those of us who feel we have not the mental or spiritual power that others have, to notice that the living sacrifice mentioned in Romans 12:1 is our 'bodies'? Of course, that includes the mental power, but does it not also include the loving, sympathizing glance, the kind, encouraging word, *the ready errand for another*, the work of our hands, opportunities for all of which come oftener in the day than for the mental power we are often tempted to envy? May we be enabled to offer willingly that which we have.

ANONYMOUS

AUGUST 23

Seekest thou great things for thyself? seek them not.
—Jeremiah 45:5

I WOULD not have the restless will
   That hurries to and fro,
Seeking for some great thing to do,
   Or secret thing to know;
I would be treated as a child,
   And guided where I go.

A. L. WARING

Oh! be little, be little, and then thou wilt be content with little. If thou feel, now and then, a check or a secret smiting,—in *that* is the Father's love. Be not over-wise, nor over-eager, in thy own willing, running, and desiring. By degrees [thou wilt] come to the knowledge of thy Guide, who will lead thee, step by step, in the path of life, and teach thee to follow. Be still, and wait for light and strength.

I. PENINGTON

Sink into the sweet and blessed littleness, where thou livest by grace alone. Contemplate with delight the holiness and goodness in God, which thou dost not find in thyself. How lovely it is to be nothing when God is all!

G. TERSTEEGEN

AUGUST 24

And that which fell among thorns are they, which, when they have heard, go forth, and are choked with cares, and riches and pleasures of this life, and bring no fruit to perfection.
—*Luke 8:14*

PRESERVE me from my calling's snare,
   And hide my simple heart above,
Above the thorns of choking care,
   The gilded baits of worldly love.
C. WESLEY

Anything allowed in the heart which is contrary to the will of God, let it seem ever so insignificant, or be ever so deeply hidden, will cause us to fall before our enemies. Any root of bitterness cherished towards another, any self-seeking, any harsh judgments indulged in, any slackness in obeying the voice of the Lord, any doubtful habits or surroundings, any one of these things will effectually cripple and paralyse our spiritual life. I believe our blessed Guide, the indwelling Holy Spirit, is always secretly discovering these things to us by continual little twinges and pangs of conscience, so that we are left without excuse.

H. W. S.

AUGUST 25

See that ye refuse not Him that speaketh.
—Hebrews 12:52

FROM the world of sin and noise
   And hurry I withdraw;
For the small and inward voice
   I wait with humble awe;
Silent am I now and still,
   Dare not in Thy presence move;
To my waiting soul reveal
   The secret of Thy love.

                   C. WESLEY

When therefore the smallest instinct or desire of thy heart calleth thee towards God and a newness of life, give it time and allow it to speak. Take care thou refuse not Him that speaketh. . . . Be retired, silent, passive, and humbly attentive to this new risen light within thee.

                   WM. LAW

It is hardly to be wondered at that he should lose the finer consciousness of higher powers and deeper feelings, not from any behaviour in itself wrong, but from the hurry, noise, and tumult in the streets of life....He had no time to think or feel.

                 G. MACDONALD

AUGUST 26

Be silent, O all flesh, before the Lord.
                    —Zechariah 2:13

———————— ⁓ ————————

BE earth, with all her scenes, withdrawn;
Let noise and vanity be gone:
In secret silence of the mind,
My heaven, and there my God, I find.
                    I. WATTS

———————— ⁓ ————————

It is only with the pious affection of the will that we can be spiritually attentive to God. As long as the noisy restlessness of the thoughts goes on, the gentle and holy desires of the new nature are overpowered and inactive.

J. P. GREAVES

There is hardly ever a complete silence in our soul. God is whispering to us wellnigh incessantly. Whenever the sounds of the world die out in the soul, or sink low, then we hear these whisperings of God. He is always whispering to us, but we do not always hear, because of the noise, hurry, and distraction which life causes as it rushes on.

F. W. FABER

The prayer of faith is a sincere, sweet, and quiet view of divine, eternal truth. The soul rests quiet, perceiving and loving God; sweetly rejecting all the imaginations that present themselves, calming the mind in the Divine presence, and fixing it only on God.

MOLINOS

AUGUST 27

Being confident of this very thing, that He which hath begun a good work in you will perform it.
—Philippians 1:6

He that endureth to the end shall be saved.
—Matthew 10:22

FILL with inviolable peace;
   Stablish and keep my settled heart;
In Thee may all my wanderings cease,
   From Thee no more may I depart:
Thy utmost goodness called to prove,
Loved with an everlasting love!

C. WESLEY

If any sincere Christian cast himself with his whole will upon the Divine Presence which dwells within him, he shall be kept safe unto the end. What is it that makes us unable to persevere? Is it want of strength? By no means. We have with us the strength of the Holy Spirit. When did we ever set ourselves sincerely to any work according to the will of God, and fail for want of strength? It was not that strength failed the will, but that the will failed first. If we could but embrace the Divine will with the whole love of ours, cleaving to it and holding fast by it, we should be borne along as upon 'the river of the water of life.' We open only certain chambers of our will to the influence of the Divine will. We are afraid of being wholly absorbed into it. And yet, if we would have peace, we must be altogether united to Him.

H. E. MANNING

AUGUST 28

They that know Thy name will put their trust in Thee: for
Thou, Lord, hast not forsaken them that seek Thee.
—Psalm 9:10

Yea, the Lord shall give that which is good.
—Psalm 85:12

IN Thee I place my trust,
  On Thee I calmly rest;
I know Thee good, I know Thee just,
  And count Thy choice the best.

H. F. LYTE

The souls that would really be richer in duty in some new
position, are precisely those who borrow no excuses from the
old one. ...Wretched and barren is the discontent that quarrels
with its tools instead of with its skill. By criticizing Providence,
discontent manages to keep up complacency with self. [We say,]
how gentle should we be, if we were not provoked; how pious,
if we were not busy; the sick would be patient, but he is not in
health; the obscure would do great things, but he is not conspic-
uous!

J. MARTINEAU

AUGUST 29

Am I my brother's keeper?

—Genesis 4:9

BECAUSE I held upon my selfish road,
And left my brother wounded by the way,
And called ambition 'duty,' and pressed on—
    O Lord, I do repent.

SARAH WILLIAMS

How many are the sufferers who have fallen amongst misfortunes along the wayside of life! 'By *chance,*' we come that way—chance, accident, Providence, has thrown them in our way. We see them from a distance, like the Priest, or we come upon them suddenly, like the Levite. Our business, our pleasure, is interrupted by the sight, is troubled by the delay. What are our feelings, what our actions towards them? . . . 'Who is thy neighbour?' It is the sufferer, wherever, whoever, whatsoever he be. Wherever thou hearest the cry of distress, wherever thou seest any one brought across thy path by the chances and changes of life (that is, by the Providence of God), whom it is in thy power to help,—he, stranger or enemy though he be,—*he* is thy neighbour.

A. P. STANLEY

AUGUST 30

Walk worthy of the vocation wherewith ye are called, with all lowliness and meekness, with long-suffering, forbearing one another in love.

—Ephesians 4:1, 2

───── ⚜ ─────

HELP us, O Lord, with patient love to bear
   Each other's faults, to suffer with true meekness;
Help us each other's joys and griefs to share,
   But let us turn to Thee alone in weakness.
                ANONYMOUS

───── ⚜ ─────

You should make a special point of asking God every morning to give you, before all else, that true spirit of meekness which He would have His children possess. You must also make a firm resolution to practise yourself in this virtue, especially in your interaction with those persons to whom you chiefly owe it. You must make it your main object to conquer yourself in this matter. Call it to mind a hundred times during the day, commending your efforts to God. It seems to me that no [gift] more than this is needed in order to subject your soul entirely to His will, and then you will become more gentle day by day, trusting wholly in His goodness. You will be very happy, my dearest child, if you can do this, for God will dwell in your heart, and where He reigns all is peace. But if you should fail, and commit some of your old faults, do not be disheartened, but rise up and go on again, as though you had not fallen.

                          FRANCIS DE SALES

AUGUST 31

But I would ye should understand, brethren, that the things
which happened unto me have fallen out rather unto the fur-
therance of the gospel; so that my bonds in Christ are manifest
in all the palace, and in all other places; and many of the
brethren in the Lord, waxing confident by my bonds, are much
more bold to speak the word without fear.

—*Philippians 1:12–14*

GO bury thy sorrow,
   The world hath its share:
Go, bury it deeply,
   Go, hide it with care
Go, bury thy sorrow,
   Let others be blest;
Go, give them the sunshine,
   And tell God the rest.

ANONYMOUS

Our veiled and terrible guest [Trouble] brings for us, if we
will accept it, the boon of fortitude, patience, self-control,
wisdom, sympathy, faith. If we reject that, then we find in our
hands the other gift,—cowardice, weakness, isolation, despair.
If your trouble seems to have in it no other possibility of good,
at least set yourself to bear it like a man. Let none of its weight
come on other shoulders. Try to carry it so that no one shall
even see it. Though your heart be sad within, let cheer go out
from you to others. Meet them with a kindly presence, considerate words, helpful acts.

G. S. MERRIAM

SEPTEMBER 1

Let them that suffer according to the will of God commit the keeping of their souls to Him in well-doing, as unto a faithful Creator.

—1 Peter 4:19

The Lord is very pitiful, and of tender mercy.

—James 5:11

ON Thy compassion I repose
   In weakness and distress:
I will not ask for greater ease,
   Lest I should love Thee less.
Oh, 'tis a blessed thing for me
   To need Thy tenderness.

A. L. WARING

Oh, look not at thy pain or sorrow, how great soever. Instead, look from them, look off them, look beyond them, to the Deliverer! His power is over them, and His loving, wise, and tender spirit is able to do thee good by them. The Lord lead thee, day by day, in the right way, and keep thy mind stayed upon Him, in whatever befalls thee. Thus, the belief of His love and hope in His mercy, when thou art at the lowest ebb, may keep up thy head above the billows.

ISAAC PENINGTON

SEPTEMBER 2

Blessed are the peacemakers: for they shall be called the children of God.

—*Matthew 5:9*

GRANT us Thy peace, down from Thy presence falling,
    As on the thirsty earth cool night-dews sweet;
Grant us Thy peace, to Thy pure paths recalling,
    From devious ways, our worn and wandering feet.

E. SCUDDER

O God, who art Peace everlasting, whose chosen reward is the gift of peace, and who hast taught us that the peacemakers are Thy children, pour Thy sweet peace into our souls, that everything discordant may utterly vanish, and all that makes for peace be sweet to us forever. Amen.

GELASIAN, A.D. 492

Have you ever thought seriously of the meaning of that blessing given to the peacemakers? People are always expecting to get peace in heaven; but you know whatever peace they get there will be ready-made. Whatever making of peace *they* can be blest for, must be on the earth here—not the taking of arms against, but the building of nests amidst its 'sea of troubles' [like the halcyons]. Difficult enough, you think? Perhaps so, but I do not see that any of us try. We complain of the want of many things—we want votes, we want liberty, we want amusement, we want money. Which of us feels or knows that he wants peace?

J. RUSKIN

SEPTEMBER 3

The eyes of all wait upon Thee; and Thou givest them their meat in due season.
—Psalm 145:15

What time I am afraid, I will trust in Thee.
—Psalm 56:3

LATE on me, weeping, did this whisper fall:
'Dear child, there is no need to weep at all!
Why go about to grieve and to despair?
Why weep now through thy Future's eyes, and bear
In vain to-day to-morrow's load of care?'

H. S. SUTTON

The crosses of the present moment always bring their own special grace and consequent comfort with them; we see the hand of God in them when it is laid upon us. But the crosses of anxious foreboding are seen out of the dispensation of God. We see them without grace to bear them; we see them indeed through a faithless spirit which banishes grace. So, everything in them is bitter and unendurable; all seems dark and helpless. Let us throw self aside. [Tolerate] no more self-interest, and then God's will, unfolding every moment in everything, will console us also every moment for all that He shall do around us, or within us, for our discipline.

FÉNELON

SEPTEMBER 4

His delight is in the law of the Lord. And he shall be like a tree planted by the rivers of water, that bringeth forth his fruit in his season; his leaf also shall not wither; and whatsoever he doeth shall prosper.

—Psalm 1:2, 3

THE wind that blows can never kill
    The tree God plants;
It bloweth east; it bloweth west;
The tender leaves have little rest,
But any wind that blows [it won't] best—
    The tree God plants
Strikes deeper root, grows higher still,
Spreads wider boughs, for God's good-will
    Meets all its wants.

LILLIE E. BARR

It is a fatal mistake to suppose that we cannot be holy except on the condition of a situation and circumstances in life such as shall suit ourselves. It is one of the first principles of holiness to leave our times and our places, our going out and our coming in, our wasted and our goodly heritage entirely with the Lord. Here, O Lord, hast Thou placed us, and we will glorify Thee here!

T. C. UPHAM

It is not by change of circumstances, but by fitting our spirits to the circumstances in which God has placed us, that we can be reconciled to life and duty.

F. W. ROBERTSON

SEPTEMBER 5

O Lord, I am oppressed; undertake for me.
—Isaiah 38:14

BEING perplexed, I say,
    Lord, make it right!
Night is as day to Thee,
    Darkness is light.
I am afraid to touch
Things that involve so much;—
    My trembling hand may shake,
    My skill-less hand may break:
    Thine can make no mistake.

ANNA WARNER

The many troubles in your household will tend to your edification, if you strive to bear them all in gentleness, patience, and kindness. Keep this ever before you, and remember constantly that God's loving eyes are upon you amid all these little worries and vexations, watching whether you take them as He would desire. Offer up all such occasions to Him, and if sometimes you are put out, and give way to impatience, do not be discouraged, but make haste to regain your lost composure.

FRANCIS DE SALES

SEPTEMBER 6

If any man will come after me, let him deny himself, and take up his cross daily, and follow me.
—Luke 9:23

THERE lies thy cross; beneath it meekly bow;
   It fits thy stature now;
Who scornful pass it with averted eye,
    'Twill crush them by and by.

           J. KEBLE

To take up the cross of Christ is no great action done once for all; it consists in the continual practice of small duties which are distasteful to us.

      J. H. NEWMAN

On one occasion an intimate friend of his was fretting somewhat at not being able to put a cross on the grave of a relation, because the rest of the family disliked it. 'Don't you see,' he said to her, 'that by giving up your own way, you will be virtually putting a cross on the grave? You'll have it in its effect. The one is but a stone cross, the other is a true spiritual cross.'

      LIFE OF JAMES HINTON

I would have you, one by one, ask yourselves, Wherein do I take up the cross daily?

      E. B. PUSEY

Every morning, receive thine own special cross from the hands of thy heavenly Father.

      L. SCUPOLI

SEPTEMBER 7

Pure religion and undefiled before God and the Father is this, To visit the fatherless and widows in their affliction, and to keep himself unspotted from the world.
—James 1:27

NOT to ease and aimless quiet
    Doth that inward answer tend,
But to works of love and duty
    As our being's end.

J. G. WHITTIER

It is surprising how practical duty enriches the fancy and the heart, and action clears and deepens the affections. Indeed, no one can have a true idea of right, until he does it; any genuine reverence for it, till he has done it often and with cost; any peace ineffable in it, till he does it always and with alacrity. Does any one complain that the best affections are transient visitors with him, and the heavenly spirit a stranger to his heart? Oh, let him not go forth on any strained wing of thought, in distant quest of them. Rather, [let him] stay at home and set his house in the true order of conscience, and of their own accord the divinest guests will enter.

J. MARTINEAU

SEPTEMBER 8

Continue in prayer, and watch in the same with thanks-giving.

—*Colossians 4:2*

Watch ye, stand fast in the faith, quit you like men, be strong.

—*1 Corinthians 16:13*

❧

WE kneel how weak, we rise how full of power.
Why therefore should we do ourselves this wrong,
Or others—that we are not always strong,
That we are ever overborne with care,
That we should ever weak or heartless be,
Anxious or troubled, when with us is prayer,
And joy and strength and courage are with Thee?

R. C. TRENCH

❧

It is impossible for us to make the duties of our lot minister to our sanctification without a habit of devout fellowship with God. This is the spring of all our life, and the strength of it. It is prayer, meditation, and converse with God that refreshes, restores, and renews the temper of our minds, at all times, under all trials, after all conflicts with the world. By this contact with the world unseen we receive continual accesses of strength. As our day, so is our strength. Without this healing and refreshing of spirit, duties grow to be burdens, the events of life chafe our temper, employments lower the tone of our minds, and we become fretful, irritable, and impatient.

H. E. MANNING

SEPTEMBER 9

This is a faithful saying, and these things I will that thou affirm constantly, that they which have believed in God might be careful to maintain good works.
—Titus 3:8

───────────❧❧───────────

FAITH'S meanest deed more favour bears
    Where hearts and wills are weighed,
Than brightest transports, choicest prayers,
    Which bloom their hour and fade.

J. H. NEWMAN

───────────❧❧───────────

One secret act of self-denial, one sacrifice of inclination to duty, is worth all the mere good thoughts, warm feelings, and passionate prayers in which idle people indulge themselves.

J. H. NEWMAN

It is impossible for us to live in fellowship with God without holiness in all the duties of life. These things act and react on each other. Without a diligent and faithful obedience to the calls and claims of others upon us, our religious profession is simply dead. To disobey conscience when it points to relative duties irritates the whole temper, and quenches the first beginnings of devotion. We cannot go from strife, breaches, and angry words, to God. Selfishness, an imperious will, want of sympathy with the sufferings and sorrows of other men, neglect of charitable offices, suspicions, and hard censures of those with whom our lot is cast, will miserably darken our own hearts and hide the face of God from us.

H. E. MANNING

SEPTEMBER 10

Lord, not my feet only, but also my hands and my head.
—John 13:9

———————— ❧ ————————

TAKE my hands, and let them move
At the impulse of Thy love.

Take my feet, and let them be
Swift and 'beautiful' for Thee.

Take my intellect, and use
Every power as Thou shalt choose.

F. R. HAVERGAL

———————— ❧ ————————

If a man may attain thereunto, to be unto God as his hand is to a man, let him be therewith content, and not seek further. That is to say, let him strive and wrestle with all his might to obey God and His commandments so thoroughly at all times, and in all things, that in him there be nothing, spiritual or natural, which opposeth God. [Let him desire] that his whole soul and body, with all their members, may stand ready and willing for that to which God hath created them—as ready and willing as his hand is to a man, which is so wholly in his power, that in the twinkling of an eye, he moveth and turneth it whither he will. And when we find it otherwise with us, we must give our whole diligence to amend our state.

THEOLOGIA GERMANICA

When the mind thinks nothing, when the soul covets nothing, and the body acteth nothing that is contrary to the will of God, this is perfect sanctification.

ANONYMOUS,
in an old Bible, 1599

SEPTEMBER 11

Thy kingdom come.

—Matthew 6:10

❧

THE kingdom of established peace,
  Which can no more remove;
The perfect powers of godliness,
  The omnipotence of love.

C. WESLEY

❧

My child, thou mayest not measure out thine offering unto me by what others have done or left undone. But [thy offering is] to seek out, even to the last moment of thine earthly life, what is the utmost height of pure devotion to which I have called *thine own self.* Remember that if thou fall short of this, each time thou utterest in prayer the words, 'Hallowed be Thy name, Thy kingdom come,' thou dost most fearfully condemn thyself. Is it not a mockery to ask for what thou wilt not seek to promote, even unto the uttermost, within the narrow compass of thine own heart and spirit?

THE DIVINE MASTER

If you do not wish for His kingdom, don't pray for it. But if you do, you must do more than pray for it; you must work for it.

J. RUSKIN

SEPTEMBER 12

She obeyed not the voice; she received not correction; she trusted not in the Lord; she drew not near to her God.
—Zephaniah 3:2

OH! let us not this thought allow;
The heat, the dust upon our brow,
Signs of the contest, we may wear;
Yet thus we shall appear more fair
   In our Almighty Master's eye,
Than if in fear to lose the bloom,
Or ruffle the soul's lightest plume,
   We from the strife should fly.

R. C. TRENCH

If God requires anything of us, we have no right to draw back under the pretext that we are liable to commit some fault in obeying. It is better to obey imperfectly than not at all. Perhaps you ought to rebuke some one dependent on you, but you are silent for fear of giving way to vehemence;—or you avoid the society of certain persons, because they make you cross and impatient. How are you to attain self-control if you shun all occasions of practising it? Is not such self-choosing a greater fault than those into which you fear to fall? Aim at a steady mind to do right, go wherever duty calls you, and believe firmly that God will forgive the faults that take our weakness by surprise in spite of our sincere desire to please Him.

JEAN NICOLAS GROU

SEPTEMBER 13

It is good that a man should both hope and quietly wait for the salvation of the Lord.

—Lamentations 3:26

Truly my soul waiteth upon God: from Him cometh my salvation.

—Psalm 62:1

NOT so in haste, my heart;
  Have faith in God, and wait—
Although He linger long,
  He never comes too late.

ANONYMOUS

The true use to be made of all the imperfections of which you are conscious is neither to justify, nor to condemn them, but to present them before God, conforming your will to His, and remaining in peace. Peace is the divine order, in whatever state we may be.

FÉNELON

You will find it less easy to uproot faults, than to choke them by gaining virtues. Do not think of your faults; still less of others' faults. In every person who comes near you look for what is good and strong: honour that; rejoice in it; and, as you can, try to imitate it. Your faults will drop off like dead leaves when their time comes.

J. RUSKIN

SEPTEMBER 14

*Call unto me, and I will answer thee, and show thee great
and mighty things which thou knowest not.*
—Jeremiah 33:3

And I have also given thee that which thou hast not asked.
— 1 Kings 3:13

NO voice of prayer to Thee can rise,
But swift as light Thy love replies;
Not always what we ask, indeed,
But, O most Kind! what most we need.

H. M. KIMBALL

If you have any trial which seems intolerable, pray,—pray that
it be relieved or changed. There is no harm in that. We may pray
for anything, not wrong in itself, with perfect freedom, if we do
not pray selfishly. One disabled from duty by sickness may pray
for health, that he may do his work; or one hemmed in by internal impediments may pray for utterance, that he may serve better the truth and the right. Or, if we have a besetting sin, we may
pray to be delivered from it, in order to serve God and man, and
not be ourselves Satans to mislead and destroy. But the answer
to the prayer may be, as it was to Paul, not the removal of the
thorn, but, instead, a growing insight into its meaning and value.
The voice of God in our soul may show us, as we look up to
Him, that His strength is enough to enable us to bear it.

J. F. CLARKE

SEPTEMBER 15

*Can ye drink of the cup that I drink of? and be baptized
with the baptism that I am baptized with?*
                    —Mark 10:38

WHATE'ER my God ordains is right;
    Though I the cup must drink
That bitter seems to my faint heart,
    I will not fear nor shrink.

                    S. RODIGAST

The worst part of martyrdom is not the last agonizing
moment; it is the wearing, daily steadfastness. Men who can
make up their minds to hold out against the torture of an hour
have sunk under the weariness and the harass of small pro-
longed vexations. And there are many Christians who have the
weight of some deep, incommunicable grief pressing, cold as
ice, upon their hearts. To bear that cheerfully and manfully is to
be a martyr. There is many a Christian bereaved and stricken in
the best hopes of life. For such a one to say quietly, 'Father, not
as I will, but as Thou wilt,' is to be a martyr. There is many a
Christian who feels the irksomeness of the duties of life, and
feels his spirit revolting from them. To get up every morning
with the firm resolve to find pleasure in those duties, and do
them well, and finish the work which God has given us to do,
that is to drink Christ's cup. The humblest occupation has in it
materials of discipline for the highest heaven.

                    F. W. ROBERTSON

SEPTEMBER 16

*Who hath measured the waters in the hollow of His hand,
and meted out heaven with the span, and comprehended the
dust of the earth in a measure, and weighed the mountains in
scales, and the hills in a balance?*
                                        —Isaiah 40:12

OH! Source divine, and Life of all,
  The Fount of Being's fearful sea,
Thy depth would every heart appal,
  That saw not love supreme in Thee.
                                        J. STERLING

He showed a little thing, the quantity of a hazel-nut, lying in
the palm of my hand, as meseemed, and it was as round as a ball.
I looked thereon with the eye of my understanding, and
thought, *'What may this be?'* It was answered generally thus, *'It
is all that is made.'* I marvelled how it might last, for methought
it might suddenly have fallen to naught for littleness. And I was
answered in my understanding, *'It lasteth, and ever shall, for
God loveth it. And so hath all things being by the Love of God.'*
In this little thing I saw three properties. The first is that God
made it. The second is that God loveth it. The third is that God
keepeth it. For this is the cause which we be not all in ease of
heart and soul—we seek rest here in this thing which is so little,
where [there is] no rest, and we know not our God who is all
Mighty, all Wise, and all Good, for He is very rest. God wills to
be known, and it pleaseth Him that we rest in Him. For all that is
beneath Him, does not satisfy us.

MOTHER JULIANA, 1373

SEPTEMBER 17

Whosoever will be great among you, shall be your minister; and whosoever of you will be the chiefest, shall be servant of all. For even the Son of man came not to be ministered unto, but to minister.

—*Mark 10:43-5*

A CHILD'S kiss
Set on thy sighing lips, shall make thee glad;
A poor man served by thee, shall make thee rich;
A sick man helped by thee, shall make thee strong,
Thou shalt be served thyself by every sense
Of service which thou renderest.

E. B. BROWNING

Let every man lovingly cast all his thoughts and cares, and his sins too, on the Will of God. Moreover, if a man, while busy in this lofty inward work, were called by some duty in the Providence of God to cease therefrom, and cook a broth for some sick person, or any other such service, he should do so willingly and with great joy. If I had to forsake such work, and go out to preach or aught else, I should go cheerfully. I would believe not only that God would be with me, but that He would grant me even greater grace and blessing in that external work undertaken out of true love in the service of my neighbour, than I should perhaps receive in my season of loftiest contemplation.

JOHN TAULER

SEPTEMBER 18

All the paths of the Lord are mercy and truth unto such as keep His covenant and His testimonies.
—Psalm 25:10

SPEAK, Lord, for Thy servant heareth,
  Speak peace to my anxious soul,
And help me to feel that all my ways
  Are under Thy wise control;

That He who cares for the lily,
  And heeds the sparrow's fall,
Shall tenderly lead His loving child;
  For He made and loveth all.

ANONYMOUS

It is not by seeking more fertile regions where toil is lighter—happier circumstances free from difficult complications and troublesome people—but by bringing the high courage of a devout soul, clear in principle and aim, to bear upon what is given to us, that we brighten our inward light, lead something of a true life, and introduce the kingdom of heaven into the midst of our earthly day. If we cannot work out the will of God where God has placed us, then why has He placed us there?

J. H. THOM

SEPTEMBER 19

Pray for us unto the Lord thy God . . . that the Lord thy God may show us the way wherein we may walk, and the thing that we may do.
> *—Jeremiah 42:2, 3*

That which I see not, teach Thou me.
> *—Job 34:32*

O FATHER, hear!
The way is dark, and I would fain discern
What steps to take, into which path to turn;
   Oh! make it clear.

CHRISTIAN INTELLIGENCER

'We can't choose happiness either for ourselves or for another; we can't tell where that will lie. We can only choose whether we will indulge ourselves in the present moment, or whether we will renounce that, for the sake of obeying the Divine voice within us,—for the sake of being true to all the motives that sanctify our lives. I know this belief is hard; it has slipped away from me again and again. But I have felt that if I let it go forever, I should have no light through the darkness of this life.'

GEORGE ELIOT

There was a care on my mind so to pass my time, that nothing might hinder me from the most steady attention to the voice of the true Shepherd.

JOHN WOOLMAN

SEPTEMBER 20

Thou shalt hide them in the secret of Thy presence from the pride of man; Thou shalt keep them secretly in a pavilion from the strife of tongues.

—*Psalm 31:20*

THE praying spirit breathe,
   The watching power impart,
From all entanglements beneath
   Call off my anxious heart.
My feeble mind sustain,
   By worldly thoughts oppressed;
Appear, and bind me turn again
   To my eternal rest.

C. WESLEY

As soon as we are with God in faith and in love, we are in prayer.

FÉNELON

If you could once make up your mind in the fear of God never to undertake more work of any sort than you can carry on calmly, quietly, without hurry or flurry, and the instant you feel yourself growing nervous and like one out of breath, would stop and take breath, you would find this simple common-sense rule doing for you what no prayers or tears could ever accomplish.

ELIZABETH PRENTISS

SEPTEMBER 21

How excellent is Thy loving-kindness, O God! Therefore the children of men put their trust under the shadow of Thy wings.

—Psalm 36:7

The eternal God is thy refuge, and underneath are the everlasting arms.

—Deuteronomy 33:27

WITHIN Thy circling arms we lie,
   O God! in Thy infinity:
Our souls in quiet shall abide,
   Beset with love on every side.

ANONYMOUS

'The Everlasting Arms.' I think of that whenever rest is sweet. How the whole earth and the strength of it, that is almightiness, is beneath every tired creature to give it rest; *holding* us, always! No thought of God is closer than that. No human tenderness of patience is greater than that which gathers in its arms a little child, and holds it, heedless of weariness. And He fills the great earth, and all upon it, with this unseen force of His love, that never forgets or exhausts itself, so that everywhere we may lie down in His bosom and be comforted.

A. D. T. WHITNEY

SEPTEMBER 22

The word is very nigh unto thee, in thy mouth, and in thy heart, that thou mayest do it.

—Deuteronomy 30:14

BUT, above all, the victory is most sure
For him, who, seeking faith by virtue, strives
To yield entire obedience to the Law
Of Conscience: Conscience reverenced and obeyed,
As God's most intimate presence in the soul,
And His most perfect image in the world.

W. WORDSWORTH

What we call Conscience is the voice of Divine love in the deep of our being, desiring union with our will; and which, by attracting the affections inward, invites them to enter into the harmonious contentment and 'fulness of joy' which attends the being joined by 'one spirit to the Lord.'

J. P. GREAVES

I rejoice that God has bestowed upon you a relish and inclination for the inner life. To be called to this precious and lofty life is a great and undeserved grace of God, to which we ought to respond with great faithfulness. God invites us to His fellowship of love, and wishes to prepare our spirit to be His own abode and temple.

GERHARD TERSTEEGEN

SEPTEMBER 23

Show me Thy ways, O Lord; teach me Thy paths.
—Psalm 25:4

———————— ❧ ————————

WHEN we cannot see our way,
Let us trust and still obey;
He who bids us forward go,
Cannot fail the way to show.
Though the sea be deep and wide,
Though a passage seem denied;
Fearless let us still proceed,
Since the Lord vouchsafes to lead.

ANONYMOUS

———————— ❧ ————————

That which is often asked of God is not so much His will and way, as His approval of our way.

S. F. SMILEY

There is nothing like the first glance we get at duty, before there has been any special pleading of our affections or inclinations. Duty is never uncertain at first. It is only after we have got involved in the mazes and sophistries of wishing that things were otherwise than they are, that it seems indistinct. Considering a duty is often only explaining it away. Deliberation is often only dishonesty. God's guidance is plain, when we are true.

F. W. ROBERTSON

SEPTEMBER 24

When I awake, I am still with Thee.
                    —Psalm 139:18

LET the glow of love destroy
Cold obedience faintly given;
Wake our hearts to strength and joy
With the flushing eastern heaven.
Let us truly rise, ere yet
    Life be set.

                    ROSENROTH

With his first waking consciousness, he can set himself to take a serious, manly view of the day before him. He ought to know pretty well on what lines his difficulty is likely to come, whether in being irritable, or domineering, or sharp in his bargains, or self-absorbed, or whatever it be. In this quiet hour he can take a good, full look at his enemy, and make up his mind to beat him. It is a good time, too, for giving his thoughts a range quite beyond himself,—beyond even his own moral struggles,—a good time, there in the stillness, for going into the realm of other lives. His wife,—what needs has she for help, for sympathy, that he can meet? His children,—how can he make the day sweeter to them? This acquaintance, who is having a hard time; this friend, who dropped a word to you yesterday that you hardly noticed in your hurry, but that comes up to you now, revealing in him some finer trait, some deeper hunger than you had guessed before,—now you can think these things over. So you get your day somewhat into right perspective and proportion before you begin it.

                    G. S. MERRIAM

SEPTEMBER 25

*Ye shall rejoice in all that ye put your hand unto, ye and
your households, wherein the Lord thy God hath blessed thee.*
—Deuteronomy 12:7

SWEET is the smile of home; the mutual look
   When hearts are of each other sure;
Sweet all the joys that crowd the household nook,
   The haunts of all affections pure.

J. KEBLE

Is there any tie which absence has loosened, or which the
wear and tear of every-day fellowship, little uncongenialities,
unconfessed misunderstandings, have fretted into the heart,
until it bears something of the nature of a fetter? Any cup at our
home-table whose sweetness we have not fully tasted, although
it might yet make of our daily bread a continual feast? Let us
reckon up these treasures while they are still ours, in thankfulness to God.

ELIZABETH CHARLES

We ought daily or weekly to dedicate a little time to the reck-
oning up of the virtues of [those to whom we] belong—wife,
children, friends,—and contemplating them then in a beautiful
collection. And we should do so now, that we may not pardon
and love in vain and too late, after the beloved one has been
taken away from us to a better world.

JEAN PAUL RICHTER

SEPTEMBER 26

Yea, though I walk through the valley of the shadow of death, I will fear no evil; for Thou art with me; Thy rod and Thy staff, they comfort me.

—*Psalm 23:4*

O WILL, that willest good alone,
   Lead Thou the way, Thou guidest best;
A silent child, I follow on,
   And trusting lean upon Thy breast.
And if in gloom I see Thee not,
   I lean upon Thy love unknown;
In me Thy blessed will is wrought,
   If I will nothing of my own.

GERHARD TERSTEEGEN

The devout soul is always safe in every state, if it makes everything an occasion either of rising up, or falling down into the hands of God, and exercising faith, trust, and resignation to Him. The pious soul that eyes only God, that means nothing but being His alone, can have no stop put to its progress; light and darkness equally assist him. In the light he looks up to God. In the darkness he lays hold on God. And so they both do him the same good.

WM. LAW

SEPTEMBER 27

When I sit in darkness, the Lord shall be a light unto me.
—Micah 7:8

There be many that say, Who will show us any good? Lord,
lift Thou up the light of Thy countenance upon us.
—Psalm 4:6

HOW oft a gleam of glory sent
   Straight through the deepest, darkest night,
   Has filled the soul with heavenly light,
With holy peace and sweet content.
               ANONYMOUS

Suppose you are bewildered and know not what is right nor what is true. Cannot you utterly and perfectly love, and rejoice to be in the dark, and gloom-beset, because that very thing is the fact of God's Infinite Being as it is to you? Cannot you take this trial also into your own heart, and be ignorant—not because you are obliged, but because that being God's will, it is yours also? Do you not see that a person who truly *loves* is one with the Infinite Being—he cannot be uncomfortable or unhappy? It is that which IS that he desires, and holds best of all to be. To know God is to utterly sacrifice self.

JAMES HINTON

SEPTEMBER 28

My little children, let us not love in word, neither in tongue; but in deed, and in truth.

—1 John 3:18

But be ye doers of the word, and not hearers only, deceiving your own selves.

—James 1:22

THRICE blest whose lives are faithful prayers.
  Whose loves in higher love endure;
  What souls possess themselves so pure,
Or is there blessedness like theirs?

A. TENNYSON

Let every creature have your love. Love, with its fruits of meekness, patience, and humility, is all that we can wish for to ourselves, and our fellow-creatures; for this is to live in God, united to Him, both for time and eternity. To desire to communicate good to every creature, in the degree we can, and that it is capable of receiving from us, is a divine temper. Thus God stands unchangeably disposed towards the whole creation.

WM. LAW

Do deeds of love for Him, to Him, following His steps. Believest thou in Christ? Do the works of Christ, that thy faith may live. Thou who sayest thou abidest in Christ, oughtest so to walk as He walked. If thou seekest thine own glory, enviest the prosperous, speakest ill of the absent, renderest evil to him who injureth thee—this did not Christ.

E. B. PUSEY

SEPTEMBER 29

Blessed are the pure in heart; for they shall see God.
—Matthew 5:8

Follow peace with all men, and holiness, without which no man shall see the Lord.
—Hebrews 12:14

SINCE Thou Thyself dost still display
   Unto the pure in heart,
Oh, make us children of the day
   To know Thee as Thou art.
For Thou art light and life and love;
   And Thy redeemed below
May see Thee as Thy saints above,
   And know Thee as they know.

               J. MONTGOMERY

Doubt, gloom, impatience, have been expelled. Joy has taken their place, the hope of heaven and the harmony of a pure heart, the triumph of self-mastery, sober thoughts, and a contented mind. How can charity towards all men fail to follow, being the mere affectionateness of innocence and peace? Thus the Spirit of God creates in us the simplicity and warmth of heart which children have, nay, rather the perfections of His heavenly hosts, high and low being joined together in His mysterious work. What are implicit trust, ardent love, and abiding purity, but the mind both of little children and of the adoring Seraphim!

              J. H. NEWMAN

SEPTEMBER 30

Lord, who shall abide in Thy tabernacle? Who shall dwell in Thy holy hill? He that walketh uprightly, and worketh righteousness, and speaketh the truth in his heart.
—Psalm 15:1, 2

HOW happy is he born or taught,
That serveth not another's will,
Whose armour is his honest thought,
And simple truth his utmost skill.
H. WOTTON

If any man compares his own soul with the picture drawn in the New Testament of what a Christian ought to be; if any man fixes his eye on the pattern of self-sacrifice, of purity, of truth, of tenderness, and measures his own distance from that standard, he might be ready to despair. But fear not, because you are far from being like the pattern set before you. Fear not because your faults are painful to think of: continue the battle and fear not. If, indeed, you are content with yourself, and are making no endeavor to rise above the poor level at which you now stand, then there is reason to fear. But if you are fighting with all your might, fear not, however often you may have fallen, however deeply, however ungratefully, however inexcusably. This one thing we can give, and this is what He asks—hearts that shall never cease from this day forward, till we reach the grave, to strive to be more like Him, to come nearer to Him, to root out from within us the sin that keeps us from Him. To such a battle, brethren, I call you in His name.

FREDERICK TEMPLE

OCTOBER 1

Be strong, all ye people of the land, saith the Lord, and
work; for I am with you, saith the Lord of hosts.
—Haggai 2:4

YET the world is Thy field, Thy garden;
   On earth art Thou still at home.
When Thou bendest hither Thy hallowing eye,
My narrow work-room seems vast and high.
Its dingy ceiling a rainbow-dome,—
Stand ever thus at my wide-swung door,
   And toil will be toil no more.

              L. LARCOM

It is possible, I dare to say, for those who will indeed draw on
their Lord's power for deliverance and victory, to live a life in
which His promises are taken as they stand, and found to be
true. It is possible to cast *every* care on Him daily, and to be at
peace amidst the pressure. It is possible to see the will of God in
everything, and to find it, as one has said, no longer a sigh, but a
song. It is possible, in the world of inner act and motion, to put
away, to get put away *all* bitterness, and wrath, and anger, and
evil speaking, daily and hourly. It is possible, by unreserved
resort to divine power, under divine conditions, to become
strongest through and through at our weakest point; to find the
thing which yesterday upset all our obligations to patience, or to
purity, or to humility, an occasion to-day, through Him who
loveth us, and worketh in us, for a joyful consent to His will, and
a delightful sense of His presence and sin-annulling power.
These are things divinely possible.

             HANDLEY C. G. MOULE

OCTOBER 2

I am purposed that my mouth shall not transgress.
              —Psalm 17:3

In the multitude of words there wanteth not sin: but he that refraineth his lips is wise.

                    —Proverbs 10:19

PRUNE thou thy words; the thoughts control
    That o'er thee swell and throng;
They will condense within thy soul,
    And change to purpose strong.
                    J. H. NEWMAN

Few men suspect how much mere talk fritters away spiritual energy. That which should be spent in action spends itself in words. Hence, he who restrains that love of talk lays up a fund of spiritual strength.

F. W. ROBERTSON

Do not flatter yourself that your thoughts are under due control, your desires properly regulated, or your dispositions subject as they should be to Christian principle, if your conversation with others consists mainly of frivolous gossip, impertinent anecdotes, speculations on the character and affairs of your neighbours, the repetition of former conversations, or a discussion of the current petty scandal of society; much less, if you allow yourself in careless exaggeration on all these points, and that grievous inattention to exact truth, which is apt to attend the statements of those whose conversation is made up of these materials.

H. WARE, JR.

OCTOBER 3

Judge not, that ye be not judged.
—Matthew 7:1

Why beholdest thou the mote that is in thy brother's eye; but perceivest not the beam that is in thine own eye?
—Luke 6:41

JUDGE not; the workings of his brain
    And of his heart thou canst not see;
What looks to thy dim eyes a stain,
    In God's pure light may only be
A scar, brought from some well-worn field,
Where thou wouldst only faint and yield.

ADELAIDE A. PROCTER

When you behold an unhappy face for whose constant gloom and frown you cannot account, whose unvarying cloud exasperates you by its apparent causelessness, be sure that there is a canker somewhere, and a canker not the less deeply corroding because concealed.

CHARLOTTE BRONTË

While we are coldly discussing a man's career, sneering at his mistakes, blaming his rashness, and labelling his opinions— 'Evangelical and narrow,' or 'Latitudinarian and Pantheistic,' or 'Anglican and supercilious'—that man, in his solitude, is perhaps shedding hot tears because his sacrifice is a hard one, because strength and patience are failing him to speak the difficult word, and do the difficult deed.

GEORGE ELIOT

OCTOBER 4

Be strong, and of a good courage; be not afraid, neither be thou dismayed: for the Lord thy God is with thee whithersoever thou goest.

—Joshua 1:9

BY Thine unerring Spirit led,
    We shall not in the desert stray;
We shall not full direction need,
    Nor miss our providential way;
As far from danger as from fear,
While love, almighty love, is near.

CHARLES WESLEY

Watch your way then, as a cautious traveller, and don't be gazing at that mountain or river in the distance and saying, 'How shall I ever get over them?' Instead, keep to the present *little inch* that is before you, and accomplish *that* in the little moment that belongs to it. The mountain and the river can only be passed in the same way. When you come to them, you will come to the light and strength that belong to them.

M. A. KELTY

Let not future things disturb thee, for thou wilt come to them, if it shall be necessary, having with thee the same reason which thou now usest for present things.

MARCUS ANTONINUS

OCTOBER 5

Say to them that are of a fearful heart, Be strong, fear not.
—Isaiah 35:4

WHY shouldst thou fill to-day with sorrow
  About to-morrow,
    My heart?
One watches all with care most true,
Doubt not that He will give thee too
    Thy part.

PAUL FLEMMING

The crosses which we make for ourselves by a restless anxiety as to the future, are not crosses which come from God. We show want of faith in Him by our false wisdom, wishing to forestall His arrangements, and struggling to supplement His Providence by our own providence. The future is not yet ours; perhaps it never will be. If it comes, it may come wholly different from what we have foreseen. Let us shut our eyes, then, to that which God hides from us, and keeps in reserve in the treasures of His deep counsels. Let us worship without seeing; let us be silent; let us abide in peace.

FÉNELON

OCTOBER 6

I had fainted, unless I had believed to see the goodness of the Lord in the land of the living.
> —*Psalm 27:13*

I will surely do thee good.
> —*Genesis 32:12*

THOU know'st not what is good for thee,
  But God doth know,—
Let Him thy strong reliance be,
  And rest thee so.

C. F. GELLERT

Let us be very careful of thinking, on the one hand, that we have no work assigned us to do, or, on the other hand, that what we have assigned to us is not the right thing for us. If ever we can say in our hearts to God, in reference to any daily duty, 'This is not my place; I would choose something dearer; I am capable of something higher;' we are guilty not only of rebellion, but of blasphemy. It is equivalent to saying not only, 'My heart revolts against Thy commands,' but 'Thy commands are unwise; Thine Almighty guidance is unskilful; Thine omniscient eye has mistaken the capacities of Thy creature; Thine infinite love is indifferent to the welfare of thy child.'

ELIZABETH CHARLES

OCTOBER 7

And because ye are sons, God hath sent the Spirit of His Son into your hearts, crying, Abba, Father.
                                        —Galatians 4:6

O LORD, forgive my sin,
  And deign to put within
A calm, obedient heart, a patient mind;
  That I may murmur not,
  Though bitter seem my lot;
For hearts unthankful can no blessing find.

                          RUTILIUS, 1604

Resignation to the Divine Will signifies a cheerful approbation and thankful acceptance of everything that comes from God. It is not enough patiently to submit, but we must thankfully receive and fully approve of everything that, by the order of God's providence, happens to us. For there is no reason why we should be patient, but what is as good and as strong a reason why we should be thankful. Whenever, therefore, you find yourselves disposed to uneasiness or murmuring at any thing that is the effect of God's providence over you, you must look upon yourself as denying either the wisdom or goodness of God.

                    WM. LAW

OCTOBER 8

Ye shall not go out with haste, for the Lord will go before you; and the God of Israel will be your reward.
—Isaiah 52:12

He that believeth shall not make haste.
—Isaiah 28:16

HOLY Spirit, Peace divine!
Still this restless heart of mine;
Speak to calm this tossing sea,
Stayed in Thy tranquillity.

S. LONGFELLOW

In whatever you are called upon to do, endeavor to maintain a calm, collected, and prayerful state of mind. Self-recollection is of great importance. 'It is good for a man to quietly wait for the salvation of the Lord.' He who is in what may be called a spiritual hurry, or rather who runs without having evidence of being spiritually sent, makes haste to no purpose.

T. C. UPHAM

There is great fret and worry in always running after work; it is not good intellectually or spiritually.

ANNIE KEARY

Whenever we are outwardly excited we should cease to act. But whenever we have a message from the spirit within, we should execute it with calmness. A fine day may excite one to act, but it is much better that we act from the calm spirit in any day, be the outward what it may.

J. P. GREAVES

OCTOBER 9

As for me and my house, we will serve the Lord.
—Joshua 24:15

O HAPPY house! and happy servitude!
   Where all alike one Master own;
Where daily duty, in Thy strength pursued,
   Is never hard or toilsome known;
Where each one serves Thee, meek and lowly,
   Whatever Thine appointment be,
Till common tasks seem great and holy,
   When they are done as unto Thee.

C. J. P. SPITTA

At Dudson there was no rushing after anything, either worldly or intellectual. It was a home of constant activity, issuing from, and retiring to, a centre of deep repose. There was an earnest application of excellent sense of the daily duties of life, to the minutest courtesy and kindness, as well as to the real interests of others. Everything great and everything little seemed done in the same spirit, and with the same degree of fidelity, because it was the will of God; and that which could not be traced to His will was not undertaken at all. . . . Nothing at Dudson was esteemed too little to be cared for, and nothing too great to be undertaken at the command of God. For this they daily exercised their mental and bodily powers on the things around them, knowing that our Lord thoroughly furnishes each of His soldiers for his work, and places before each the task he has to do.

M. A. SCHIMMELPENNINCK

OCTOBER 10

Now the Lord of peace Himself give you peace always, by all means.

—*2 Thessalonians 3:16*

The Lord will give strength unto His people; the Lord will bless His people with peace.

—*Psalm 29:11*

IN the heart's depths a peace serene and holy
   Abides, and when pain seems to have its will,
Or we despair,—oh, may that peace rise slowly,
   Stronger than agony, and we be still.

S. JOHNSON

But if a man ought and is willing to lie still under God's hand, he must and ought also to lie still under all things, whether they come from God, himself, or the creatures, nothing excepted. And he who would be obedient, resigned, and submissive to God, must and ought to be also resigned, obedient, and submissive to all things, in a spirit of yielding, and not of resistance; and take them in silence, resting on the hidden foundations of his soul, and having a secret inward patience, that enableth him to take all chances or crosses willingly. Whatever befalleth, he ought neither to call for nor desire any redress, or deliverance, or resistance, or revenge, but always in a loving, sincere humility to cry, 'Father, forgive them, for they know not what they do!'

THEOLOGIA GERMANICA

OCTOBER 11

And when the people complained, it displeased the Lord.
—Numbers 11:1

———— ❧ ————

WHEN thou hast thanked thy God
   For every blessing sent,
What time will then remain
   For murmurs or lament?

R. C. TRENCH

———— ❧ ————

Let him, with a cheerful and thankful spirit, yield himself up to suffer whatever God shall appoint unto him, and to fulfill, according to his power, by the grace of God, all His holy will to the utmost that he can discern it. Let him never complain of his distresses but to God alone with entire and humble resignation, praying that he may be strong to endure all his sufferings according to the will of God.

JOHN TAULER

He who complains, or thinks he has a right to complain because he is called in God's Providence to suffer, has something within him which needs to be taken away. A soul whose will is lost in God's will can never do this. Sorrow may exist, but complaint never.

CATHERINE ADORNA

OCTOBER 12

Singing and making melody in your heart to the Lord.
—Ephesians 5:19

Sanctify the Lord God in your hearts.
—1 Peter 3:15

THERE are in this loud stunning tide
   Of human care and crime,
With whom the melodies abide
   Of th' everlasting chime;
Who carry music in their heart
   Through dusky lane and wrangling mart,
Plying their daily task with busier feet,
Because their secret souls a holy strain repeat.

J. KEBLE

   Strive to carry thyself with a total resignation to the Divine will, that God may do with thee and all thine according to His heavenly pleasure, relying on Him as on a kind and loving Father. Never recall that intention, and though thou beest taken up about the affairs of the condition wherein God hath placed thee, yet thou wilt still be in prayer, in the presence of God, and in perpetual acts of resignation. 'A just man leaves not off to pray unless he leaves off to be just.' He always prays who always does well. The good desire is prayer, and if the desire be continued, so also is the prayer.

M. MOLINOS

OCTOBER 13

*We desire that every one of you do show the same diligence
to the full assurance of hope unto the end.*
                    —Hebrews 6:2

*The Lord is faithful, who shall stablish you, and keep you
from evil.*
                    —2 Thessalonians 3:3

LONG though my task may be,
   Cometh the end.
God 'tis that helpeth me,
His is the work, and He
   New strength will lend.

ANONYMOUS

Set yourself steadfastly to those duties which have the least
attractive exterior. It matters not whether God's holy will be fulfilled in great or small matters. Be patient with yourself and your
own failings. Never be in a hurry, and do not yield to longings
after that which is impossible to you. My dear sister, go on
steadily and quietly—if our dear Lord means you to run, He will
'strengthen your heart.'

FRANCIS DE SALES

Always begin by doing that which costs me most, unless the
easier duty is a pressing one. Examine, classify, and determine at
night the work of the morrow; arrange things in the order of
their importance, and act accordingly. Dread, above all things,
bitterness and irritation. Never say, or indirectly recall anything
to my advantage.

MADAME SWETCHINE

OCTOBER 14

He that sinneth against Me wrongeth his own soul: all they that hate Me love death.

—Proverbs 8:36

But now being made free from sin, and become servants to God, ye have your fruit unto holiness, and the end everlasting life. For the wages of sin is death; but the gift of God is eternal life through Jesus Christ our Lord.

—Romans 6:22, 23

O SOVEREIGN Love, to Thee I cry!
Give me Thyself, or else I die!
Save me from death; from hell set free!
Death, hell, are but the want of Thee.
Quickened by Thy imparted flame,
Saved when possessed of Thee I am:
My life, my only heaven Thou art;
O might I feel Thee in my heart!

C. WESLEY

Sin itself is hell, and death, and misery to the soul, as being a departure from goodness and holiness itself; I mean from God, in conjunction with whom the happiness, and blessedness, and heaven of a soul doth consist. Avoid it, therefore, as you would avoid being miserable.

SAMUEL SHAW

'I couldn't live in peace if I put the shadow of a wilful sin between myself and God.'

GEORGE ELIOT

Unholy tempers are always unhappy tempers.

JOHN WESLEY

OCTOBER 15

Mine iniquities have taken hold upon me, so that I am not able to look up; therefore my heart faileth me. Be pleased, O Lord, to deliver me; O Lord, make haste to help me.
—Psalm 40:12, 13

Sin shall not have dominion over you.
—Romans 6:14

O THOU, to whose all-searching sight
The darkness shineth as the light!
Search, prove my heart; it pants for Thee:
Oh, burst these bonds, and set it free!
G. TERSTEEGEN

Yes, this sin which has sent me weary-hearted to bed and desperate in heart to morning work, that has made my plans miscarry until I am a coward, that cuts me off from prayer, that robs the sky of blueness and the earth of spring-time, and the air of freshness, and human faces of friendliness,—this blasting sin which perhaps has made my bed in hell for me so long,—*this can be conquered*. I do not say annihilated, but, better than that, *conquered*, captured and transfigured into a *friend:* so that I at last shall say, 'My temptation has become my strength! for to the very fight with it I owe my force.'

W. C. GANNETT

Henceforth my soul should fight with the prestige of victory, with the courage that comes of having striven and won, trusted and not been confounded.

JULIANA H. EWING

OCTOBER 16

I am not worthy of the least of all the mercies, and of all the truth, which Thou hast showed unto Thy servant.
—*Genesis 32:10*

SOME murmur if their sky is clear,
   And wholly bright to view,
If one small speck of dark appear
   In their great heaven of blue:
And some with thankful love are filled,
   If but one streak of light,
One ray of God's good mercy, gild
   The darkness of their night.

R. C. TRENCH

Habitual sufferers are precisely those who least frequently doubt the Divine benevolence, and whose faith and love rise to the serenest cheerfulness. Possessed by no idea of a prescriptive right to be happy, their blessings are not benumbed by anticipation, but come to them fresh and brilliant as the first day's morning and evening light to the dwellers in Paradise. With the happy it is their constant peace that seems to come by nature, and to be blunted by its commonness,—and their griefs to come from God, sharpened by their sacred origin. With the sufferer, it is his pain that appears to be a thing of course, and to require no explanation, while his relief is reverently welcomed as a divine interposition, and, as a breath of Heaven, caresses the heart into melodies of praise.

J. MARTINEAU

OCTOBER 17

Hath the Lord as great delight in burnt-offerings and sacrifices, as in obeying the voice of the Lord? Behold, to obey is better than sacrifice.
—1 Samuel 15:22

Fear ye not, stand still, and see the salvation of the Lord, which He will show to you to-day.
—Exodus 14:13

THE folded hands seem idle:
   If folded at His word,
'Tis a holy service, trust me,
   In obedience to the Lord.

ANNA SHIPTON

It is not the multitude of hard duties, it is not constraint and contention that advance us in our Christian course. On the contrary, it is the yielding of our wills without restriction and without choice, to tread cheerfully every day in the path in which Providence leads us, to seek nothing, to be discouraged by nothing, to see our duty in the present moment, to trust all else without reserve to the will and power of God.

FÉNELON

Godliness is the devotion of the soul to God, as to a living person whose will is to be its law, whose love is to be its life. It is the habit of living before the face of God, and not simply doing certain things.

J. B. BROWN

OCTOBER 18

Except your righteousness shall exceed the righteousness of the scribes and Pharisees, ye shall in no case enter into the kingdom of heaven.

—Matthew 5:20

THE freedom from all wilful sin,
  The Christian's daily task,—
Oh these are graces far below
  What longing love would ask!
Dole not thy duties out to God.

F. W. FABER

You perhaps will say that all people fall short of the perfection of the Gospel, and therefore you are content with your failings. The question is not whether Gospel perfection can be fully attained, but whether you come as near it as a sincere intention and careful diligence can carry you; whether you are not in a much lower state than you might be if you sincerely intended and carefully laboured to advance yourself in all Christian virtues.

WM. LAW

OCTOBER 19

Thus saith the Lord, thy Redeemer, the Holy One of Israel; I am the Lord thy God who teacheth thee to profit, who leadeth thee by the way thou shouldest go.
—Isaiah 48:17

I SEEK Thy aid, I ask direction,
    Teach me to do what pleaseth Thee;
I can bear toil, endure affliction,
    Only Thy leadings let me see.

ANONYMOUS

Of all paths a man could strike into, there *is,* at any given moment, a *best path* for every man; a thing which, here and now, it were of all things *wisest* for him to do. Could he but be led or driven to do it, he were then doing 'like a man,' as we phrase it. His success, in such case, were complete, his felicity a maximum. To find this path, and walk in it, is the one thing needful for him.

T. CARLYLE

Every man has his own vocation. There is one direction in which all space is open to him. He has faculties silently inviting him thither to endless exertion. He is like a ship in a river: he runs against obstructions on every side but one; on that side all obstruction is taken away, and he sweeps serenely over a deepening channel into an infinite sea.

R. W. EMERSON

OCTOBER 20

Be not overcome of evil, but overcome evil with good.
—Romans 12:21

COME, in this accepted hour;
   Bring Thy heavenly kingdom in;
Fill us with Thy glorious power,
   Rooting out the seeds of sin.

               C. WESLEY

If we wish to overcome evil we must overcome it by good. There are doubtless many ways of overcoming the evil in our own hearts, but the simplest, easiest, most universal, is to overcome it by active occupation in some good word or work. The best antidote against evil of all kinds, against the evil thoughts which haunt the soul, against the needless perplexities which distract the conscience, is to keep hold of the good we have. Impure thoughts will not stand against pure words, prayers, and deeds. Little doubts will not avail against great certainties. Fix your affections on things above, and then you will be less and less troubled by the cares, the temptations, and the troubles of things on earth.

               A. P. STANLEY

OCTOBER 21

I am the Almighty God; walk before me, and be thou perfect.

—Genesis 17:1

Consecrate yourselves to-day to the Lord.

—Exodus 32:29

❧

TAKE my life, and let it be
Consecrated, Lord, to Thee.

Take my moments and my days;
Let them flow in ceaseless praise.

F. R. HAVERGAL

❧

I have noticed that wherever there has been a faithful following of the Lord in a consecrated soul, several things have inevitably followed, sooner or later. Meekness and quietness of spirit become in time the characteristics of the daily life. A submissive acceptance of the will of God as it comes in the hourly events of each day; pliability in the hands of God to do or to suffer all the good pleasure of His will; sweetness under provocation; calmness in the midst of turmoil and bustle; yieldingness to the wishes of others, and an insensibility to slights and affronts; absence of worry or anxiety; deliverance from care and fear;—all these, and many similar graces, are invariably found to be the natural outward development of that inward life which is hid with Christ in God.

H. W. S.

OCTOBER 22

Father, if Thou be willing, remove this cup from me; never-
theless, not my will, but Thine, be done.
                              —Luke 22:42

JUST as Thou wilt is just what I would will;
Give me but this, the heart to be content,
And, if my wish is thwarted, to lie still,
Waiting till puzzle and till pain are spent,
And the sweet thing made plain which the Lord meant.
                              SUSAN COOLIDGE

Let your will be one with His will, and be glad to de disposed
of by Him. He will order all things for you. What can cross your
will, when it is one with His will, on which all creation hangs,
round which all things revolve? Keep your hearts clear of evil
thoughts; for as evil choices estrange the will from His will, so
evil thoughts cloud the soul and hide Him from us. Whatever
sets us in opposition to Him makes our will an intolerable torment. So long as we will one thing and He another, we go on
piercing ourselves through and through with a perpetual
wound. ...

H. E. MANNING

OCTOBER 23

Teach me to do Thy will; for Thou art my God: Thy spirit is good; lead me into the land of uprightness.
—Psalm 143:10

THE battle of our life is won,
    And heaven begun,
When we can say, 'Thy will be done!'
    But, Lord, until
These restless hearts in Thy deep love are still,
We pray Thee, 'Teach us how to do Thy will!'
                LUCY LARCOM

You are seeking your own will, my daughter. You are seeking some good other than the law you are bound to obey. But how will you find good? It is not a thing of choice; it is a river that flows from the foot of the Invisible Throne, and flows by the path of obedience. I say again, man cannot choose his duties. You may choose to forsake your duties, and choose not to have the sorrow they bring. But you will go forth, and what will you find, my daughter? Sorrow without duty—bitter herbs, and no bread with them.

GEORGE ELIOT

However dark and profitless, however painful and weary existence may have become; however any man, like Elijah, may be tempted to cast himself down beneath the juniper-tree and say, 'It is enough, O Lord!'—life is not done, and our Christian character is not won, so long as God has anything left for us to suffer, or anything left for us to do.

F. W. ROBERTSON

OCTOBER 24

The Lord is my strength, and my shield; my heart trusted in Him, and I am helped: therefore my heart greatly rejoiceth; and with my song will I praise Him.
—Psalm 28:7

WELL may Thy happy children cease
　　From restless wishes, prone to sin,
And, in Thy own exceeding peace,
　　Yield to Thy daily discipline.

A. L. WARING

Talk of hair-cloth shirts, and scourgings, and sleeping on ashes as means of saintship! There is no need of them in our country. Let a woman look at her domestic trials as her hair-cloth, her ashes, her scourges,—accept them,—rejoice in them,—smile and be quiet, silent, patient, and loving under them,—the convent can teach her no more than that; she is a victorious saint.

H. B. STOWE

Perhaps it is a greater energy of Divine Providence which keeps the Christian from day to day, from year to year—praying, hoping, running, believing—against all hindrances—which maintains him as a *living* martyr, than that which bears him up for an hour in sacrificing himself at the stake.

R. CECIL

OCTOBER 25

For I am persuaded that neither death, nor life, nor angels, nor principalities, nor powers, nor things present, nor things to come, nor height, nor depth, nor any other creature, shall be able to separate us from the love of God, which is in Christ Jesus our Lord.

—Romans 8:38, 39

I KNOW not what the future hath
   Of marvel or surprise,
Assured alone that life and death
   His mercy underlies.

J. G. WHITTIER

Be of good faith, my dear Friends. Look not out at any thing; fear none of those things ye may be exposed to suffer, either outwardly or inwardly. But trust the Lord over all, and your life will spring, and grow, and refresh you, and ye will learn obedience and faithfulness daily more and more, even by your exercises and sufferings. Yea, the Lord will teach you the very mystery of faith and obedience: the wisdom, power, love, and goodness of the Lord ordering *every* thing for you, and ordering *your* hearts in every thing.

J. PENINGTON

OCTOBER 26

Turn you to the stronghold, ye prisoners of hope.
—Zechariah 9:12

Their strength is to sit still.
—Isaiah 30:7

❧

O POWER to do; O baffled will!
  O prayer and action! ye are one.
Who may not strive, may yet fulfil
The harder task of standing still,
  And good but wished with God is done.

J. G. WHITTIER

❧

That God has circumscribed our life may add a peculiar element of trial, but often it defines our way and cuts off many tempting possibilities that perplex the free and the strong. It leaves intact the whole body of spiritual reality, with the Beatitude thereon, 'that if we know these things, happy are we if we do them.' We know that God orders the lot; and to meet it with the energies it requires and permits, neither more nor less,—to fill it at every available point with the light and action of an earnest and spiritually inventive mind, though its scene be no wider than a sick chamber, and its action narrowed to patient suffering, and gentle, cheerful words, and all the light it can emit the thankful quiet of a trustful eye. Without chafing, as though God had misjudged our sphere and placed us wrong and did not know where we could best serve Him,—this is what, in that condition, we *have to do.*

J. H. THOM

OCTOBER 27

Therefore I take pleasure in infirmities, in reproaches, in necessities, in persecutions, in distresses for Christ's sake: for when I am weak, then am I strong.

—*2 Corinthians 12:10*

WHATE'ER God does is well!
In patience let us wait;
He doth Himself our burdens bear,
   He doth for us take care,
And He, our God, knows all our weary days.
   Come, give Him praise.

                 B. SCHMOLCKE

Nothing else but this of seeing God in everything will make us loving and patient with those who annoy and trouble us. They will then be to us only the instruments for accomplishing His tender and wise purposes towards us, and we shall even find ourselves at last inwardly thanking them for the blessings they bring us. Nothing else will completely put an end to all murmuring or rebelling thoughts.

                 H. W. S.

The subjection of the will is accomplished by calmly resigning thyself up in everything that internally or externally vexes thee. It is thus only that the soul is prepared for the reception of divine influences. Prepare the heart like clean paper, and God will imprint on it characters to His own liking.

                 M. MOLINOS

OCTOBER 28

I know the thoughts that I think toward you, saith the Lord,
thoughts of peace, and not of evil, to give you an expected end.
—Jeremiah 29:11

THY thoughts are good, and Thou art kind,
    E'en when we think it not;
How many an anxious, faithless mind
    Sits grieving o'er its lot,
And frets, and pines by day and night,
As though God had lost it out of sight,
    And all its wants forgot.

P. GERHARDT

You are never to complain of your birth, your training, your
employments, your hardships; never to fancy that you could be
something if only you had a different lot and sphere assigned
you. God understands His own plan, and He knows what you
need a great deal better than you do. The very things that you
most deprecate, as fatal limitations or obstructions, are probably
what you most need. What you call hindrances, obstacles, or
discouragements, are probably God's opportunities. Bring
down your soul, or, rather, bring it up to receive God's will
and do His work, in your lot, in your sphere, under your cloud
of obscurity, against your temptations—and then you shall find
that your condition is never opposed to your good, but really
consistent with it.

H. BUSHNELL

OCTOBER 29

Behold, I have refined thee, but not with silver; I have chosen thee in the furnace of affliction.
—Isaiah 48:10

BE patient, suffering soul! I hear thy cry.
The trial fires may glow, but I am nigh.
  I see the silver, and I will refine
  Until My image shall upon it shine.
Fear not, for I am near, thy help to be;
Greater than all thy pain, My love for Thee.

              H. W. C.

God takes a thousand times more pains with us than the artist with his picture, by many touches of sorrow and many colours of circumstance, to bring man into the form which is the highest and noblest in His sight—if only we received His gifts and myrrh in the right spirit. . . . But when the cup is put away, and these feelings are stifled or unheeded, a greater injury is done to the soul than can ever be amended. No heart can conceive in what surpassing love God giveth us this myrrh; yet this which we ought to receive to our soul's good, we suffer to pass by us in our sleepy indifference, and nothing comes of it. Then we come and complain: 'Alas, Lord! I am so dry, and it is so dark within me!' I tell thee, dear child, open thy heart to the pain, and it will do thee more good than if thou wert full of feeling and devoutness.

              J. TAULER

OCTOBER 30

That good thing which was committed unto thee, keep by the Holy Ghost which dwelleth in us.
—2 Timothy 1:14

OH that the Comforter would come!
   Nor visit as a transient guest,
But fix in me His constant home,
   And keep possession of my breast;
And make my soul His loved abode,
The temple of indwelling God!

C. WESLEY

Thy spirit should become, while yet on earth, the peaceful throne of the King of Heaven. Think, then, how quiet, how gentle and pure, how reverent, thou shouldst be.

GERHARD TERSTEEGEN

I cannot tell you how much I love you. But that which of all things I have most at heart, with regard to you, is the real progress of your soul in the divine life. Heaven seems to be awakened in you. It is a tender plant. It requires stillness, meekness, and the unity of the heart, totally given up to the unknown workings of the Spirit of God, which will do all its work in the calm soul, that has no hunger or desire but to escape out of the mire of its earthly life into its lost union and life in God. I mention this out of a fear of your giving in to an eagerness about many things, which, though seemingly innocent, yet divide and weaken the workings of the divine life within you.

WM. LAW

OCTOBER 31

And Enoch walked with God; and he was not; for God took him.

—Genesis 5:24

OH for a closer walk with God,
    A calm and heavenly frame;
A light to shine upon the road
    That leads me to the Lamb!

W. COWPER

Is it possible for any of us in these modern days to so live that we may walk with God? Can we walk with God in the shop, in the office, in the household, and on the street? When men exasperate us, and work wearies us, and the children fret, and the servants annoy, and our best-laid plans fall to pieces, and our castles in the air are dissipated like bubbles that break at a breath, then can we walk with God? That religion which fails us in the everyday trials and experiences of life has somewhere in it a flaw. It should be more than a plank to sustain us in the rushing tide, and land us exhausted and dripping on the other side. It ought, if it comes from above, to be always, day by day, to our souls as the wings of a bird, bearing us away from and beyond the impediments which seek to hold us down. If the Divine Love be a conscious presence, an indwelling force with us, it will do this.

CHRISTIAN UNION

NOVEMBER 1

Of whom the whole family in heaven and earth is named.
—Ephesians 3:15

———————— ❧ ————————

ONE family, we dwell in Him;
    One church above, beneath;
Though now divided by the stream,—
    The narrow stream of death.

One army of the living God,
    To His command we bow:
Part of His host has crossed the flood.
    And part is crossing now.

                C. WESLEY

———————— ❧ ————————

It is right that we should have an aim of our own, determined
by our individuality and our surroundings. But this may readily
degenerate into exclusive narrowness, unless it has for a background the great thought that there is a Kingdom of God within
us, around us, and above us. Toward the forwarding of this
silent, ever-advancing Kingdom, our little work, whatever it be,
if good and true, may contribute something. This thought lends
to any calling, however lowly, a consecration. But even if our
aim should be frustrated and our work come to naught, yet the
failure of our most cherished plans may be more than compensated. In the thought that we are members of this Kingdom—
already begun here and now, yet reaching forward through all
time—we shall have a reserve of consolation which is better
than any [that is provided by temporal] success.

                JOHN CAMPBELL SHAIRP

NOVEMBER 2

0Wherefore seeing we also are compassed about with so great a cloud of witnesses, let us lay aside every weight, and the sin which doth so easily beset us, and let us run with patience the race that is set before us.
                    —Hebrews 12:1

❦

WHEN the powers of hell prevail
    O'er our weakness and unfitness,
Could we lift the fleshly veil,
    Could we for a moment witness
Those unnumbered hosts that stand
    Calm and bright on either hand;

Oh, what joyful hope would cheer,
    Oh, what faith serene would guide us!
Great may be the danger near,
    Greater are the friends beside us.
                    ANONYMOUS

❦

We are compassed about by a cloud of witnesses, whose hearts throb in sympathy with every effort and struggle, and who thrill with joy at every success. How should this thought check and rebuke every worldly feeling and unworthy purpose, and enshrine us, in the midst of a forgetful and unspiritual world, with an atmosphere of heavenly peace! They have overcome—have risen—are crowned, glorified; but...in every hour of darkness their voice speaks to us: 'So we grieved, so we struggled, so we fainted, so we doubted; but we have overcome, we have obtained, we have seen, we have found,—and in our victory behold the certainty of thy own.'

H. B. STOWE

NOVEMBER 3

Wherefore putting away lying, speak every man truth with
his neighbour: for we are members one of another.
                                   —*Ephesians 4:25*

IN conversation be sincere;
Keep conscience as the noontide clear;
Think how All-seeing God thy ways
And all thy secret thoughts surveys.
                     THOMAS KEN

The essence of lying is in deception, not in words. A lie may
be told by silence, by equivocation, by the accent on a syllable,
by a glance of the eye attaching a peculiar significance to a sentence. All these kinds of lies are worse and baser by many
degrees than a lie plainly worded. No form of blinded conscience is so far sunk as that which comforts itself for having
deceived because the deception was by gesture or silence,
instead of utterance.

                     J. RUSKIN

He that is habituated to deceptions and artificialities in trifles,
will try in vain to be true in matters of importance. Truth is a
thing of habit rather than of will. You cannot in any given case,
by any sudden and single effort, will to be true if the habit of
your life has been insincerity.

                     F. W. ROBERTSON

NOVEMBER 4

A soft answer turneth away wrath: but grievous words stir up anger.

—Proverbs 15:1

Doest thou well to be angry?

—Jonah 4:4

RENEW Thine image, Lord, in me,
Lowly and gentle may I be;
   No charms but these to Thee are dear;
No anger mayest Thou ever find,
No pride in my unruffled mind,
   But faith, and heaven-born peace be there.

P. GERHARDT

Neither say nor do aught displeasing to thy neighbour. If thou hast been wanting in charity, seek his forgiveness, or speak to him with gentleness. Speak always with mildness and in a low tone of voice.

L. SCUPOLI

Injuries hurt not more in the receiving than in the remembrance. A small injury shall go as it comes; a great injury may dine or sup with me; but none at all shall lodge with me. Why should I vex myself because another hath vexed me? Grief for things past that cannot be remedied, and care for things to come that cannot be prevented, may easily hurt, but can never benefit me. I will therefore commit myself to God in both, and enjoy the present.

JOSEPH HALL

NOVEMBER 5

The temple of God is holy, which temple ye are.
—1 Corinthians 3:17

NOW shed Thy mighty influence abroad
On souls that would their Father's image bear;
Make us as holy temples of our God,
Where dwells forever calm, adoring prayer.

C. J. P. SPITTA

This pearl of eternity is the church or temple of God within thee, the consecrated place of divine worship, where alone thou canst worship God in Spirit and in truth. When once thou art well grounded in this inward worship, thou wilt have learned to live unto God above time and place. For every day will be Sunday to thee, and wherever thou goest, thou wilt have ... a church, and an altar along with thee. For when God has all that He should have of thy heart, when thou art wholly given up to the obedience of the light and spirit of God within thee, to will only in His will, to love only in His love, to be wise only in His wisdom, then it is that everything thou dost is as a song of praise, and the common business of thy life is a conforming to God's will on earth as angels do in heaven.

WM. LAW

NOVEMBER 6

He will fulfil the desire of them that fear Him: He also will hear their cry, and will save them.
—*Psalm 145:19*

Delight thyself also in the Lord; and He shall give thee the desires of thine heart.
—*Psalm 37:4*

THOUGH to-day may not fulfil
All thy hopes, have patience still;
For perchance to-morrow's sun
Sees thy happier days begun.

P. GERHARDT

His great desire and delight is God; and by desiring and delighting, he hath Him. *Delight thou in the Lord, and He shall give thee thy heart's desire,*—HIMSELF; and then surely thou shall have all. Any other thing *commit it to Him,* and He shall bring it to pass.

R. LEIGHTON

All who call on God in true faith, earnestly from the heart, will certainly be heard, and will receive what they have asked and desired, although not in the hour or in the measure, or the very thing which they ask. They will obtain something greater and more glorious than they had dared to ask.

MARTIN LUTHER

NOVEMBER 7

I was not disobedient unto the heavenly vision.
—Acts 26:19

The Lord our God will we serve, and His voice will we obey.
—Joshua 24:24

I WILL shun no toil or woe,
Where Thou leadest I will go,
   Be my pathway plain or rough;
If but every hour may be
Spent in work that pleases Thee,
   Ah, dear Lord, it is enough!

                 G. TERSTEEGEN

All these longings and doubts, and this inward distress, are the voice of the Good Shepherd in your heart, seeking to call you out of all that is contrary to His will. Oh, let me entreat you not to turn away from His gentle pleadings.

                 H. W. S.

The fear of man brings a snare. By halting in our duty and turning back in the time of trial, our hands grow weaker, our ears grow dull as to hearing the language of the true Shepherd. Then when we look at the way of the righteous, it seems as though it was not for us to follow them.

               J. WOOLMAN

NOVEMBER 8

Lo, I come to do Thy will, O God.
                        —Hebrews 10:9

Teach me to do Thy will, for Thou art my God.
                        —Psalm 143:10

———————————— ∽⌘∾ ————————————

LO! I come with joy to do
   The Father's blessed will;
Him in outward works pursue,
   And serve His pleasure still.
Faithful to my Lord's commands,
   I still would choose the better part;
Serve with careful Martha's hands,
   And loving Mary's heart.

                        C. WESLEY

———————————— ∽⌘∾ ————————————

A soul cannot be regarded as truly subdued and consecrated in its will, and as having passed into union with the Divine will, until it has a disposition to do promptly and faithfully all that God requires, as well as to endure patiently and thankfully all that He imposes.

                        T. C. UPHAM

When we have learned to offer up every duty connected with our situation in life as a sacrifice to God, a settled employment becomes just a settled habit of prayer.

                        THOMAS ERSKINE

'Do *the duty which lies nearest thee,*' which thou knowest to be a duty. The second duty will already have become clearer.

                        T. CARLYLE

NOVEMBER 9

And she called the name of the Lord that spake unto her,
Thou God seest me: for she said, Have I also here looked after
Him that seeth me?

—Genesis 16:13

AMONG so many, can He care?
Can special love be everywhere?
A myriad homes,—a myriad ways,—
And God's eye over every place?

I asked: my soul bethought of this;—
In just that very place of His
Where He hath put and keepeth you,
God hath no other thing to do!

A. D. T. WHITNEY

Give free and bold play to those instincts of the heart which
believe that the Creator must care for the creatures He has
made, and that the only real effective care for them must be
that which takes each of them into His love, and knowing it
separately surrounds it with His separate sympathy. There is
not one life which the Life-giver ever loses out of His sight; not
one which sins so that He casts it away; not one which is not so
near to Him that whatever touches it touches Him with sorrow
or with joy.

PHILLIPS BROOKS

NOVEMBER 10

In Him we live, and move, and have our being.
—Acts 17:28

Whither shall I go from Thy spirit? or whither shall I flee from Thy presence?

—Psalm 139:7

YEA! In Thy life our little lives are ended,
　　Into Thy depths our trembling spirits fall;
In Thee enfolded, gathered, comprehended,
　　As holds the sea her waves—Thou hold'st us all.
　　　　　　　E. SCUDDER

Where then is *our* God? You say, He is *everywhere:* then show me *anywhere* that you have met Him. You declare Him *everlasting:* then tell me *any moment* that He has been with you. You believe Him ready to soccour them that are tempted, and to lift those that are bowed down: then in what passionate hour did you subside into His calm grace? In what sorrow lose yourself in His 'more exceeding' joy? These are the testing questions by which we may learn whether we too have raised our altar to an 'unknown God' and pay the worship of the blind; or whether we commune with Him 'in whom we live, and move, and have our being.'

J. MARTINEAU

NOVEMBER 11

Walk worthy of the Lord unto all pleasing, being fruitful in every good work, and increasing in the knowledge of God; strengthened with all might, according to His glorious power, unto all patience and long-suffering with joyfulness.
                                        —Colossians 1:10, 11

TO be the thing we seem,
To do the thing we deem
   Enjoined by duty;
To walk in faith, nor dream
Of questioning God's scheme
   Of truth and beauty.

                     ANONYMOUS

To shape the whole Future is not our problem; but only to shape faithfully a small part of it, according to rules already known. It is perhaps possible for each of us, who will with due earnestness inquire, to ascertain clearly what he, for his own part, ought to do; this let him do, with true heart, and continue doing. The general issue will, as it has always done, rest well with a Higher Intelligence than ours. ...This day thou knowest ten commanded duties, seest in thy mind ten things which should be done for every one that thou doest! *Do* one of them. This of itself will show thee ten others which can and shall be done.

               T. CARLYLE

NOVEMBER 12

I must work the works of Him that sent me, while it is day;
the night cometh, when no man can work.
                                        —John 9:4

Wherefore have ye not fulfilled your task?
                                        —Exodus 5:14

HE who intermits
The appointed task and duties of the day
Untunes full oft the pleasures of the day;
Checking the finer spirits that refuse
To flow, when purposes are lightly changed.
                        W. WORDSWORTH

By putting off things beyond their proper times, one duty
treads upon the heels of another, and all duties are felt as irksome
obligations,—a yoke beneath which we fret and lose our peace. In
most cases the consequence of this is that we have no time to do
the work as it ought to be done. It is therefore done precipitously,
with a greater desire simply to get it done than to do it well, and
with very little thought of God throughout.

                        F. W. FABER

Sufficient for each day is the *good* thereof, equally as the evil.
We must do at once, and with our might, the merciful deed that
our hand findeth to do,—otherwise it will never be done, for the
hand will find other tasks. And every unconsummated good feeling, every unfulfilled purpose that His Spirit has prompted, shall
one day charge us as faithless and recreant before God.

                        J. H. THOM

NOVEMBER 13

*Blessed is the man whom Thou chastenest, O Lord, and
teachest him out of Thy law.*
>   *—Psalm 94:12*

Truly this is a grief, and I must bear it.
>   *—Jeremiah 10:19*

HOLD in thy murmurs, heaven arraigning!
> The patient see God's loving face;
Who bear their burdens uncomplaining,
> 'Tis they that win the Father's grace.
>   ANONYMOUS

Do not run to this and that for comfort when you are in trouble, but bear it. Be uncomfortably quiet—be uneasily silent—be patiently unhappy.

> J. P. GREAVES

Hard words *will* vex; unkindness *will* pierce; neglect *will* wound; threatened evils *will* make the soul quiver; a sharp pain or weariness *will* rack the body, or make it restless. But what says the Psalmist? 'When my heart is vexed, I will complain.' To whom? Not *of* God, but *to* God.

> E. B. PUSEY

NOVEMBER 14

Thou art my servant; I have formed thee; thou art my servant; O Israel, thou shalt not be forgotten of me.
—Isaiah 44:21

OH, give Thy servant patience to be still,
    And bear Thy will;
Courage to venture wholly on the arm
    That will not harm;
The wisdom that will never let me stray
    Out of my way;
The love, that, now afflicting, knoweth best
    When I should rest.

J. M. NEALE

Accept His will entirely, and never suppose that you can serve Him better in any other way. You can never serve Him well, save in the way He chooses. Supposing that you were never to be set free from such trials, what would you do? You would say to God, 'I am Thine—if my trials are acceptable to Thee, give me more and more.' I have full confidence that this is what you would say, and then you would not think more of it—at any rate, you would not be anxious. Well, do the same now. Make friends with your trials as though you were always to live together. You will see that when you cease to take thought of your own deliverance, God will take thought for you. When you cease to help yourself eagerly, He will help you.

FRANCIS DE SALES

Ah, if you knew what peace there is in accepted sorrow!

MADAME GUYON

NOVEMBER 15

Fear thou not; for I am with thee: be not dismayed; for I am thy God: I will strengthen thee; yea, I will help thee; yea, I will uphold thee with the right hand of my righteousness.
—Isaiah 41:10

LORD, be Thou near and cheer my lonely way;
   With Thy sweet peace my aching bosom fill;
Scatter my cares and fears; my griefs allay,
   And be it mine each day
   To love and please Thee still.

                  P. CORNEILLE

What if the wicked nature, which is as a sea casting out mire and dirt, rage against thee? There is a river, a sweet, still, flowing river, the streams whereof will make glad thy heart. Learn in quietness and stillness to retire to the Lord, and wait upon Him. In Him thou shalt feel peace and joy, in the midst of thy trouble from the cruel and vexatious spirit of this world. So wait to know thy work and service to the Lord every day, in thy place and station. The Lord make thee faithful therein, and thou wilt lack neither help, support, nor comfort.

            I. PENINGTON

NOVEMBER 16

Thou wilt keep him in perfect peace, whose mind is stayed on Thee; because he trusteth in Thee.
                    —Isaiah 26:3

WHAT comforts, Lord, to those are given,
    Who seek in Thee their home and rest!
They find on earth an opening heaven,
    And in Thy peace are amply blest.
                    W. C. DESSLER

God is a tranquil Being, and abides in a tranquil eternity. So must thy spirit become a tranquil and clear little pool, wherein the serene light of God can be mirrored. Therefore shun all that is disquieting and distracting, both within and without. Nothing in the whole world is worth the loss of thy peace; even the faults which thou hast committed should only humble, but not disquiet thee. God is full of joy, peace, and happiness. Endeavour then to obtain a continually joyful and peaceful spirit. Avoid all anxious care, vexation, murmuring, and melancholy, which darken the soul and render thee unfit for the friendship of God. If thou dost perceive such feelings arising, turn gently away from them.

                    G. TERSTEEGEN

NOVEMBER 17

Every day will I bless Thee, and I will praise Thy name for ever and ever.

　　　　　　　　—*Psalm 145:2*

Commit thy works unto the Lord, and thy thoughts shall be established.

　　　　　　　　—*Proverbs 16:3*

LORD, I my vows to Thee renew;
Disperse my sins as morning dew;
Guard my first springs of thought and will,
And with Thyself my spirit fill.

　　　　　　　　THOMAS KEN

Morning by morning think, for a few moments, of the chief employments of the day, any one thing of greater moment than others, thine own especial trial, any occasions of it which are likely to come that day, and by one short strong act commend thyself beforehand in all to God. Offer all thy thoughts, words, and deeds to Him—to be governed, guided, accepted by Him. …Choose some great occasions of the day, such as bring with them most trial to thee, on which, above others, to commend thyself to God.

　　　　　　　　E. B. PUSEY

Will you not, before venturing away from your early quiet hour, 'Commit thy works' to Him definitely, the special things you have to do to-day, and the unforeseen work which He may add in the course of it?

　　　　　　　　F. R. HAVERGAL

NOVEMBER 18

Hereby know we that we dwell in Him, and He in us,
because He hath given us of His Spirit.
—1 John 4:13

WITHIN! within, oh turn
    Thy spirit's eyes, and learn
Thy wandering senses gently to control;
Thy dearest Friend dwells deep within thy soul,
    And asks thyself of thee,
That heart, and mind, and sense, He may make whole
    In perfect harmony.

G. TERSTEEGEN

Wait patiently, trust humbly, depend only upon, seek solely the God of Light and Love, of Mercy and Goodness, of Glory and Majesty, who dwells in the inmost depth and spirit of your soul. There you have all the secret, hidden, invisible Upholder of all the creation, whose blessed operation will always be found by a humble, faithful, loving, calm, patient introversion of your heart to Him. He has His hidden heaven within you, and it will open itself to you as soon as your heart is left wholly to His eternal, ever-speaking word, and ever-sanctifying spirit within you. Beware of all eagerness and activity of your own natural spirit and temper. Run not in any hasty ways of your own. Be patient under the sense of your own vanity and weakness. And patiently wait for God to do His own work, in His own way.

WM. LAW

NOVEMBER 19

If any man among you seem to be religious, and bridleth not his tongue, but deceiveth his own heart, this man's religion is vain.

—James 1:26

I said, I will take heed to my ways, that I sin not with my tongue.

—Psalm 39:1

NO sinful word, nor deed of wrong,
    Nor thoughts that idly rove;
But simple truth be on our tongue,
    And in our hearts be love.

ST. AMBROSE

Let us all resolve,—First, to attain the grace of SILENCE. Second, to deem all FAULT-FINDING that does no good a SIN, and to resolve, when we are happy ourselves, not to poison the atmosphere for our neighbours by calling on them to remark every painful and disagreeable feature of their daily life. Third, to practice the grace and virtue of PRAISE.

HARRIET B. STOWE

Surrounded by those who constantly exhibit defects of character and conduct, if we yield to a complaining and impatient spirit, we shall mar our own peace without having the satisfaction of benefiting others.

T. C. UPHAM

NOVEMBER 20

Ye have need of patience, that, after ye have done the will of God, ye might receive the promise.
—Hebrews 10:36

❧

SWEET Patience, come:
Not from a low and earthly source,—
Waiting, till things shall have their course,—
Not as accepting present pain
In hope of some hereafter gain,—
Not in a dull and sullen calm,—
But as a breath of heavenly balm,
Bidding my weary heart submit
To bear whatever God sees Fit;
    Sweet Patience, come!

HYMNS OF THE
CHURCH MILITANT

❧

Patience endues their scholars with content of mind and evenness of temper, preventing all repining, grumbling, impatient desires, and inordinate affections. Disappointments to her are not crosses, and all anxious thoughts are disarmed of their sting. In her habitations dwell quietness, submission, and long-suffering; all fierce, turbulent inclinations are hereby allayed. The eyes of the patient fixedly wait the inward power of God's providence, and they are thereby mightily enabled towards their salvation and preservation.

THOMAS TRYON

NOVEMBER 21

Man shall not live by bread alone, but by every word that proceedeth out of the mouth of God.
— *Matthew 4:4*

A man's life consisteth not in the abundance of the things which he possesseth.
— *Luke 12:15*

WHATE'ER God does is well,
Whether He gives or takes!
And what we from His hand receive
    Suffices us to live.
He takes and gives, while yet He loves us still.
    Then love His will.

B. SCHMOLCK

Is that beast better, that hath two or three mountains to graze on, than a little bee that feeds on dew or manna, and lives on what falls every morning from the storehouse of heaven, clouds, and providence?

JEREMY TAYLOR

Something is wrong when the Christian cannot rejoice in all the dear dispensations of his Father's providence.

ISABELLA CAMPBELL, 1825

Every lot is happy to a person who bears it with tranquillity.

BOËTHIUS

NOVEMBER 22

Your Father knoweth what things ye have need of.
—Matthew 6:8

Seek ye first the kingdom of God, and His righteousness,
and all these things shall be added unto you.
—Matthew 6:33

THY kingdom come, with power and grace,
   To every heart of man;
Thy peace, and joy, and righteousness
   In all our bosoms reign.

             C. WESLEY

God bids us, then, by past mercies, by present grace, by fears
of coming ill, by hopes in His goodness, earnestly, with our
whole hearts, to seek Him and His righteousness. All these
things, all ye need for soul and body, peace, comfort, joy, and
the overflowing of His consolations, shall be added over and
above you.

             E. B. PUSEY

Grant us, O Lord, we beseech Thee, always to seek Thy kingdom and righteousness; and of whatsoever Thou seest us to
stand in need, mercifully grant us an abundant portion. Amen.

Be content to be a child, and let the Father proportion out
daily to thee what light, what power, what exercises, what
straits, what fears, and what troubles He sees fit for thee.

             I. PENINGTON

NOVEMBER 23

I have taught thee in the way of wisdom; I have led thee in right paths.

—Proverbs 4:11

WE know not what the path may be
    As yet by us untrod;
But we can trust our all to Thee,
    Our Father and our God.

WM. J. IRONS

We have very little command over the circumstances in which we may be called by God to bear our part—we have unlimited command over the temper of our souls, but next to no command over the outward forms of trial. The most energetic will cannot order the events by which our spirits are to be tested. Powers quite beyond our reach—death, accident, misfortune, another's sin—may change in a moment all the conditions of our life. With to-morrow's sun, existence may have new and awful aspects for any of us.

J. H. THOM

Oh, my friend, look not *out* at what stands in the way—what if it look dreadfully as a lion, is not the Lord stronger than the mountains of prey? Look *in*, where the law of life is written and the will of the Lord revealed, that thou mayest know what is the Lord's will concerning thee.

I. PENINGTON

NOVEMBER 24

Be of good courage, and He shall strengthen your heart, all ye that hope in the Lord.
　　　　　　　　—Psalm 31:24

Let not your heart be troubled, neither let it be afraid.
　　　　　　　　—John 14:27

IN heavenly love abiding,
　No change my heart shall fear;
And safe is such confiding,
　For nothing changes here.

　　　　　A. L. WARING

A true Christian, that hath power over his own will, may live nobly and happily, and enjoy perpetually a clear heaven within the serenity of his own mind. When the sea of this world is most rough and tempestuous about him, then can he ride safely at anchor within the haven, by a sweet compliance of his will with God's will. He can look about him, and with an even and indifferent mind behold the world either to smile or frown upon him. He that hath got the mastery over his own will feels no violence from without, finds no contests within. When God calls for him out of this state of mortality, he finds in himself a power to lay down his own life—it is not so much taken from him, as quietly and freely surrendered up by him.

　　　　　DR. JOHN SMITH

NOVEMBER 25

And the Lord, He it is that doth go before thee; He will be with thee, He will not fail thee, neither forsake thee: fear not, neither be dismayed.

—Deuteronomy 31:8

KNOW well, my soul, God's hand controls
    Whate'er thou fearest;
Round Him in calmest music rolls
    Whate'er thou hearest.

J. G. WHITTIER

The lessons of the moral sentiment are an emancipation from that anxiety which takes the joy out of all life. It teaches a great peace. It comes itself from the highest place. It is that, which being in all sound natures, and strongest in the best and most gifted men, we know to be implanted by the Creator of men. It is a commandment at every moment, and in every condition of life, to do the duty of that moment, and to abstain from doing the wrong.

R. W. EMERSON

Fight like a good soldier. If thou sometimes fall through frailty, take again greater strength than before, trusting in My more abundant grace.

THOMAS À KEMPIS

NOVEMBER 26

Behold, I am with thee, and will keep thee in all places whither thou goest.

—Genesis 28:15

BE quiet, soul:
Why shouldst thou care and sadness borrow,
Why sit in nameless fear and sorrow,
    The livelong day?
God will mark out thy path to-morrow
    In His best way.

ANONYMOUS

I had hoped, Madame, to find you here, and was rejoicing in that hope; but God has sent you elsewhere. The best place is wherever He puts us, and any other would be undesirable, all the worse because it would please our fancy and be of our own choice. Do not think about distant events. This uneasiness about the future is unwholesome for you. We must leave to God all that depends on Him, and think only of being faithful in all that depends upon ourselves. When God takes away that which He has given you, He knows well how to replace it, either through other means or by Himself.

FÉNELON

NOVEMBER 27

The Lord hath been mindful of us: He will bless us.
—Psalm 115:12

MY Father! what am I, that all
Thy mercies sweet like sunlight fall
   So constant o'er my way?
That Thy great love should shelter me,
And guide my steps so tenderly
   Through every changing day!

ANONYMOUS

What a strength and spring of life, what hope and trust, what glad, unresting energy, is in this one thought,—to serve Him who is 'my Lord,' ever near me, ever looking on. He sees my intentions before He beholds my failures; knows my desires before He sees my faults; cheers me to endeavour greater things, and yet accept the least; invites my poor service, and above all, He is content with my poorer love. Let us try to realize this, whatsoever, wheresoever we be. The humblest and the simplest, the weakest and the most encumbered, may love Him not less than the busiest and strongest, the most gifted and laborious. If our heart be clear before Him, if He be to us our chief and sovereign choice, dear above all, and beyond all desired, then all else matters little. That which concerneth us He will perfect in stillness and in power.

H. E. MANNING

NOVEMBER 28

Yea, I have loved thee with an everlasting love; therefore with lovingkindness have I drawn thee.
—Jeremiah 31:3

ON the great love of God I lean,
Love of the Infinite, Unseen,
With nought of heaven or earth between.
   This God is mine, and I am His;
   His love is all I need of bliss.

H. BONAR

If ever human love was tender, self-sacrificing, and devoted; if ever it could bear and forbear; if ever it could suffer gladly for its loved ones; if ever it was willing to pour itself out in lavish abandonment for the comfort or pleasure of its objects; then infinitely more is Divine love tender, self-sacrificing, devoted, glad to bear and forbear, to suffer, and to lavish its best of gifts and blessings upon the objects of its love. Put together all the tenderest love you know of, the deepest you have ever felt and the strongest that has ever been poured out upon you, and heap upon it all the love of all the loving human hearts in the world, and then multiply it by infinity, and you will begin, perhaps, to have some faint glimpse of what the love of God is.

H. W. S.

NOVEMBER 29

*My sons, be not now negligent: for the Lord hath chosen you
to stand before Him, to serve Him.*
                                                —2 Chronicles 29:11

BRIGHT be my prospect as I pass along;
    An ardent service at the cost of all,—
Love by untiring ministry made strong,
    And ready for the first, the softest call.
                                    A. L. WARING

There are many things that appear trifles, which tend greatly
to enervate the soul and hinder its progress in the path to virtue
and glory. The habit of indulging in things which our judgment
cannot thoroughly approve, grows stronger and stronger by
every act of self-gratification. We are led on by degrees to an
excess of luxury which must greatly weaken our hands in the
spiritual warfare. If we do not endeavour to do that which is
right in every particular circumstance, though trifling, we shall
be in great danger of letting the same negligence take place in
matters more essential.

MARGARET WOODS

The will can only be made submissive by my frequent self-
denials, which must keep in subjection its sallies and inclinations. Great weakness is often produced by indulgences which
seem of no importance.

M. MOLINOS

NOVEMBER 30

Why art thou cast down, O my soul? and why art thou disquieted in me? hope thou in God; for I shall yet praise Him for the help of His countenance.

—Psalm 42:5

We are troubled on every side, yet not distressed.
—2 Corinthians 4:8

⁓

OH, my soul, why art thou vexed?
   Let things go e'en as they will;
Though to thee they seem perplexed,
   Yet His order they fulfil.

A. H. FRANCKE

⁓

The vexation, restlessness, and impatience which small trials cause arise wholly from our ignorance and want of self-control. We may be thwarted and troubled, it is true, but these things put us into a condition for exercising patience and meek submission, and the self-abnegation wherein alone the fullness of God is to be found.

DE RENTY

Every day deny yourself some satisfaction, bearing all the inconveniences of life (for the love of God)—cold, hunger, restless nights, ill health, unwelcome news, the faults of servants, contempt, ingratitude of friends, malice of enemies, calumnies, our own failings, lowness of spirits, the struggle in overcoming our corruptions;—bearing all these with patience and resignation to the will of God. Do all this unto God, with the greatest privacy.

BISHOP WILSON

DECEMBER 1

Charity envieth not . . . thinketh no evil.
—1 Corinthians 8:4, 5

Why dost thou judge thy brother? or why dost thou set at
nought thy brother?
—Romans 14:10

He that despiseth his neighbour, sinneth.
—Proverbs 14:21

LOOK thou with pity on a brother's fall,
But dwell not with stern anger on his fault;
The grace of God alone holds thee, holds all;
Were that withdrawn, thou too wouldst swerve and halt.

J. EDMESTON

Let us be very watchful on hearing of the fall of a brother,
however differing or severed from us, lest we feel the least inclination to linger over it, instead of hiding it in grief and shame or
veiling it in the love which covereth a multitude of sins. Let us
also be watchful in seeing a joy or a grace or an effective service
given to others, if we do not rejoice, but feel depressed. The
most diabolical of passions may mask itself as humility, or zeal
for the glory of God.

ELIZABETH CHARLES

Love taketh up no malign elements. Its spirit prompteth it to
cover in mercy all things that ought not to be exposed, to
believe all of good that can be believed, to hope all things that a
good God makes possible, and to endure all things that the hope
may be made good.

J. H. THOM

DECEMBER 2

Therefore thou art inexcusable, O man, whosoever thou art that judgest: for wherein thou judgest another, thou condemnest thyself; for thou that judgest doest the same things.
—*Romans 2:1*

SEARCH thine own heart. What paineth thee
   In others, in thyself may be;
All dust is frail, all flesh is weak;
   Be thou the true man thou dost seek.
          J. G. WHITTIER

A saint's life in one man may be less than common honesty in another. From *us,* whose consciences He has reached and enlightened, God may look for a martyr's truth, a Christian's unworldly simplicity, before He will place us on a level even with the average of the exposed classes. We perhaps think our lives at least harmless. We do not consider what He may think of them, when compared with the invitations of His that we have slighted, with the aims of His providence we are leaving without our help, with the glory for ourselves we are refusing and casting away, with the vast sum of blessed work that daily faithfulness could rear in time without overwork on any single day.

J. H. THOM

DECEMBER 3

Now the God of hope fill you with all joy and peace in believing, that ye may abound in hope, through the power of the Holy Ghost.

—*Romans 15:13*

———— ❧ ————

TO heaven I lift my waiting eyes;
    There all my hopes are laid;
The Lord that built the earth and skies
    Is my perpetual aid.

I. WATTS

———— ❧ ————

Grovel not in things below, among earthly cares, pleasures, anxieties, toils, if thou wouldst have a good strong hope on high. Lift up thy cares with thy heart to God, if thou wouldst hope in Him. Then see what in thee is most displeasing to God. This it is which holdeth thy hope down. Strike firmly, repeatedly, in the might of God, until it give way. Thy hope will soar at once with thy thanks to God who delivereth thee.

E. B. PUSEY

The snares of the enemy will be so known to thee and discerned, the way of help so manifest and easy that their strength will be broken, and the poor entangled bird will fly away singing from the nets and entanglements of the fowler. Praises and great love in thy heart will spring up to the Forgiver and Redeemer.

I. PENINGTON

DECEMBER 4

Fight the good fight of faith, lay hold on eternal life, where-unto thou art also called.
>   —*1 Timothy 6:12*

OH, dream no more of quiet life;
Care finds the careless out; more wise to vow
    Thy heart entire to faith's pure strife;
So peace will come, thou knowest not when or how.
>   LYRA APOSTOLICA

Who art thou that complainest of thy life of toil? Complain not. Look up, my wearied brother. See thy fellow-workmen there in God's Eternity; they alone surviving, sacred band of the Immortals, celestial body-guard of the empire of mankind. To thee Heaven, though severe, is *not* unkind. Heaven is kind;—as that noble Spartan mother said while she gave her son his shield, 'With it, my son, or upon it.' Thou too shalt return to thy far-distant Home in honour, doubt it not,—if in the battle thou keep thy shield!

>   T. CARLYLE

DECEMBER 5

The God of all grace, who hath called us unto His eternal glory by Christ Jesus, after that ye have suffered a while, make you perfect, stablish, strengthen, settle you.
—1 Peter 5:10

Take heed, and be quiet; fear not, neither be faint-hearted.
—Isaiah 7:4

HOW shalt thou bear the cross that now
 So dread a weight appears?
Keep quietly to God, and think
 Upon the Eternal Years.

F. W. FABER

God forgive them that raise an ill report upon the sweet cross of Christ. It is our weak and dim eyes that look but to the black side, that make us mistake. Those that can take that crabbed tree handsomely upon their backs, and fasten it on securely, shall find it such a burden as wings unto a bird or sails to a ship.

S. RUTHERFORD

Blessed is any weight, however overwhelming, which God has been so good as to fasten with His own hand upon our shoulders.

F. W. FABER

We cannot say that this or that trouble shall not befall us. Yet we may, by help of the Spirit, say that nothing that doth befall shall make me do that which is unworthy of a Christian.

R. SIBBES

DECEMBER 6

This God is our God for ever and ever: He will be our guide even unto death.
                                        —Psalm 48:14

For the Lord shall be thy confidence.
                                        —Proverbs 3:26

BE still, my soul! Thy God doth undertake
　To guide the future, as He has the past:
Thy hope, thy confidence, let nothing shake,
　All now mysterious shall be bright at last.
                          J. BORTHWICK

He has kept and folded us from ten thousand ills when we did not know it. In the midst of our security we should have perished every hour, but He sheltered us 'from the terror by night and from the arrow that flieth by day'—from the powers of evil that walk in darkness, and from snares of our own evil will. He has kept us even against ourselves, and saved us even from our own undoing. Let us read the traces of His hand in all our ways, in all the events, the chances, the changes of this troubled state. It is He that folds and feeds us, that makes us to go in and out, to be faint or to find pasture, to lie down by the still waters, or to walk by the way that is parched and desert.

H. E. MANNING

We are never without help. We have no right to say of any good work, 'it is too hard for me to do,' or of any sorrow, 'it is too hard for me to bear;' or of any sinful habit, 'it is too hard for me to overcome.'

ELIZABETH CHARLES

DECEMBER 7

Acquaint now thyself with Him, and be at peace.
—Job 22:21

All thy children shall be taught of the Lord, and great shall
be the peace of thy children.
—Isaiah 54:13

UNITE, my roving thoughts, unite
   In silence soft and sweet;
And thou, my soul, sit gently down
   At thy great Sovereign's feet.

P. DODDRIDGE

Yes! blessed are those holy hours in which the soul retires
from the world to be alone with God. God's voice, as Himself, is
everywhere. Within and without, He speaks to our souls if we
would hear. Only the din of the world, the tumult of our own
hearts, deafens our inward ear to it. Learn to commune with
Him in stillness, and He, whom thou hast sought in stillness, will
be with thee when thou goest abroad.

E. B. PUSEY

Open wide every avenue of your being to receive the blessed
influences your Divine Husbandman may bring to bear upon
you. Bask in the sunshine of His love. Drink in of the waters of
His goodness. Keep your face upturned to Him. You need make
no efforts to grow. But let your efforts instead be all concentrat-
ed on this, that you abide in the Vine.

H. W. S.

DECEMBER 8

Blessed be the God and Father of our Lord Jesus Christ, who hath blessed us with all spiritual blessings.
—Ephesians 1:3

As sorrowful, yet always rejoicing.
—2 Corinthians 6:10

There is something sweet and pure,
Through life, through death it may endure;
With steady foot I onward press,
And long to win that Blessedness.

LOUISA J. HALL

The elements of *happiness* in this present life no man can command, even if he could command himself, for they depend on the action of many wills, on the purity of many hearts, and by the highest law of God the holiest must ever bear the sins and sorrows of the rest. But, over the *blessedness* of one's own spirit, circumstance need have no control. God has given an unlimited power to the means of preservation, of grace and growth, which is at every man's command.

J. H. THOM

There is in man a higher than love of happiness: he can do without happiness, and instead thereof find blessedness.

T. CARLYLE

DECEMBER 9

For this shall every one that is godly pray unto Thee in a time when Thou mayest be found: surely in the floods of great waters they shall not come nigh unto him.
        —Psalm 32:6

BE not o'ermastered by thy pain,
    But cling to God, thou shalt not fall.
The floods sweep over thee in vain,
    Thou yet shalt rise above them all;
For when thy trial seems too hard to bear,
Lo! God, thy King, hath granted all thy prayer.
        Be thou content.

        P. GERHARDT

It is the Lord's mercy to give thee longings after life and cries unto Him against that which oppresseth thee. Happy wilt thou be when He shall fill thy soul with that which He hath given thee to long after. Be not troubled. If troubles abound, and there be tossing, storms, and tempests, and no peace, nor anything visible left to support—yet, lie still till a secret hope stir, which will stay the heart in the midst of all these. The Lord will administer comfort. He knows how and what relief to give to the weary traveller, who knows not where it is, nor which way to look, nor where to expect a path.

        I. PENINGTON

DECEMBER 10

Behold, we count them happy which endure.
—James 5:11

If ye endure chastening, God dealeth with you as with sons.
—Hebrews 12:7

TRIALS must and will befall;
　　But with humble faith to see
Love inscribed upon them all,
　　This is happiness to me.

　　　　　　　　　W. COWPER

Be not afraid of these trials which God may see fit to send upon thee. It is with the wind and storm of tribulation that God separates the true wheat from the chaff. Always remember, therefore, that God comes to thee in thy sorrows, as really as in thy joys. He lays low, and He builds up. Thou wilt find thyself far from perfection if thou dost not find God in everything.

M. MOLINOS

God hath provided a sweet and quiet life for His children, could they improve and [rise to] use it. [He wants them to have] a calm and firm conviction in all the storms and troubles that are about them, however things go; to find content, and be careful for nothing.

R. LEIGHTON

DECEMBER 11

Oh that Thou wouldest bless me indeed, and that Thine hand might be with me, and that Thou wouldest keep me from evil, that it may not grieve me!

—1 Chronicles 4:10

Ye shall serve the Lord your God, and He shall bless thy bread and thy water.

—Exodus 23:25

———————— ❧❧ ————————

WHAT I possess, or what I crave,
   Brings no content, great God, to me,
If what I would, or what I have,
   Be not possest, and blest, in Thee;
   What I enjoy, O make it mine,
   In making me that have it, Thine.

J. QUARLES

———————— ❧❧ ————————

Offer up to God all pure affections, desires, regrets, and all the bonds which link us to home, kindred, and friends, together with all our works, purposes, and labours. These things, which are not only lawful, but sacred, become then the matter of thanksgiving and offering. Memories, plans for the future, wishes, intentions; works just begun, half done, all but completed; emotions, sympathies, affections,—all these things throng tumultuously and dangerously in the heart and will. The only way to master them is to offer them up to Him, as once ours, [now] under Him, always His by right.

H. E. MANNING

DECEMBER 12

I delight to do Thy will, O my God: yea, Thy law is within my heart.

—*Psalm 40:8*

A PATIENT, a victorious mind,
That life and all things casts behind,
   Springs forth obedient to Thy call;
A heart that no desire can move,
But still to adore, believe, and love,
   Give me, my Lord, my Life, my All.

P. GERHARDT

That piety which sanctifies us, and which is a true devotion to God, consists in doing all His will precisely at the time, in the situation, and under the circumstances, in which He has placed us. Perfect devotedness requires not only that we do the will of God, but that we do it with love. God would have us serve Him with delight; it is our hearts that He asks of us.

FÉNELON

Devotion is really neither more nor less than a general inclination and readiness to do that which we know to be acceptable to God. It is that 'free spirit,' of which David spoke when he said, 'I will run the way of Thy commandments, when Thou hast set my heart at liberty.' People of ordinary goodness walk in God's way, but the devout run in it, and at length they almost fly therein. . . . To be truly devout, we must not only do God's will, but we must do it cheerfully.

FRANCIS DE SALES

DECEMBER 13

So teach us to number our days, that we may apply our hearts unto wisdom.

—Psalm 90:12

Seek not ye what ye shall eat, or what ye shall drink, neither be ye of doubtful mind.

—Luke 12:29

OUR days are numbered: let us spare
Our anxious hearts a needless care:
'Tis Thine to number out our days;
'Tis ours to give them to Thy praise.

MADAME GUYON

Every day let us renew the consecration to God's service. Every day let us, in His strength, pledge ourselves afresh to do His will, even in the veriest trifle, and to turn aside from anything that may displease Him. . . . He does not bid us bear the burdens of to-morrow, next week, or next year. Every day we are to come to Him in simple obedience and faith, asking help to keep us and aid us through that day's work. To-morrow, and to-morrow, and to-morrow, through years of long to-morrows, it will be but the same thing to do; leaving the future always in God's hands, sure that He can care for it better than we. Blessed trust! that can thus confidingly say, 'This hour is mine with its present duty; the next is God's, and when it comes, His presence will come with it.'

ANONYMOUS

DECEMBER 14

And as many as walk according to this rule, peace be on them, and mercy, and upon the Israel of God.
—Galatians 6:16

❦

LORD, I have given my life to Thee,
 And every day and hour is Thine,—
What Thou appointest let them be;
 Thy will is better, Lord, than mine.

A. WARNER

❦

Begin at once. Before you venture away from this quiet moment, ask your King to take you wholly into His service, and place all the hours of this day quite simply at His disposal. Ask Him to make and keep you *ready* to do just exactly what He appoints. Never mind about to-morrow; one day at a time is enough. Try it to-day, and see if it is not a day of strange, almost curious peace, so sweet that you will be only too thankful, when to-morrow comes, to ask Him to take it also,—till it will become a blessed habit to hold yourself simply and 'wholly at Thy commandment for *any* manner of service.' The 'whatsoever' is not necessarily active work. It may be waiting (whether half an hour or half a lifetime), learning, suffering, or sitting still. Let us ask Him to prepare us for all that He is preparing for us.

F. H. HAVERGAL

DECEMBER 15

*Return unto thy rest, O my soul; for the Lord hath dealt
bountifully with thee.*
—Psalm 116:7

We which have believed do enter into rest.
—Hebrews 4:3

REST is not quitting
   The busy career;
Rest is the fitting
   Of self to its sphere.

'Tis loving and serving
   The highest and best!
'Tis onwards, unswerving,—
   And that is true rest.

J. S. DWIGHT

As a result of this strong faith, the inner life of Catherine of
Genoa was characterized, in a remarkable degree, by what may
be termed rest or quietude. This is only another form of expression for true interior peace. It was not, however, the quietude of
a lazy inaction, but the quietude of an inward acquiescence. Not
a quietude which feels nothing and does nothing, but that higher and divine quietude which exists by feeling and acting in the
time and degree of God's appointment and God's will. It was a
principle in her conduct to give herself to God in the discharge
of duty, and to leave all results without worry in His hands.

T. C. UPHAM

DECEMBER 16

Thou understandest my thought afar off.
　　　　　　　—Psalm 139:2

*Who can understand his errors? cleanse Thou me from
secret faults.*
　　　　　　　　—Psalm 19:12

MY newest griefs to Thee are old;
　My last transgression of Thy law,
Though wrapped in thought's most secret fold,
　Thine eyes with pitying sadness saw.
　　　　　　H. M. KIMBALL

Lord our God, great, eternal, and wonderful in glory, Thou
keepest covenant and promises for those that love Thee with
their whole heart. Thou art the Life of all, the Help of those that
flee unto Thee, the Hope of those who cry unto Thee. Cleanse
us from our sins, secret and open, and from every thought displeasing to Thy goodness. Cleanse our hearts and consciences,
so that with a pure heart and a clear soul, with perfect love and
calm hope, we may venture confidently and fearlessly to pray
unto Thee. Amen.

　　　　　　COPTIC LITURGY OF ST. BASIL

The dominion of any sinful habit will fearfully estrange us
from His presence. A single consenting act of inward disobedience in thought or will is enough to let fall a cloud between Him
and us, and to leave our hearts cheerless and dark.

　　　　　　H. E. MANNING

DECEMBER 17

The fruit of the Spirit is love, joy, peace, long-suffering, gentleness, goodness, faith, meekness, temperance.
—Galatians 5:22, 23

Herein is my Father glorified, that ye bear much fruit; so shall ye be my disciples.
—John 15:8

O BREATH from out the Eternal Silence! blow
    Softly upon our spirits' barren ground;
The precious fullness of our God bestow,
    That fruits of faith, love, reverence may abound.
          G. TERSTEEGEN

Is it possible that we should be ignorant about whether we feel contrary to love or not?—whether we rejoice always, or are burdened and bowed down with sorrow?—whether we have a praying, or a dead, lifeless spirit?—whether we can praise God, and be resigned in all trials, or feel murmurings, fretfulness, and impatience under them?—It is easy to know if we feel anger at provocations, or whether we feel our tempers mild, gentle, peaceable, and easy to be entreated, or feel stubbornness, self-will, and pride. [We know] whether we have slavish fears, or are possessed of that perfect love which casteth out all fear that hath torment.

        HESTER ANN ROGERS

DECEMBER 18

We trust in the living God.
—1 Timothy 4:10

THY secret judgment's depths profound
   Still sings the silent night;
The day, upon his golden round,
   Thy pity infinite.

I. WILLIAMS, *Translated from Latin*

Now that I have no longer any sense for the transitory and perishable, the universe appears before my eyes under a transformed aspect. The dead, heavy mass which did but stop up space has vanished, and in its place there flows onward, with the rushing music of mighty waves, an eternal stream of life, power, and action, which issues from the original source of all life,—from Thy life, O Infinite One! for all life is Thy life, and only the religious eye penetrates to the realm of true Beauty.

J. G. FICHTE

What is nature? Art thou not the 'Living Garment' of God? O Heavens, He that ever speaks through thee, [He who] lives and loves in thee, [He also] lives and loves in me. Sweeter than dawn to the shipwrecked, …like the mother's voice to her little child that strays bewildered …like soft streamings of celestial music to my too exasperated heart, came this Good Word—the universe is not dead and demoniacal, a charnel-house with spectres; [it is] my Father's.

T. CARLYLE

DECEMBER 19

O Lord, be gracious unto us; we have waited for Thee.
—Isaiah 33:2

And now, Lord, what wait I for? my hope is in Thee.
—Psalm 39:7

HE never comes too late;
    He knoweth what is best;
Vex not thyself in vain;
    Until He cometh, rest.

B. T.

We make mistakes, or what we call such. The nature that could fall into such mistakes needs, and in the goodness of the dear God is given, the living out of them. In the patient living out of our mistakes we come to find that we have fallen, not into hopeless confusion of our own wild, ignorant making, but that the finger of God has been at work among our lives, and that the emerging [from our mistakes] is into His blessed order. He is forever making up for us our own undoings. [In fact,] He makes them up beforehand; He evermore restoreth our souls.

A. D. T. WHITNEY

The Lord even knows how to make stepping-stones for us of our defects. It is what He lets them be for. He remembereth that we are but dust; the dust of earth out of which He *chose* to make something little lower than the angels.

A. D. T. WHITNEY

DECEMBER 20

Take no thought how or what ye shall speak: for it shall be given you in that same hour what ye shall speak.
—Matthew 10:19

JUST to follow hour by hour
    As He leadeth;
Just to draw the moment's power
    As it needeth.

F. R. HAVERGAL

You have a disagreeable duty to do at twelve o'clock. Do not blacken nine, ten, eleven, and all between, with the colour of twelve. Do the work of each, and reap your reward in peace. So when the dreaded moment in the future becomes the present, you shall meet it walking in the light, and that light will overcome its darkness. The best preparation is the present well seen to, the last duty done. For this will keep the eye so clear and the body so full of light that the right action will be perceived at once, the right words will rush from the heart to the lips, and the man, full of the Spirit of God because he cares for nothing but the will of God, will trample on the evil thing in love, and be sent, it may be, in a chariot of fire to the presence of his Father, or stand unmoved amid the cruel mockings of the men he loves.

G. MACDONALD

DECEMBER 21

Hast thou not known? hast thou not heard, that the ever-lasting God, the Lord, the Creator of the ends of the earth, fainteth not, neither is weary? He giveth power to the faint; and to them that have no might he increaseth strength.
—Isaiah 40:28, 29

WORKMAN of God! Oh, lose not heart,
But learn what God is like;
And in the darkest battle-field
Thou shalt know where to strike.
F. W. FABER

For the rest, let that vain struggle to read the mystery of the Infinite cease to harass us. It is a mystery which, through all ages, we shall only read here a line of, there another line of. Do we not already know that the name of the Infinite is GOOD, is GOD? Here on earth we are as soldiers, fighting in a foreign land, who understand not the plan of the campaign, and have no need to understand it. We see well what is at our hand to be done. Let us do it like soldiers, with submission, with courage, and with a heroic joy. Behind each one of us lie six thousand years of human effort, human conquest. Before us is boundless Time, with its as yet uncreated and unconquered continents and Eldorados, which we have to conquer and create. And from the bosom of Eternity there shine for us celestial guiding stars.

T. CARLYLE

DECEMBER 22

I will wait upon the Lord, that hideth His face from the house of Jacob, and I will look for Him.
—*Isaiah 8:17*

WHAT heart can comprehend Thy name,
    Or, searching, find Thee out?
Who art within, a quickening flame,
    A presence round about.

Yet though I know Thee but in part,
    I ask not, Lord, for more:
Enough for me to know Thou art,
    To love Thee and adore.

F. L. HOSMER

Stand up, O heart! and yield not one inch of thy rightful territory to the usurping intellect. Hold fast to God in spite of logic, and yet not quite blindly. Be not torn from thy grasp upon the skirts of His garments by any wrench of atheistic hypothesis that seeks only to hurl thee into utter darkness. But do not refuse to let thy hands be gently unclasped by that loving and pious teaching that seeks to draw thee from the feet of God only to place thee in His bosom. Trustfully, though tremblingly, let go the robe, and thou shalt rest upon the heart and clasp the very living soul of God.

JAMES HINTON

DECEMBER 23

Thou, therefore, endure hardness, as a good soldier of Jesus Christ.

—2 Timothy 2:3

WHERE our Captain bids us go,
'Tis not ours to murmur, 'No.'
   He that gives the sword and shield,
   Chooses too the battle-field
On which we are to fight the foe.

              ANONYMOUS

Of nothing may we be more sure than this: if we cannot sanctify our present lot, we could sanctify no other. Our heaven and our Almighty Father are there, or nowhere. The obstructions of that lot are given for us to heave away by the concurrent touch of a Holy Spirit, and labour of strenuous will. Its gloom we are to tint with some celestial light. Its mysteries are for our worship; its sorrows for our trust; its perils for our courage; its temptations for our faith. Soldiers of the cross, it is not for us, but for our Leader and our Lord to choose the field. It is ours, taking the station which He assigns, to make it the field of truth and honour, [even] though it [may] be the field of death.

            J. MARTINEAU

DECEMBER 24

*Giving thanks unto the Father, who hath made us meet to
be partakers of the inheritance of the saints in light.*
—Colossians 1:12

THE souls most precious to us here
    May from this home have fled;
But still we make one household dear;
    One Lord is still our head.
Midst cherubim and seraphim
    They mind their Lord's affairs;
Oh! if we bring our work to Him
    Our work is one with theirs.

                  T. H. GILL

To 'give thanks to Him for all things,' is indeed a very difficult
duty. It includes giving thanks for trials of all kinds—for suffering
and pain, for languor and weariness, for the crossing of our
wills, for contradiction, for reproaches, for loneliness, and for
privations. Yet they who have learned submission will not find it
a hard duty. They will so entirely love all that God wills and
appoints, that they will see it is the very best thing for them.
Hereafter they will see all the links of the chain, and how won-
derfully those have fitted, which at the time seemed to have no
adaptation or agreement. This belief enables them to praise Him
and give thanks *now* for each thing, assured that as it has been,
so it will be—that the God of love will do all things well.

                  PRISCILLA MAURICE

DECEMBER 25

That ye, being rooted and grounded in love, may be able to comprehend with all saints what is the breadth, and length, and depth, and height; and to know the love of Christ, which passeth knowledge, that ye might be filled with all the fulness of God.

—Ephesians 3:17-19

O LOVE that passeth knowledge, thee I need;
   Pour in the heavenly sunshine; fill my heart;
Scatter the cloud, the doubting, and the dread,—
   The joy unspeakable to me impart.

                H. BONAR

To examine its evidence is not to try Christianity. To admire its martyrs is not to try Christianity. To compare and estimate its teachers is not to try Christianity. To attend its rites and services with more than Mahometan punctuality is not to try or know Christianity. But for one week, for one day, to have lived in the pure atmosphere of faith and love to God, of tenderness to man; to have beheld earth annihilated, and heaven opened to the prophetic gaze of hope; to have seen evermore revealed behind the complicated troubles of this strange, mysterious life, the unchanged smile of an eternal Friend, and everything that is difficult to reason solved by that reposing trust which is higher and better than reason,—to have known and felt this, I will not say for a *life,* but for a single blessed hour, *that,* indeed, is to have made experiment of Christianity.

                WM. ARCHER BUTLER

DECEMBER 26

*The peace of God, which passeth all understanding, shall
keep your hearts and minds through Christ Jesus.*
—Philippians 4:7

Let the peace of God rule in your hearts.
—Colossians 3:15

DROP Thy still dews of quietness,
    Till all our strivings cease;
Take from our souls the strain and stress,
And let our ordered lives confess
    The beauty of Thy peace.

J. G. WHITTIER

'These things write we unto you, that your joy may be full.'
What is fullness of joy but *peace?* Peace is the privilege of those
who are 'filled with the knowledge of the glory of the Lord, as the
waters cover the sea.' 'Thou wilt keep him in perfect peace,
whose mind is stayed on Thee, because he trusteth in Thee.' It is
peace, springing from trust and innocence, and then overflowing
in love towards all around him. He who is anxious thinks of himself, is suspicious of danger, speaks hurriedly, and has no time for
the interests of others. He who lives in peace is at leisure, wherever his lot is cast.

J. H. NEWMAN

Through the spirit of Divine Love let the violent, obstinate
powers of thy nature be quieted, the hardness of thy affections
softened, and thine intractable self-will subdued. As often as anything contrary stirs within thee, immediately sink into the blessed
Ocean of meekness and love.

G. TERSTEEGEN

DECEMBER 27

Wherefore thou art no more a servant, but a son; and if a son, then an heir of God through Christ.
—Galatians 4:7

NOT by the terrors of a slave
    God's sons perform His will,
But with the noblest powers they have
    His sweet commands fulfil.

ISAAC WATTS

Did not Jesus say, "I am the door of the sheepfold"? What to us is the sheepfold, dear children? It is the heart of the Father, whereunto Christ is the Gate that is called Beautiful. O children, how sweetly and how gladly has He opened that door into the Father's heart, into the treasure-chamber of God! And there within He unfolds to us the hidden riches, the nearness and the sweetness of companionship with Himself.

JOHN TAULER

Whatever we are, high or lowly, learned or unlearned, married or single, in a full house or alone, charged with many affairs or dwelling in quietness, we have our daily round of work—our duties of affection, obedience, love, mercy, industry, and the like. That which makes one man to differ from another is not so much what things he does, as his manner of doing them.

H. E. MANNING

DECEMBER 28

*Now the God of peace make you perfect in every good work,
to do His will, working in you that which is well-pleasing in
His sight.*

—Hebrews 13:20, 21

Be ready to every good work.

—Titus 3:1

SO, firm in steadfast hope, in thought secure,
   In full accord to all Thy world of joy,
May I be nerved to labours high and pure,
   And thou Thy child to do Thy work employ.

J. STERLING

Be with God in thy outward works, refer them to Him, offer
them to Him, seek to do them in Him and for Him, and He will
be with thee in them. They shall not hinder, but rather invite His
presence in thy soul. Seek to see Him in all things, and in all
things He will come nigh to thee.

E. B. PUSEY

Nothing less than the majesty of God and the powers of the
world to come can maintain the peace and sanctity of our
homes, the order and serenity of our minds, the spirit of patience and tender mercy in our hearts. Then will even the merest drudgery of duty cease to humble us, when we transfigure it
by the glory in our own spirit.

J. MARTINEAU

DECEMBER 29

Finally, brethren, whatsoever things are true, whatsoever things are honest, whatsoever things are just, whatsoever things are pure, whatsoever things are lovely, whatsoever things are of good report,—think on these things.
                                        —Philippians 4:8

STILL may Thy sweet mercy spread
A shady arm above my head,
About my paths; so shall I find
The fair centre of my mind
Thy temple, and those lovely walls
Bright ever with a beam that falls
Fresh from the pure glance of Thine eye,
Lighting to eternity.

R. CRASHAW

The way to think of God so as to know Him, is to think of Christ. Then we see Him, and can understand how tender and merciful and good He is. We see that if He sends us sorrows and difficulties, He only sends them because they are the true blessings, the things that are truly good. He would have us like Himself, with a happiness like His own, and nothing below it. As His own happiness is in taking sorrow and infirmity, and ever assisting, giving and sacrificing Himself, He gives us sorrows too, and weaknesses, which are not the evils that we think them, but are what we should be most happy in, if we were perfect and had knowledge like Him. So there is a use and a service in all we bear, in all we do, which we do not know, but which He knows, and which in Christ He shows to us. It is a use *for others,* a hidden use, but one which makes all our life rich, and that richness which is most like Christ's.

JAMES HINTON

DECEMBER 30

O Lord, I know that the way of man is not in himself; it is not in man that walketh to direct his steps.
—*Jeremiah 10:23*

I will direct all his ways.
—*Isaiah 45:13*

COME, Light serene and still!
Our darkened spirits fill
　　With thy clear day:
Guide of the feeble sight,
Star of grief's darkest night,
Reveal the path of right,
　　Show us Thy way.

ROBERT II. OF FRANCE

There had been solemn appointed seasons in Anna's life, when she was accustomed to enter upon a full and deliberate survey of her business in this world. The claims of each relationship, and the results of each occupation, were then examined in the light of eternity. It was then, too, her fervent prayer to be enabled to discern the will of God far more perfectly, not only in the indications given of it for her guidance through each day's occupations, but as it might concern duties not yet brought home to her conscience, and therefore unprovided for in her life.

ANNA, OR PASSAGES
FROM HOME LIFE

DECEMBER 31

Forgetting those things which are behind, and reaching forth unto those things which are before, I press toward the mark.

—Philippians 3:13, 14

    YET I argue not
Against Heaven's hand or will, nor bate a jot
Of heart or hope; but still bear up and steer
Right onward.

                J. MILTON

It is not by regretting what is irreparable that true work is to be done, but by making the best of what we are. It is not by complaining that we have not the right tools, but by using well the tools we have. What we are, and where we are, is God's providential arrangement,—God's doing, though it may be man's misdoing. The manly and the wise way is to look your disadvantages in the face and see what can be made out of them. Life, like war, is a series of mistakes, and he is not the best Christian nor the best general who makes the fewest false steps. He is the best who wins the most splendid victories by the retrieval of mistakes. Forget mistakes; organize victory out of mistakes!

                F. W. ROBERTSON

INDEX OF AUTHORS
OF THE POETICAL SELECTIONS

INDEX OF AUTHORS
OF THE PROSE SELECTIONS